TARTINE ALL DAY

TAR TINE ALL DAY

MODERN RECIPES FOR THE HOME COOK

ELISABETH PRUEITT

WITH JESSICA WASHBURN AND MARIA ZIZKA
PHOTOGRAPHS BY PAIGE GREEN

LORENA JONES BOOKS
An imprint of TEN SPEED PRESS
California | New York

TO MY BELOVED ARCHER
AND CHAD

CONTENTS

APPETIZERS AND SNACKS

SOUPS

SALADS, VEGETABLES, AND SIDES

MAINS

GATHERINGS

DESSERTS

WHY THIS BOOK NOW

I remember once hearing that cookbooks are the novels of choice for working parents. That they are bedside reading, blueprints for a fantasy time when afternoons would be free enough to bake a cake or when flavor could be considered an equal to convenience in the morning.

Before becoming a parent and business owner, I found this utterly depressing. Of course, I understood indulging in a cookbook's pleasurable writing, but to only read and not cook from a cookbook? One café, two restaurants, and one nine-year-old daughter later, and I understand that limitations on time can reduce the family meal to a slapdash event on most days. I know that it's often easy to forget to pause to really taste the food, and this is despite the fact that I know how to cook well.

   You see, there's no way around it: cooking is work. Work in that it requires forethought, a modicum of skill, and time. Work in that you must use your hands, stand on your feet, wash the dishes. (And, full disclosure: for my husband, Chad, and me, cooking *is* work. It is how we earn our living.) Your simple hope is that while sitting around the table to share the fruits of your labors, the effort fades to memory. Or better yet, the effort becomes part of a meal's pleasure, and that the experience of transforming ingredients into a sum greater than their parts connects you to the food in a far more profound way than any recipe lets on. That is the ideal, and to fess up to my own biases, I believe wholeheartedly that it's attainable.

Chad and I first met at culinary school in Hyde Park, New York, but we really started to come into our own as cooks when we studied with innovative bakers and pastry chefs, from Massachusetts to France to California. After more than a decade of baking, Chad began to make the bread he was after: a loaf with an "old soul." That is, bread with a caramel-colored crust, a moist crumb, and the slightly sour aroma of the natural leaven. I combined classic French pastry techniques with a California aesthetic, drawing upon seasonal fruit and flowers as inspiration. And though this may come as a surprise, I created all of my pastry recipes that would later become favorites at our bakery while tending to a gluten intolerance.

I realize now, after several years of abstaining entirely from gluten (except for naturally leavened breads, like Chad's), how physically uncomfortable I truly was. But I discovered this intolerance years before autoimmune disorders were understood, and long before a gluten-free diet was in fashion. Had my intolerance been identified today, I may very well have abandoned wheat early on. But I found an imperfect way to cope with it—mastering pastry recipes one minuscule bite at a time. It's said that limitations often become the best teachers. And it's true. I was forced to cultivate an acute awareness of how the slightest shift in technique or ingredient altered a pastry's outcome.

I've brought this same attention to detail and experimentation to working with nongluten flours. It is not an exaggeration to say that there is infinite potential in new recipes and techniques by the very fact that we now have access to such high-quality and diverse flours. I consider myself fortunate that today I can reference my classical training while also abandoning it freely to experiment. Wheat-based recipes, I should say, will always serve as my original reference point. They are what I learned to make first. But a young cook today could happily achieve similarly light textures, crisp crusts, and friable cookies without ever knowing how wheat itself behaves. And that's an exciting development.

However, it's certainly worthwhile to know how wheat works, so that we can confidently use ingredients and techniques that do not incorporate it. After all, wheat in all of its forms—from varietals to types of flour—thrives in a bakery setting for a reason. When wheat flour is kneaded, or worked at all, gluten, a substance found in wheat, creates an elastic network between its constituent proteins. This in turn solidifies when heated, giving structure to the baked good. The desired texture and structure are quite different for a loaf of bread than for a piecrust, for example, so the baker works to either develop or minimize the gluten, which helps to achieve the intended form. The baker can also choose from different wheat flours with either low- or high-protein content, which will further aid in this highly manipulative process. While there is no one exact replacement for wheat, its effects can be replicated. For this, we look to an incredible array of nongluten flours to work with, made from grains, legumes, roots, nuts, and in the case of coconut flour, a fruit. Each has unique properties that translate well to particular recipes and often work successfully when combined.

Working with new ingredients is like learning a new language. The basic grammar is the same whether baking with wheat flour or nongluten flours, but the vocabulary is wildly different. And just like the moment when, while learning a new language, you discover a word that has no exact English translation but that opens a world unto itself, baking with nongluten flours has opened my palate to exciting possibilities that I couldn't have thought of when baking only with wheat.

In facing my intolerance, I've learned one final lesson: it's not just ingredients that matter; it's also technique. A few years ago, our friend and renowned journalist Michael Pollan was in the midst of writing his book, *Cooked*. He was studying naturally leavened breads, like Chad's, and was coming upon research that suggested that such breads, made with heirloom grains and natural leaven, might be suitable for a person like me: gluten-sensitive but without celiac disease. Chad and I recalled how years ago during our stay in the Savoie region of France, I could eat the bread he was baking with his mentor without issue. Any other wheat-based food in France, and in the States when I returned, caused too much discomfort to be worth eating. Michael's research highlighted the link between enhanced digestibility and the fermentation enacted by a natural leaven, suggesting that such breads might actually work for me. Miraculously, it is true. I can eat Chad's bread, and any other made in the same way. Science is finally answering our decades-old question, and it turns out it has everything to do with both ingredient and technique. For example, our friend, producer/director J.D. McLelland, is working on a project (and film) known as Ingrained. The project is focused on grain breeding, growing, and processing, as new insights and science emerge to reveal just how much more there is to know about the subject.

In this book, I want to share the many small and large discoveries I've made as a professional chef in the role of a home cook. I want a book that inspires experimentation and delivers gratifying moments of success, a cookbook that is as useful to you as *Joy of Cooking* felt to me, decades ago. I cannot claim it is anywhere as comprehensive as that tome, but I've selected favorite recipes from across the seasons, using eggplants, quince, blood oranges, and spring peas. I've included my current preferred ways of cooking staple ingredients, like a whole chicken or a piece of salmon, while also including approachable methods for tackling more intimidating projects: a leg of lamb, or that impossible holiday bird, a turkey. In a time when recipes are infinite, I've selected ones that will ensure that your efforts are met with success. When I've come upon practical tips that feel indispensable to the recipe, or just fascinating for the curious cook, I've shared them right after I introduce the recipe. And, inspired by two classic books, *Joy of Cooking* and Julia Child's *Mastering the Art of French Cooking,* I've written the recipes so that the ingredients are alongside the

instructions, appearing next to the text right when needed. I have always preferred this way of reading a recipe. I find it easier to track. If I leave the page to juice a lemon or slice an onion, it's easier to find my place upon return. I have a theory, too, that I tend to learn the ins and outs of a recipe faster in this format because it reads as a continuous narrative. Ultimately, internalizing the general concept of any recipe is a worthwhile goal, for when you know it, the recipe can be altered on a whim. I decided to write the recipes in this way because this book is meant to be a steadfast guide. This style may feel new at first, but I promise, its advantages will soon become clear.

While the recipes, ingredients, and techniques shared here are intended for the modern home cook, I'd be remiss to not credit my time at our bakery. I came into my own as a chef at Tartine, where I witnessed firsthand the seasonal flavors that speak to people every day. When we first opened Tartine in San Francisco, we were swept up in the city's creative spirit, hanging local art on our walls as we became a part of a dynamic burgeoning food scene. We had no way of anticipating how well our bakery would be received. Even today, lines continue to snake out the door and around the corner of Tartine's modest space. As our work has matured, so too has the food world. People have come to expect quality ingredients innovatively prepared, drawing upon an ever-widening source of inspiration. The home kitchen, too, has become a different place. The divide that separated health from deliciousness has nearly disappeared. Fat is no longer the demon, salt no longer a dirty word. There's an understanding that food can be both healthful and flavorful and that a crucial step to cultivating wellness is creating a sense of richness out of elemental foods prepared with intention. Home cooking at its best seeks to strike a balance between everyday sustenance and celebratory foods, while spice, acid, and fermentation have become accessible tools for amping up taste. By wonderful coincidence, these very elements happen to make a food's nutritious qualities more available.

But it is not only the food world that has changed. In Tartine's tenure, San Francisco has become the hub of an international tech culture. The very role of technology looms larger than ever in our lives. And, while it has its many advantages, Chad and I are faced with the same quandary as all parents. We want to show our daughter, Archer, that the skills of generations gone by are still relevant today, and that in its own way, there can be as much collective knowledge in a loaf of bread as there is in a smartphone. By using our hands to prepare food for our family and friends, a cultural knowledge is transmitted that no technology can replicate.

Cultural knowledge—family history, where we live, and the influence of friends and others—informs and distinguishes every cookbook. In my case, I lean toward Middle Eastern cooking (having spent my childhood near Atlantic Avenue in Brooklyn, where my parents often browsed the spice-filled shops buying spinach and meat pies, baklava, and halvah). My grandmother was from Sweden and was a prolific baker. The flavors and foods I remember from her are cardamom, pickled herring, gravlax, and roasts. My father, being from Kentucky, brought fried chicken, preserves, and pickles to the culinary legacy that has been passed on to me.

That is where this book comes in. When I look at my bookshelves, what I want is an up-to-date, all-purpose cookbook that reflects this new landscape, an inspiring guide to integrating new ingredients and old techniques into the daily tempos of our busy lives. Between us, Chad and I have written three cookbooks. *Tartine All Day* marks a new kind of book for us: it is a collection of recipes that we like to cook every day. This book, an accumulation of the lessons learned by a working parent with decades of culinary experience, is a companion for every kind of cook. Years from now, I hope that it will be stained and dog-eared, appreciated most for the good food it helps to get on the table night after night. Let other books stack up on the bedside stand—this one belongs in the kitchen.

BASICS

GREMOLATA

Makes $\frac{1}{4}$ cup/10g

Gremolata is a classic Italian condiment of finely chopped lemon zest, parsley, and garlic. Depending on the dish you're finishing, you may substitute another bold ingredient for one of the three components or add it to the mix. Add horseradish to Gremolata when used to finish beef stew, for example, or capers when serving with grilled fish. Gremolata can be made in less than 5 minutes with ingredients you are likely to have on hand and adds a lovely flavor lift to both rich and simple dishes.

1 lemon

1 bunch flat-leaf parsley, leaves stripped from stems

2 cloves garlic, peeled

Pinch of sea salt

Finely grate the zest of the lemon into a small bowl. Finely chop the parsley and garlic. Add the parsley, garlic, and salt to the bowl and stir to blend. Use immediately.

AIOLI

Makes about $1\frac{1}{4}$ cups/300g

The necessary labor required to make aioli belies its utter simplicity, both in ingredients and presentation. If you're making it alone, there are a few tricks that can help, and the outcome is entirely worth the effort. Aioli, which comes from the Provençal words *ai,* meaning "garlic," and *oli,* meaning "oil," is traditionally used as the central condiment in a Grand Aioli, a Provençal meal at which blanched vegetables, potatoes, and salt cod are served. Aioli unites textures and flavors in anything from a complex seafood stew to simple summer tomatoes on toast. Traditionally it is made only of oil and garlic, and occasionally with egg. I sometimes like to add a splash of lemon juice or vinegar, which makes it more of a proper mayonnaise.

📖 Make sure that all of the ingredients are at room temperature.

📖 A good-quality olive oil is a must. Choose one that is mild and fruity, rather than a grassy or peppery oil. →

📖 Winter garlic will be stronger flavored than spring and summer garlic, so adjust the amount as necessary. If the cloves have little green germs in them (particularly in winter), remove them as they'll make the aioli sharper in flavor.

📖 Purists shy away from adding lemon juice or vinegar, but I tend to like a splash of either because a little acidity goes well with the richness of the sauce.

📖 To ease the whisking process, dampen a kitchen towel and place it under the bowl you are using to anchor it. Alternatively, use the traditional mortar and pestle (although your yield will be limited to the capacity of your mortar).

1 or 2 cloves garlic

Sea salt

1 large egg yolk, at room temperature

$\frac{2}{3}$ cup/160ml olive oil

$\frac{1}{3}$ cup/80ml neutral-flavored vegetable oil, such as safflower, sunflower, or grapeseed oil

1 to 2 tsp water, at room temperature, or more as needed (optional)

Splash of lemon juice or white vinegar (optional)

Place the garlic and a couple of pinches of salt in a mortar and pound with a pestle to make a smooth paste. Transfer to a bowl, add the egg yolk, and use a whisk or mortar to mix in a few drops of the olive oil. Continue whisking and adding the olive oil drop by drop until you have a thick mixture, and then gradually pour in the vegetable oil in a slow, thin stream. The finished sauce should have the same consistency as lightly whipped cream. If it gets thicker than that, you can thin it by adding water 1 tsp at a time until it reaches the desired consistency. Add the splash of lemon juice or vinegar and stir in. Taste and adjust the seasoning.

Store, tightly covered, in the refrigerator for up to 2 days.

BAGNA CAUDA

Makes about 1 cup/240ml

Literally translated, *bagna cauda* means "hot bath." This Piedmontese sauce of anchovy and garlic is an ingenious melding of ingredients that are warmed over low heat in olive oil and butter until melting, which may seem an unusual pair, but the butter smoothes the pungent edges perfectly. The traditional accompaniments of raw vegetables are sublime when dipped in the warm sauce, rich in cooked salty bits of fish and garlic. I love to make this when I have the first asparagus of the year, a head of Romanesco, or bright gypsy peppers. Bagna Cauda is also delicious drizzled over cooked greens, such as spigarello, broccoli rabe, or kale. Cooked beans, such as Scarlet Runner or navy beans, are equally good dressed with it. You could make a whole meal of boiled potatoes, Romano beans, and hard-cooked eggs, and good crusty bread with warm Bagna Cauda (made complete with a glass of a young Piedmontese wine).

📖 Make sure the garlic doesn't color while in the pan. If it does, an acrid flavor will permeate the sauce.

4 cloves garlic 8 olive oil- or salt-packed anchovies, rinsed $\frac{1}{2}$ tsp sea salt	Combine the garlic, anchovies, and salt in a mortar and pound to a paste using a pestle.
$\frac{3}{4}$ cup/180ml olive oil $\frac{1}{4}$ cup/60g unsalted butter	In a small saucepot, warm the oil and butter together over low heat. Once the butter has melted, stir in the garlic-anchovy paste and cook gently but not so long that the garlic sizzles. Serve warm or hot.
	Store, tightly covered, in the refrigerator for up to 5 days.

SALSA VERDE

Makes about $\frac{1}{2}$ cup/120ml

It amazes me how many seemingly simple dishes come alive when served with Salsa Verde. While some sauces are clearly best suited for either beef or fowl, pork or fish, this Italian standard seems to renounce categorization. Traditionally made with parsley, any number of herbs can be added to shift its flavors to best fit whatever you're pairing it with. If I were planning to serve it with chicken or fish, I might add tarragon. With lamb, oregano, marjoram, or mint would become the central herb. Salsa Verde brings out the inherent sweetness of grilled vegetables and even works alongside a fresh cheese, such as feta or mozzarella, with a summery tomato salad or an omelet; use it liberally and without hesitation. →

½ cup/10g flat-leaf parsley leaves, finely chopped

2 Tbsp chopped tender fresh herbs (such as tarragon, basil, sorrel, chervil, cilantro, or watercress)

½ cup/120ml olive oil, plus more as needed

1 small clove garlic, minced, or 1 Tbsp finely chopped shallot

1 Tbsp salt-packed capers, rinsed, chopped (optional)

Pinch of sea salt

Mix the parsley, the 2 Tbsp additional herbs, olive oil, garlic or shallot, capers, and salt together in a bowl with a wooden spoon. If the sauce is too thick to pour, add up to another ¼ cup/60ml olive oil.

Store, tightly covered, in the refrigerator for up to 5 days.

Basil Salsa Verde: Substitute ½ cup/10g basil leaves, finely chopped, for the parsley and use parsley instead of basil in the fresh herb mix.

CHIMICHURRI SAUCE

Makes about 2 cups/360ml

Chimichurri is the herbaceous green sauce found throughout Argentina and Uruguay. Its name is said to originate from the Basques who settled there in the nineteenth century and translates to "a mixture of several things in no particular order." Because it traditionally calls for oregano and has the addition of a fresh or dried chile, chimichurri is earthier and more piquant than Salsa Verde (page 13) and punches up the inherent flavors of rich foods, such as beef or lamb. Try it with corona beans (page 172) or alongside grilled steak, roasted chicken, or even 9-minute hard-cooked eggs (see Mollet Eggs, page 92) for a quick, satiating snack.

I've recently started adding the salt to a small amount of water, effectively making a brine, which is a trick I learned from Francis Mallmann, the Argentinian chef known for his Patagonian open-fire barbecues. Adding the brine keeps the color vibrant, while also seasoning the sauce. →

1 cup/20g flat-leaf parsley leaves	Finely chop the herbs and place them in a medium bowl.
$\frac{1}{4}$ cup/5g cilantro leaves	
$\frac{1}{4}$ cup/5g oregano leaves	
1 Tbsp finely chopped shallot or onion	Add the shallot or onion, garlic, pequin chiles or jalapeño or red pepper flakes, olive oil, and red wine vinegar. In a separate bowl, combine the salt and water and stir until the salt has dissolved. Stir the salt water into the olive oil mixture.
3 cloves garlic, minced	
2 pequin chiles or $\frac{1}{2}$ jalapeño, finely chopped, or $\frac{1}{2}$ tsp red pepper flakes	
$\frac{3}{4}$ cup/180ml olive oil	
$\frac{1}{4}$ cup/60ml red wine vinegar	
$\frac{3}{4}$ tsp sea salt	
$\frac{1}{2}$ cup/120g hot water	
	Store, covered, in the refrigerator for up to 5 days.

YOGURT SAUCE

Makes $\frac{1}{2}$ cup/120ml

Yogurt's natural sourness pairs well with lemon, garlic, and salt to make a sauce that cools a dish and cuts through richness, as it does for Roasted Baby Eggplant (page 182), Spatchcocked Roasted Chicken (page 228), and Lamb Kofta (page 245).

$\frac{1}{2}$ cup (4 oz)/115g Greek yogurt	In a small bowl, mix together the yogurt, garlic, lemon juice, and salt. Add the water and stir in more, 1 tsp at a time to thin, until the sauce drizzles when spooned. Serve immediately.
1 clove garlic, minced	
1 Tbsp lemon juice	
Pinch of sea salt	
1 tsp water, or more as needed	
	Store, covered, in the refrigerator for up to 3 days.

TZATZIKI

Makes about 2 cups/360ml

This traditional Greek sauce of cucumber, yogurt, and dill (which also works as a dip) can be used in endless ways—alongside fresh tomatoes, grilled eggplant, a bowl of chickpeas, or roast lamb, to name a few. Cucumbers and yogurt are a natural pair as they are both cooling, and the crunch of the cucumber contrasts nicely with the creaminess of yogurt. Because cucumbers retain so much water, it's necessary to salt the grated cucumber beforehand to draw out the excess moisture. Use Tzatziki to sauce Leg of Lamb (page 279) or Lamb Kofta (page 245) or as a dip for vegetables or pita bread.

1 large cucumber (about 10 oz/280g)

$\frac{1}{4}$ tsp sea salt

Using the large holes of a box grater, grate the cucumber. Sprinkle the salt over the cucumber and set aside for about 10 minutes. Wring out the moisture with your hands.

1 clove garlic, minced

Pinch of black pepper

1 cup (8 oz)/230g Greek yogurt

2 Tbsp flat-leaf parsley, finely chopped

3 Tbsp fresh dill, finely chopped

2 tsp white wine vinegar or lemon juice

3 Tbsp olive oil

In a serving bowl, combine the garlic, black pepper, yogurt, parsley, dill, vinegar or lemon juice, and olive oil. Add the cucumber, mix it in well, and serve.

Store, covered, in the refrigerator for up to 3 days.

TOMATILLO SALSA

Makes 2½ cups/590ml

Tomatillos resemble small green tomatoes, but while they're in the same nightshade family, they're even more closely related to Cape gooseberries, another husk-covered fruit. When you roast half of the tomatillos and leave the other half raw, you end up with a more vibrant, fresh sauce but still have the smooth texture and good, charred flavor from the roasted ones. This salsa is often served in tacos with carnitas, but try it with poached eggs or tri-tip. Tomatillos are used in braising liquid, too, so this salsa could also be spooned over chicken or pork for braising.

📖 Tomatillos are high in pectin. If there is salsa left over, it may become thick once refrigerated. Just let it come to room temperature, give it a good stir, and it should return to its more liquid consistency. An extra squeeze of lime always gives leftover salsa a fresh, bright flavor.

1 lb/455g tomatillos, husked and halved

½ large white onion or 1 small onion, cut into 1-inch/2.5cm pieces

2 cloves garlic

½ jalapeño, seeded

2 Tbsp olive oil

½ tsp sea salt

Preheat the oven to 450°F/230°C. Toss half of the tomatillos, onion, garlic, jalapeño, olive oil, and salt in a bowl. Spread the mixture on a sheet pan in a single layer and roast in the oven until the tomatillos are soft and a little charred on top, about 10 minutes. Transfer the mixture to a blender, add the rest of the tomatillos, and blend until broken down and chunky (that is, not too finely). Transfer the salsa to a serving bowl.

½ lime

Pinch of sea salt

½ bunch cilantro, coarsely chopped

Squeeze the lime over the salsa. Stir in the lime juice, salt, and cilantro, and serve.

Store in the refrigerator, covered, for up to 3 days.

Tomatillo-Avocado Salsa: Add ½ avocado, scooped out in coarse chunks, to the blender along with the roasted vegetables. This variation is best eaten the day it is made because the avocado will discolor when stored overnight.

SPICED NUT-DATE SAUCE

Makes 1 cup/250g

This sweet, nutty condiment was inspired by a very fond food memory of a trip to Paris with Chad more than twenty years ago. We visited a friend there whose grandmother made legendary *b'steeya* (Moroccan pastry stuffed with spiced meat). Our friend's grandmother shipped her frozen packages of it. It was the balance of sweetness, spice, and rich flavor from the meat (traditionally pigeon) that I wanted to re-create without the lengthy process of making pastry to envelop it all. Serve it with lamb, duck or other game birds, turkey, or pork. Because the sauce is thick rather than runny, it also makes an unexpected and delicious contribution to a cheese plate, particularly with a tangy sheep's milk cheese or nutty Gouda.

$\frac{1}{2}$ cup/70g almonds, toasted, coarsely chopped

$\frac{1}{4}$ cup/30g pine nuts, toasted

4 dates, pitted, cut into $\frac{1}{3}$-inch/8mm pieces

1 Tbsp sesame seeds, lightly toasted

1 Tbsp honey

$\frac{1}{4}$ to $\frac{1}{2}$ tsp hot sauce

4 grinds black peppercorns

1 Tbsp plus 2 tsp sherry vinegar or apple cider vinegar

2 Tbsp olive oil

Pinch of ground cinnamon

Pinch of sea salt

Combine the almonds, pine nuts, dates, sesame seeds, honey, hot sauce, peppercorns, sherry vinegar or apple cider vinegar, olive oil, cinnamon, and salt in a bowl and mix well. Serve at room temperature.

Store, covered, in the refrigerator for up to 5 days.

BUTTERMILK-HERB DRESSING

Makes about 1 cup/240ml

On a hot day, when you want something more substantial than a vinaigrette and less involved than a composed salad, cool and crunchy romaine with this tangy dressing hits the spot. Or serve breaded and pan-fried or grilled fish with a wedge of lemon on the side and a spoonful of this dressing, to which I add an additional handful of parsley, chervil, or tarragon.

📖 This is not an exact formula. Any combination of cultured dairy, including crème fraîche, sour cream, yogurt (Greek or plain full-fat), or buttermilk, and herbs will be delicious, so use what you have on hand. If using Greek yogurt, the mixture may be perfectly thick for a dip but a little stiff for a dressing. If this is the case, thin the dressing with 1 to 2 tsp of water or a mixture of water and lemon juice.

$\frac{1}{4}$ cup/60g mayonnaise

$\frac{1}{2}$ cup/120ml buttermilk

$\frac{1}{3}$ cup/7g tender herbs (such as flat-leaf parsley, thyme, chervil, tarragon, carrot tops, or any combination), chopped

1 Tbsp minced shallot or yellow onion

1 Tbsp lemon juice

Pinch of red pepper flakes

Sea salt

Ground black pepper

Combine the mayonnaise, buttermilk, herbs, shallot or onion, lemon juice, and red pepper flakes in a bowl. Mix well, and then taste and season with salt and pepper to your liking. Serve chilled or at room temperature.

Store in an airtight container in the refrigerator for up to 1 week.

LEMON-GARLIC-HERB DRESSING

Makes about ¾ cup/180ml

I make this dressing to accompany the Seafood Salad (page 219) and the Dark Leafy Greens (page 168). With a piquant and savory balance, this is a dressing to make often, varying the herb depending on the application. The relative plainness of a potato salad would brighten when dressed with this, and if I were serving it with fish or chicken, I might shift the flavors by replacing the marjoram with dill or parsley. Spooned over roasted vegetables or even added to cooked grains, such as rice or farro, this would banish the quotidian from any dish.

3 Tbsp lemon juice, plus more as needed

½ cup/120ml olive oil

1 or 2 cloves garlic, thinly sliced

2 tsp fresh marjoram leaves, coarsely chopped

½ medium shallot, thinly sliced

Sea salt and ground black pepper

In a small bowl, whisk the lemon juice into the olive oil, and then whisk in the garlic, marjoram, and shallot. Season with salt and pepper to taste, adding more lemon juice if you like. Serve at room temperature.

Store, covered, in the refrigerator for up to 5 days.

GREENEST GODDESS DRESSING AND DIP

Makes 2½ cups/600ml

I'd always thought that green goddess salad dressing was so named for its reliance upon an abundance of tender, bright green herbs but, in fact, it was created at the San Francisco Palace Hotel in 1923, after a popular play of that era, *The Green Goddess*. Similar to other creamy dressings, it is made with half mayonnaise and half sour cream or yogurt and a large amount of herbs, chief among them being tarragon, a woefully underused herb. The aniselike tarragon and chives or scallions lend a mild bite. I add a ripe avocado to my version; the traditional recipe is the same as mine but without the avocado. This verdant, refreshing dressing is perfect on crunchy romaine lettuce, but it can also be served as a dip for crudité or boiled, roasted, or fried potatoes and roasted chicken.

📖 Carrot tops are too often tossed away, but when they are tender they are quite delicious raw, their flavor being somewhere between parsley, lovage, and carrots themselves. If you're without tender carrot tops, just add more parsley, chervil, or a combination of both to equal 3 Tbsp total. The remaining herbs (tarragon and parsley) can be replaced with other tender green herbs you have on hand, such as basil, dill, or chervil.

$\frac{3}{4}$ cup/180g mayonnaise or Aioli (page 10)

$\frac{3}{4}$ cup/180g sour cream or Greek yogurt

3 Tbsp finely chopped tarragon

$\frac{1}{4}$ cup/5g finely chopped flat-leaf parsley

2 Tbsp finely chopped chives or scallions

Juice of 1 lemon

2 olive oil- or salt-packed anchovies, rinsed, finely chopped

1 ripe avocado, halved, pitted, peeled, and cut into quarters

3 Tbsp finely chopped carrot tops

$\frac{1}{4}$ tsp sea salt

Ground black pepper

Combine the mayonnaise, sour cream or yogurt, tarragon, parsley, chives or scallions, lemon juice, and anchovies, avocado, carrot tops, and salt in a blender and blend until smooth. Taste and adjust the seasoning, adding pepper to taste. Serve immediately.

Store in a jar with a tight-fitting lid in the refrigerator for up to 1 week.

APPLESAUCE

Makes 5 cups/1.2kg

Like chicken stock, applesauce is always remarkably better when made at home. Apples range from tart to candy sweet, so I've included a small amount of both lemon juice and sugar to balance the flavors. It's important to taste as you season, finding just the right amount of lemon juice and sugar to amplify the apple taste. Salt is by no means necessary, but just a pinch enhances. When serving applesauce with pork—a winning pair—I prefer it to be chunkier, so I just let it cook without mashing. Fully pureed, it is a wonderful baby food (minus the sugar), and left chunky, served with cool unsweetened cream, it makes a comforting dessert. The apples in homemade applesauce retain more of their subtlety and floral characteristics and show the differences of the apple varieties that are hard to distinguish in commercially made sauce.

📖 I generally favor using a mix of tart and sweet apple varieties to build flavor and complexity. I often include a few Granny Smiths for their acidity, and then I grab whatever else appeals—Fuji, Gala, Golden Delicious, Gravenstein, Jonathan, Pink Lady, or Pippin. Were I to choose just one apple for saucemaking, it would be Pink Lady, which has wonderful flavor and a good balance between sweetness and acidity. However, it is really interesting and worth the experiment to try one variety at a time and taste the characteristics of each variety.

📖 Consider using this in Spiced Apple-Walnut Cake (page 300), instead of the apples, but use it prior to pureeing, when the fruit is still in bigger chunks.

1 cup/240ml water

3 to 4 lb/1.3 to 1.8kg apples (about 8 large), peeled, cored, cut into eighths

2 to 3 Tbsp/45ml lemon juice, or more as needed

$\frac{1}{4}$ cup/50g granulated sugar, or more as needed

1 cinnamon stick (optional)

$\frac{1}{4}$ tsp sea salt (optional)

Combine the water, apples, lemon juice, sugar, cinnamon stick, and salt in a large pot and bring to a boil. Decrease the heat to low, cover the pot and simmer for 30 to 40 minutes, until the apple pieces are tender and some are falling apart. →

Remove and discard the cinnamon stick. For a very chunky sauce, mash with a potato masher. If you prefer a smoother sauce, use an immersion blender or transfer to a blender and blend to desired smoothness or just process partially, depending on your preference. If transferring to a blender, blend the hot applesauce in 2 or 3 batches, filling the blender no more than halfway and taking care not to burn yourself.

Taste for sweetness and add more sugar accordingly; if the sweetness needs to be balanced, add a little more lemon juice.

Let cool, and then store, covered, in the refrigerator for up to 10 days.

Pear Applesauce: Use pears for up to half of the apples.

SAUTÉED APPLES

Makes 2 cups/380g

I make these apples to pair with the Buckwheat Dutch Baby (page 83), but they just as easily complement savory foods, particularly roasted or sautéed pork. While Applesauce (page 27) and Apple Butter (page 60) are classic accompaniments to pork, I love the texture and relative speed of a quick sauté.

📖 I like to use a combination of tart and sweet apples. Pink Lady apples are a favorite, but use whatever you have on hand. Golden Russets get applesauce-soft with just a little cooking and are nice and tart.

📖 Leaving on the apples' skins heightens the flavor and adds texture, unless the apples have been stored for a long time, which toughens their skins. Peel them if that's the case.

2 Tbsp unsalted butter	Melt the butter in a 10-inch/25cm heavy-bottomed pan with a lid over medium heat. Add the apples so they are in a single layer on the bottom of the pan.
2 cups/200g coarsely chopped apples (2 apples), skin on	
Pinch of sea salt	Add the salt and apple cider or water. Cover the pot and increase the heat to high. Cook for 2 to 3 minutes and then check for doneness. The apples should be cooked all the way through, with a soft texture easily pierced by a fork. If necessary, continue cooking, adding a splash more apple cider or water if it has fully evaporated, and turning the apples over.
3 Tbsp apple cider or water, plus more as needed	
2 Tbsp maple syrup or honey	When the apples are cooked completely, drizzle with the maple syrup or honey and gently stir to coat evenly. Remove from the heat and serve immediately.

ROMESCO SAUCE

Makes 1¾ cups/410g

This Catalonian sauce is named after the romesco pepper, which when dried, forms the basis of this piquant mixture of nuts and pepper. The romesco pepper is difficult to find, so a combination of roasted red peppers and Spanish paprika can take its place. As often happens with regional specialties, there are as many versions as there are cooks. Romesco can be made with almonds or hazelnuts or both. Garlic, olive oil, and bread add dimension and body, and sherry vinegar adds acidity. This sauce most famously accompanies grilled calçots—wintered-over onions that are something between a scallion and a leek—during the Catalonian calçotada festivals in early spring. Delicious with grilled vegetables of any kind, romesco is also a natural with shellfish, calamari, fish, or lamb.

📖 The garlic becomes more pronounced as the romesco sits, so I use 2 cloves if I'm going to use it within an hour or two. If I am not using the sauce right away, I use just 1 clove. Of course, if you prefer a robust garlic flavor, you can always add more after the sauce has had a chance to settle. →

2 large red peppers, roasted, peeled, seeds and stem removed, or 1 (8 oz/225g) jar roasted red peppers, drained

$\frac{1}{4}$ cup/30g hazelnuts, toasted, chopped

$\frac{1}{4}$ cup/35g almonds, toasted, chopped

1 or 2 cloves garlic, peeled

1 ($\frac{1}{2}$-inch/12mm-thick) slice of baguette, toasted, cut into chunks (optional)

Combine the roasted peppers, hazelnuts, almonds, garlic, and bread in the bowl of a food processor fitted with a metal blade. Blend until combined but still slightly chunky.

5 Tbsp/75ml olive oil

1 Tbsp sherry vinegar

1 tsp sweet Spanish paprika (pimentón dulce)

1 tsp sea salt, plus more as needed

Add the olive oil, vinegar, paprika, and salt to the pepper mixture and blend to incorporate. Taste and adjust the seasoning to your liking, adding more salt as needed. Serve at room temperature.

Store, covered, in the refrigerator for up to 5 days.

QUICK TOMATO SAUCE

Makes about 3 cups/720ml

A tomato sauce made from quality canned tomatoes is one of those few additions to a meal that for some reason seems perfectly okay coming from a can, like sardines and coconut milk. This sauce is quickly made with pantry ingredients and ready to go on pasta, polenta, or the Ricotta Dumplings on page 214. Add torn pieces of fresh basil just before serving, or a pinch of red pepper flakes (or a whole, dried pepper) if you like some heat.

2 Tbsp olive oil

$\frac{1}{2}$ large yellow onion, finely diced

$\frac{1}{2}$ tsp sea salt

Heat the olive oil in a medium saucepan over medium heat. Add the onion and salt and cook, stirring often, until translucent, 4 to 5 minutes. Take care to not let the onion brown. →

2 cloves garlic, sliced	Add the garlic and sauté for 1 to 2 minutes, until softened but not at all browned.
1 bay leaf 1 (28 oz/800g) can crushed tomatoes	Add the bay leaf and tomatoes and cook for about 10 minutes. Taste and add more salt, if needed. Cook for 30 minutes more for deeper flavor.
Fresh basil leaves, torn (optional) Pinch of red pepper flakes (optional)	Stir in the basil leaves and season with the red pepper flakes just before serving.
	Store, covered, in the refrigerator for up to 5 days.
	Rich Tomato Sauce: For a version inspired by one of Marcella Hazan's sauces, halve the onion and add it plus 5 Tbsp/70g unsalted butter (omitting the olive oil) to the tomatoes and cook for 45 minutes.

CHICKEN STOCK

Makes 6 qt/5.7L

Classically speaking, there are two kinds of chicken stock: a light stock, made from a whole chicken that is boiled for a couple of hours at most, and a dark stock, for which bones are roasted and then simmered for at least several hours, producing a richer broth. Both have their place in cooking. The recipes in this book call only for a light stock. Because the entire bird is cooked, the stock is slightly more gelatinous than a bone-only one.

📖 To allow the water to penetrate bones and cartilage more easily, I cut up the bird before cooking, but you could ask your butcher to do the same.

📖 If I am planning to use the meat afterward, I'll remove the breast from the pot as soon as it is fully cooked, so it doesn't become tough and dried out. Combined with the remaining dark meat (which withstands longer cooking), the breast meat can be used for any chicken salad or soup. I particularly like to use this meat in the Chicken–Celery Root Salad (page 163).

1 whole chicken (about 3 lb/1.4kg), cut into large pieces

3 stalks celery with tops, coarsely chopped

3 carrots, coarsely chopped

1 yellow onion, quartered

4 to 6 sprigs thyme

1 bay leaf

1 $\frac{1}{2}$ tsp sea salt

1 tsp black peppercorns

Fill a large stockpot with cold water and add the chicken, celery, carrots, onion, thyme, bay leaf, salt, and peppercorns. Over medium heat, bring to a gentle boil and then decrease to low heat and simmer. After approximately 15 minutes, remove the chicken breasts and set aside to cool, while the stock continues to cook, approximately 2 hours longer. Remove the pot from the heat and let the ingredients cool to room temperature.

Place a colander over a large bowl and strain the stock into the bowl, reserving the meat and vegetables in the colander. Transfer the bowl to the refrigerator for 2 hours or up to overnight. Meanwhile remove the chicken meat from the bones and reserve for another use.

When completely cool, skim any fat off the surface and then use the stock.

Store, tightly covered, in the refrigerator for up to 7 days or in the freezer for up to 3 months.

RICOTTA CHEESE

Makes about 1 cup/240g

Ricotta, literally meaning "recooked," refers to its Italian origins as a fresh cheese made from whey, the by-product of milk making. When whey is heated and an acid is introduced, it forms the soft curds of ricotta. Italy's ricotta, whether from cow's or sheep's milk, is perhaps the most famous whey cheese and is made all over the world as an ingenious way to waste nothing. Many people use buttermilk or cream to make ricotta or even whole milk, as this home version does. The distilled vinegar might seem very strong, but it does its curdling job and then leaves the ricotta during the draining step. →

When I want to use the ricotta for a dessert, I generally use lemon juice; for all other uses, I use vinegar. Serve the ricotta on toast, drizzled with honey and olive oil and seasoned with black pepper, alongside dressed arugula, or in a classic lasagna or in a cake (such as the Cornmeal-Ricotta Upside-Down Cake, page 305).

📖 Ultra-pasteurized milk (also known as UHT pasteurized) is not recommended for making ricotta, because it will not curdle as easily as flash pasteurized. To make a creamier (nontraditional) ricotta, add $\frac{3}{4}$ cup/180ml cream to the milk. If using buttermilk as the acid agent, use $\frac{1}{2}$ cup/120ml.

📖 The draining time depends on how you plan to use the ricotta. If eating the cheese fresh, briefly drain for only 5 minutes. If making ravioli or lasagna, the ricotta should be drier, so drain it for at least 1 hour and up to overnight. The cheese, once refrigerated, will separate like yogurt does, forming a pool of whey on the surface. Just stir it back in, or if you want drier cheese, pour off the surface liquid. To drain, set a colander over a large bowl and line the colander with several layers of dampened cheesecloth. (Alternatively, you can use a fine-mesh strainer set over a large bowl.)

1 qt/1L whole milk

$\frac{1}{4}$ cup/60ml distilled white vinegar, white wine vinegar, lemon juice, or $\frac{1}{2}$ tsp citric acid dissolved in 1 Tbsp hot water

$\frac{1}{2}$ tsp sea salt

Combine the milk, vinegar or lemon juice or citric acid, and salt in a medium saucepan and heat until the liquid reaches 165°F/74°C. Curds will begin to form before the mixture reaches 165°F/74°C, but the whey will still look milky. The ricotta is ready when the whey is a translucent, pale yellow, and there is a pronounced separation of curds and whey.

Let the mixture sit undisturbed off the heat for 3 to 5 minutes. Line a fine-mesh strainer with cheesecloth and set the strainer over a bowl. Pour the mixture into the strainer and set aside to drain as long as needed for the planned use. Drain for 5 minutes if serving immediately. For spreadable, small curds, which are ideal for filling pasta, drain for 1 hour. For dry, crumbly curds to use in cake batter, drain overnight.

The ricotta can be used after draining or covered and stored in the refrigerator for up to 5 days.

CREAM CHEESE DOUGH

Makes enough for 2 (9-inch/23cm or 10-inch/25cm) single-crust pie, or one double-crust pie

This is a favorite all-purpose dough, inspired by a classic rugelach, in which cream cheese combines with butter to make an extra pliable and slightly tangy dough. Rugelach is an Ashkenazi Jewish sweet with roots in Eastern Europe. The dough is usually spread with a filling of raisins or nuts and rolled into crescents. Because the dough is half the treat and is meant to be both tender and durable, I saw the potential for a gluten-free version to become a successful all-purpose pastry. I credit gluten-free cook and author Shauna James Ahern for the basic ratio of flours in this recipe, which is a blend that I've found works best for a variety of uses. Given its versatility, it is a dough that I find myself using again and again—a go-to for pies, galettes, bars, and even savory pastries.

$\frac{3}{4}$ cup plus 1 Tbsp/115g brown rice flour

$\frac{1}{3}$ cup/60g potato starch

$\frac{1}{2}$ cup/60g tapioca flour/starch

1 $\frac{1}{2}$ cups/180g oat flour

In the bowl of a food processor fitted with the metal blade, combine the brown rice flour, potato starch, tapioca flour/starch, and oat flour. Blend to mix well.

1 cup (8 oz)/227g cream cheese, very cold

1 cup/220g unsalted butter, very cold, cut into $\frac{1}{4}$-inch-/6mm-thick slices

1 tsp sea salt

Add the cream cheese, butter, and salt. Pulse approximately 15 times and then let the food processor run just until the dough begins to come together in a ball but is not completely smooth, about 20 seconds. You should still be able to see some butter and cream cheese chunks.

Divide the dough into 2 equal balls and shape each ball into a disk about 1 inch/2.5cm thick. Wrap well in plastic wrap and chill for at least 2 hours or for up to overnight.

Cornstarch or tapioca flour/starch, for rolling

To roll out, place a dough disk on a surface lightly dusted with cornstarch or tapioca flour/starch. Roll to $\frac{1}{8}$ inch/3mm thick, rolling from the center evenly out in all directions. Dust with additional cornstarch or tapioca flour/starch as needed to discourage sticking. Cut out a circle or rectangle 2 inches/5cm larger than the pan the recipe calls for. Carefully lift and transfer to the pan, easing the dough into the bottom and sides. Do not stretch or press too firmly, or it will shrink during baking. If the dough tears, just patch it, pressing gently to adhere. Trim the dough level with the top of the pan. (Leftover dough scraps can be frozen for future use or used as a simple cookie dough.) Place the dough shell in the refrigerator to chill for 15 minutes.

Preheat the oven to 325°F/165°C.

Using a fork, prick the bottom of the dough shell approximately every 2 inches/5cm. For a partially baked shell, bake for 5 to 10 minutes, depending on the size of the dough shell, until lightly golden and dry. For a fully baked shell, continue baking for an additional 5 to 7 minutes, until golden brown.

Let the baked shell cool completely on a wire rack before filling or storing.

The pastry shell will keep, well wrapped, for up to 1 week in the refrigerator or for up to 2 weeks in the freezer.

CRÈME FRAÎCHE

Makes 2 cups/480g

Start this recipe a day before you plan to use the crème fraîche. In the early days of Tartine Bakery, crème fraîche was one of the first cultured products we made ourselves. We use it in our quiche →

recipe, which I learned to do while working in France. Like buttermilk in panna cotta or lemon in ice cream, crème fraîche's acidity cuts through richness, making a dish more complex and satisfying. A main difference between crème fraîche and its American cousin, sour cream, is that its fat content is higher and therefore it can be cooked without curdling. Along with Gravlax (page 120), dark bread, and thin slices of onion, it makes a satisfying meal. When making a quick pan sauce after sautéing pork chops or fish, a spoonful of crème fraîche added to the reducing wine will thicken the sauce slightly and amplify the sauce's flavors.

📖 Long before pasteurization, crème fraîche was made with raw cream. If you have access to raw cream and feel comfortable using it, the live beneficial bacteria still present in the cream will accelerate the culturing process. Flash-pasteurized milk or cream is just called pasteurized while UHT pasteurized containers are labeled as such.

2 cups/480ml heavy cream (preferably pasteurized, not ultra-pasteurized)

2 generous Tbsp buttermilk or store-bought crème fraîche

Pour the cream into a nonreactive container with a lid. (If you use a canning jar, use a 1½-pt/700ml jar, because a pint jar will be filled to the brim.) Stir in the buttermilk or crème fraîche, cover with cheesecloth or a porous clean kitchen towel, and let rest at room temperature, between 60°F/15°C and 75°F/24°C, out of direct sunlight, for 8 to 24 hours. Check periodically to see if the mixture has thickened and a slight skin has formed on top. If you used Jersey cream, this skin might have a perfectly normal yellowish tint. The cultures will be more active and transform the cream more quickly in a warmer environment, but if the room is too hot or humid (above 80°F/26°C), the cream may spoil and will smell more like milk that has gone bad than like yogurt.

Once the crème fraîche has reached a consistency comparable to that of regular cow's milk yogurt (not quite as thick as Greek-style yogurt), stir well to incorporate the top layer, cover with a lid, and refrigerate. Crème fraîche will keep in the refrigerator for up to 10 days.

PRESERVED LEMONS

Makes 2 (1-pt/450g) jars

I find it miraculous that only two ingredients—lemons and salt—can make everything taste a hundred times better. Preserved lemons have a long history in Moroccan cuisine, in which their peels infuse the famed tagines with a distinctly soft lemon flavor that is not at all sour. Their natural season is winter. Preserving them in salt allowed cooks of earlier times to relish them throughout the year. While some recipes call for flavorings, such as bay leaf or coriander, I prefer to leave mine plain. To preserve lemons takes little active time, but a few weeks of waiting. Slice preserved lemons thinly on top of poached eggs, yogurt, or a bowl of black beans, or mince and stir into chickpeas or add to lamb tagine; and you'll lighten the savory flavors of each dish.

📖 No matter the variety of lemon, the preserved peel will taste superb. Meyer lemons, however, with their thinner skins, require less time and should be checked for doneness after 2 weeks. Organic lemons are preferable, because you'll be eating the fruit's exterior. You can tell they are done by their uniform soft texture and easily sliced peels.

📖 In the professional kitchen, we use everything until there's nothing left to use. The by-products of these lemons are no exception. The pulp of the preserved lemons can be used to marinate fish. The salty lemon juice in the jar can be reused to make the next batch of preserved lemons. It's also delicious in a cocktail.

8 to 10 lemons, scrubbed	Cut each lemon vertically from one pointed end to within $\frac{1}{2}$ inch/12mm of the other end, almost cutting the fruit into quarters but leaving it attached at the bottom.
$\frac{3}{4}$ **cup/110g sea salt** **Lemon juice, as needed to cover**	Rub about 1 Tbsp of the salt over the cut surfaces of each lemon, then reshape the fruits and pack them tightly into two 1-pt/480ml jars, pressing down to release the lemon juice. Sprinkle a little more salt between the lemons as you add them to the jar. If the lemons are not completely submerged in their own juices when packed in the jars, add lemon juice to cover. →

Close the jars with tight-fitting lids and set them aside at cool room temperature (between 60°F/15°C and 70°F/21°C) for 3 to 4 weeks, shaking the jars to redistribute the salt every day or so. The lemons are done preserving when the peels have softened and can be easily pierced with a fork. Transfer the jars to the refrigerator until ready to use.

To cook with preserved lemon, simply rinse the fruit under cool running water. Scrape out and discard the pulp or reserve it for another use. Thinly slice the peel and add to your dish.

Store the jarred preserved lemons in the refrigerator for up to 1 year.

Preserved Lemons with Fennel: For anise-scented preserved lemons, pack a fennel frond or two (I use wild fennel) into the jars with the lemon and salt.

PRESERVED QUINCE

Makes 6 (8 oz/225g) jars

This recipe came about as a way to make use of the fruit leftover from making quince jelly. I wanted to find a new use for this underused fruit, the pulp of which still retains its particular scent even after it is used to make jelly. One might turn this remaining fruit into *membrillo* (Spanish quince paste), though I prefer to use the whole fruit to make it pectin rich. Adding a little black pepper, wine, and vinegar is a quick way to make a fall/winter preserve to go with game birds, chicken with Indian spices, cheese, pâté, pork, and, of course, lamb, its frequent companion in many classic Middle Eastern and Moroccan recipes.

Like little pieces of core left on baked apples, quince inevitably have tough spots on their flesh that remain hard even after cooking. Be sure to run your fingers along the surface of the cooked segments to feel for any hard spots, and remove them with a paring knife. Don't try to do this before cooking, when the hard spots are more difficult to find and remove.

2 3/4 lb/1.25kg cooked and strained quince from making Quince Jelly (page 58)

Trim any tough spots so that all the fruit is uniformly soft and perfect looking.

To prepare the jars and lids, preheat the oven to 250°F/120°C. Wash the jars and lids with hot, soapy water and set on a rimmed baking sheet. Place in the oven for at least 10 minutes and up to 1 hour.

2 cups/480ml water

2/3 cup/200g quince jelly

5 Tbsp/75ml apple cider vinegar

1/2 cup/120ml dry rosé or white wine

1/2 cup/100g granulated sugar

3 to 5 grinds black peppercorns

Pinch of sea salt

Combine the quince, water, quince jelly, apple cider vinegar, dry rosé or white wine, sugar, pepper, and salt in a preserving pan or large, heavy-bottomed saucepan. Bring to a simmer and cook for 15 minutes.

When the quince is ready, carefully transfer the fruit and syrup to the hot, sterilized jars, leaving 1/4-inch/6mm headspace. Wipe the jar rims with a clean, dampened towel and close the jars with the hot, sterilized lids. Place the jars upright in a large stockpot of water, adding more water as needed to cover the jars by at least 2 inches/5cm. Bring the water to a boil. Leave the jars in the boiling water to process for 10 minutes. Lift the jars out of the water and set them to cool in a protected spot where they will not be moved or bumped for 12 hours.

Check the seal of each jar. Any jars that did not seal should be transferred to the refrigerator and eaten within 2 weeks. Label the jars that did seal and store in a cool, dark place for up to 1 year. Once opened, store in the refrigerator and eat within 2 weeks.

5-DAY SAUERKRAUT

Makes about 6 cups/1.35kg (three 1-qt/960ml jars or crocks)

With just a little practice, I've learned that making sauerkraut is not at all difficult—once you know what's most important in the process. Make sure that the brine covers the sauerkraut completely, preventing any exposure to air. *Lactobacilli,* the beneficial bacteria that make sauerkraut what it is, thrive in an anaerobic environment. Their proliferation gives sauerkraut its characteristic tang and makes the kraut acidic enough so that harmful bacteria cannot survive. Store your sauerkraut in a cool place as it ferments. If its temperature is too warm, pectin-digesting enzymes will activate, and the sauerkraut will taste vinegary and will lose its crunch. I make many sauerkraut variations, but this is the basic one that I return to again and again. The carrots add a hint of sweetness, and leaving them in larger pieces makes them a treat to eat, like a pickle. If you can get your hands on multicolored carrots, use them, as they tint the neighboring cabbages and juice a beautiful sunset orange. Adding caraway seeds is classic, although they are an acquired taste for some kids.

While there are crocks made for fermenting, any large jar can be used. If you are using a jar, do not tighten the lid. Carbon dioxide needs to be able to escape once the fermentation begins, or the jar could explode. Alternatively, a kitchen towel or piece of wax paper may be loosely tied around the top. There are jars and crocks specifically designed so that carbon dioxide can escape without allowing any oxygen in, but these are unnecessary for the occasional fermenter. I most often use a jar with a lid when I don't want to make a huge batch of sauerkraut.

Five days is the minimum amount of time for fermenting, at which point you will have a fresh "green" sauerkraut. Let it go longer and see when you like it the most. Two to three weeks of fermentation creates a lovely kraut with well-developed flavors. There are so many variables, including the strength of the brine, how finely cut your vegetables or cabbage are, and the temperature of the room. There are jars in my refrigerator that I started last year that are more and more delicious each time I try them. Once they are refrigerated, →

fermentation does continue but at a snail's pace. If you want to know more after making this simple sauerkraut, I highly recommend *The Art of Fermentation* by Sandor Katz for an in-depth guide to fermenting, with recipes and methods from around the world.

📖 Use 1½ to 2 tsp salt per 1 lb/455g of cabbage or vegetables. Additional brine ratio (if you need more to submerge cabbage): Use ¾ to 1 tsp salt per 1 cup/240ml water.

📖 The best temperature is under 70°F/21°C. If you are in a warm climate, check the fermentation after a few days and reduce the fermentation period as needed.

📖 After the jar is filled with the salted cabbage (and extra brine if necessary) place a large cabbage leaf on top and weigh it down with a small plate, ramekin, or a smaller jar filled with water or pie weights (this is particularly effective for a widemouthed Mason jar). The force of the weight should bring the brine level just above the top cabbage leaf. Very lightly twist on the lid or loosely drape cheesecloth or a clean kitchen towel over the opening so that air can escape but nothing can contaminate the cabbage. If the top layer of cabbage develops an off-flavor or mold, just remove it and replace the weight to weigh down the remaining cabbage.

📖 1½ lb/680g cabbage fills a 1-qt/960ml jar with enough space left to weigh down the top.

1 large or 2 small heads (4 lb/1.8kg) white cabbage	Discard any dried or damaged outer leaves from the cabbages. Remove 4 or 5 large, fresh leaves and set aside for later use. Cut each cabbage in half, remove and discard the core, and then cut each half in half. Working with one-quarter at a time, slice the cabbage into ¼-inch/6mm-wide strips and place in a large bowl.
5 small or 2 large/ 500g carrots	Cut the carrots lengthwise and then crosswise into halves, if they are small, or into quarters, if they are large.
2 Tbsp noniodized salt **2 tsp caraway seeds (optional)**	Sprinkle the salt evenly over the cabbage. Using your hands, massage the salt into the cabbage, gently pressing and squeezing the cabbage for several minutes, until it releases its juices. Once

a good amount of liquid has been released, mix in the caraway seeds and then pack the mixture into three 1-qt/960ml jars or crocks. Slip the carrots in along one side and press down to release any pockets of air. The liquid should cover the cabbage-carrot mixture completely. If it does not, make additional brine by dissolving $\frac{3}{4}$ to 1 tsp of salt in 1 cup/240ml of room-temperature water and add enough to cover. Alternatively, use 2-qt/2L jars or crocks and pack them three-quarters full.

Place the whole cabbage leaves (from the first step) over the cabbage-carrot mixture to create a lid, cutting them to fit the size of your containers. On top of this, place a small plate or ramekin that fits snugly inside the jars or crocks. Set them in a cool, dark place and let ferment at room temperature for 5 days.

Check the sauerkraut periodically, returning the lids and weights so it can continue to ferment without being exposed to air if you want it to ferment longer. You may hear gurgling coming from the jars or crocks. This is a good sign, indicating active fermentation. At this point, you will have a lightly fermented sauerkraut. If you favor a more pronounced fermented flavor, the sauerkraut can be left to ferment for a few more days or weeks. Once you are happy with the flavor, transfer the sauerkraut to clean glass jars and cover tightly with lids.

Store indefinitely in the refrigerator, covered tightly with a lid.

QUICK VEGETABLE PICKLES

Makes 2 cups/280g

This versatile pickle—our original recipe developed for the bakery—is served alongside our hot-pressed sandwiches. Because the simmered pickling liquid is poured over the vegetables and left to sit off the heat, the pickles remain pleasantly crisp. Just as a cornichon cuts through a rich pâté, these pickles brighten any meat or roast, from cured meats to chicken, pork, and beef. I like to slice the pickles paper-thin and add them to sandwiches, or finely chop and fold them into a slaw. The recipe itself is malleable, too. If you're after a sweeter, bread-and-butter–style pickle, add 2 tsp of sugar. Vary the spices, as well as the vegetables, to your liking. I favor fermenting, but a quick pickle is good when you need a sandwich or picnic pickup.

1 cup/240ml white wine vinegar or champagne vinegar

1 cup/240ml water

2 cloves garlic, crushed

$\frac{1}{4}$ tsp black peppercorns

6 allspice berries (optional)

6 whole cloves (optional)

$\frac{1}{4}$ tsp red pepper flakes

1 bay leaf

Pinch of granulated sugar

1 tsp sea salt

Combine the white wine vinegar or champagne vinegar, water, garlic, peppercorns, allspice berries, whole cloves, red pepper flakes, bay leaf, sugar, and salt in a small saucepot and bring to a boil. Lower the heat and simmer for 5 minutes.

2 cups/280g sliced vegetables (such as small, hot peppers of any kind, bell peppers, red or yellow onion, cauliflower, small carrots, radishes, Persian cucumbers, or any combination of these vegetables)

Place the vegetables in a 1-qt/960ml jar and then pour in the hot pickling brine. Let cool to room temperature. Use immediately or refrigerate for later use.

Store, covered, in the refrigerator for up to 3 weeks.

STRAWBERRY-ORANGE JAM

Makes 6 (8 oz/220g) jars

As with so many food preoccupations, my love of preserving began with my mother. When we left Brooklyn for upstate New York, we gained a quarter acre of land. My mom planted it densely with fruits and vegetables, and then we ate the fresh produce, baked, pickled, and put up jars throughout the seasons. My mom taught me that jamming need not be an all-day process; she would often quickly turn her small harvests into preserves. Small batches are also easier to control. I use the orange in this recipe for several reasons: The naturally high pectin content of oranges ensures a nice set. The flavors of orange and strawberries go well together. And strawberries help winter fruit trampoline into spring, when the first berries often aren't as flavorful as the midsummer ones.

📖 Many recipes use the method of placing a spoonful of cooking jam on a chilled plate to see if it has reached the desired consistency. I prefer to go by thermometer—I like its definitive answer—but the advantage of using the plate method is that you learn the visual cues of when a jam is ready. I've included both methods so you can find your preferred technique.

📖 You may skip the sterilizing and water bath boiling processes if you plan to keep the jarred jam in your refrigerator, where it can be stored safely for several months.

1 orange 2 cups/480ml water	Cut the orange in half through the middle and then cut each half into 6 wedges. Slice each wedge crosswise as thinly as possible. Place in a saucepan with the water and simmer for 20 minutes.
	To sterilize the jars and lids, preheat the oven to 350°F/180°C. Wash the jars and lids with hot, soapy water and set them on a rimmed baking sheet. Place in the oven for at least 10 minutes and up to 1 hour.
2½ lb/1.2kg strawberries, hulled 4 cups/800g granulated sugar 2 Tbsp lemon juice	Meanwhile, crush the strawberries using your hands or a potato masher. Place the strawberries in a wide, heavy-bottomed pot with the sugar, lemon juice, and the cooked orange along with the orange cooking water.

Cooked orange, with liquid (from the first step)

Bring the mixture to a full boil over high heat, then skim the pale orange foam that rises to the surface. Cook for 15 to 25 minutes, until the jam gels and reaches 221°F/105°C. If you don't have a thermometer, put a small plate in the freezer and, when you think the jam is close to done, remove from the heat and spoon about $\frac{1}{2}$ tsp of jam onto the cold plate. Return the plate to the freezer for 1 minute, then check to see if the jam has gelled. If not, continue cooking and testing until it does gel.

When the jam is ready, carefully ladle it into the hot, sterilized jars, leaving $\frac{1}{4}$-inch/6mm headspace. Wipe the jar rims with a clean, dampened kitchen towel and close the jars with the sterilized lids. Place the jars upright in a large stockpot of water, adding more water as needed to cover the jars by at least 2 inches/5cm. Bring the water to a boil. Leave the jars in the boiling water to process for 10 minutes. Using canning tongs or cooking tongs, lift the jars out of the water and allow them to cool in a protected spot.

Check the seal of each jar by tapping on the lid; if you hear a hollow sound, the jar did not seal. Any that did not seal should be transferred to the refrigerator, and eaten within 2 weeks. Label the jars that did seal and store in a cool, dark place for up to 1 year. Once opened, store in the refrigerator. Because this is a high-sugar jam (sugar is a preservative), it keeps for up to 3 months in the refrigerator.

BLUEBERRY JAM

Makes 5 (8 oz/220g) jars

There are many ways to make jam, but I tend to use the simplest method I know that yields predictable and delicious results. I've come to a ratio that works for most of the fruit jams I make: $2\frac{1}{4}$ lb/1kg fruit, 3 cups/600g of granulated sugar, and the juice of 2 lemons. I find that these quantities produce a jam that is well balanced and →

gels consistently. (For comparison, most classic jam recipes call for twice the amount of sugar.) Blueberry jam is a great match with cornbread and a natural on muffins and yogurt.

📖 When selecting any fruit for making jam, include a small amount of under ripe fruit. This ensures more pectin in the jam, making the gelling process easier. If your fruit has become ripe, or even slightly overripe, the finished jam may be slightly looser (but the flavor will be just as good).

📖 The lemon juice plays an essential role in jam-making and is not just a flavor addition. When fruit is exposed to heat, acid, and sugar, it activates the fruit's pectin, making it gel without having to add additional commercial pectin. This is why the sugar content is what it is. The more sugar, the more easily a jam gels, and believe it or not, the amount of sugar in this recipe is about as low as it can be and still achieve a natural set. Many recipes call for a 1-to-1 ratio. Finally, a small word of caution: Every once in a while, despite having the right proportions of ingredients, a jam just doesn't want to set. This doesn't happen often, but when it does, I designate that batch for syrup and love serving it with Any Day Pancakes (page 82) or spooning it into yogurt.

$2\frac{1}{4}$ lb/1kg blueberries

3 cups/600g granulated sugar

Juice of 2 lemons

Mix the blueberries, sugar, and lemon juice in a wide, heavy-bottomed pot. Bring to a boil over medium-high heat, skimming any brownish foam off the top. Cook, stirring from time to time as the juice reduces, until the jam reaches 221°F/105°C on an instant-read thermometer, 15 to 20 minutes.

To sterilize the jars and lids, preheat the oven to 350°F/180°C. Wash the jars and lids with hot, soapy water and set them on a rimmed baking sheet. Place in the oven for at least 10 minutes and up to 1 hour.

When the jam is ready, carefully ladle it into the hot, sterilized jars, leaving $\frac{1}{4}$-inch/6mm headspace. Wipe the jar rims with a clean, dampened kitchen towel and close the jars with the sterilized lids.

Place the jars upright in a large stockpot of water, adding more water as needed to cover the jars by at least 2 inches/5cm. Bring the water to a boil. Leave the jars in the boiling water to process for 10 minutes. Using canning tongs or cooking tongs, lift the jars out of the water and allow them to cool in a protected spot. →

Check the seal of each jar. Any that did not seal should be transferred to the refrigerator and eaten within 2 weeks. Label the sealed jars and store in a cool, dark place for up to 1 year. Once opened, store in the refrigerator. Because this is a high-sugar jam, it keeps for up to 3 months in the refrigerator.

Mixed Berry Jam: Using the same amount of fruit ($2\frac{1}{4}$ lb/1kg), substitute any combination of blackberries, blueberries, raspberries, huckleberries, olallieberries, Tayberries, and boysenberries. The cooking time may change slightly depending on the fruit you use, but the jam will still be ready when it reaches 221°F/105°C on an instant-read thermometer.

PEACH JAM

Makes 8 (8 oz/220g) jars

There is no fruit more emblematic of summer than a peach. Mostly, I make simple desserts when I have a handful of ripe peaches, or I just eat them out of hand. But I also want to preserve their beguiling sweetness for the coming year, when a winter morning will be immeasurably brightened with a bit of jam on toast. I like a little texture in the finished jam, so I let the peaches remain in chunks when cooking—a reminder of the original fruit's form. Plain yogurt with a dollop of peach jam is a favorite way of mine to enjoy this recipe, as are popovers with a little butter and jam. Use peaches that are full of flavor and natural acidity. The character of each peach variety will show in the finished product.

📖 Usually, yellow peaches are more acidic than white, and I'd recommend using them for this recipe and the white peaches for eating fresh in desserts.

$4\frac{1}{2}$ lb/2kg yellow peaches (about 8 large)

Bring a saucepan of water to a boil. Peel the peaches by dipping each one in boiling water for about 20 seconds, setting them aside until cool enough to handle, and then removing the skin with a paring knife. The skin will peel off easily. Halve and pit the peaches, cut into eighths, and then into 1-inch/2.5cm pieces. Put the peaches in a wide, heavy-bottomed pot.

6 cups/1.2kg granulated sugar

Juice of 3 lemons

Add the sugar and lemon juice to the peaches and mix well. Bring to a boil over medium-high heat, skimming any brownish foam off the top. Cook, stirring from time to time as the juice reduces, until the jam registers 221°F/105°C on an instant-read thermometer, 25 to 30 minutes. If you do not have a thermometer, use the plate test (see page 51).

To sterilize the jars and lids, preheat the oven to 350°F/180°C. Wash the jars and lids with hot, soapy water and set them on a rimmed baking sheet. Place in the oven for at least 10 minutes and up to 1 hour.

Carefully ladle the jam into the hot, sterilized jars, leaving $\frac{1}{4}$-inch/6mm headspace. Wipe the jar rims with a clean, dampened kitchen towel and close the jars with the sterilized lids.

Place the jars upright in a large stockpot of water, adding more water as needed to cover the jars by at least 2 inches/5cm. Bring the water to a boil. Leave the jars in the water to process for 10 minutes. Using canning tongs or cooking tongs, lift the jars out of the water and allow them to cool in a protected spot.

Check the seal of each jar by tapping on the lid; if you hear a hollow sound, the jar did not seal. Any that did not seal should be transferred to the refrigerator and eaten within 2 weeks. Label the jars that did seal and store in a cool, dark place for up to 1 year. Once opened, store in the refrigerator. Because this is a high-sugar jam, it keeps for up to 3 months in the refrigerator.

Mixed Stone Fruit Jam: In place of all or some of the peaches, use nectarines or plums (peels left on) or a combination.

QUINCE JELLY

Makes 8 (4-oz/110g) jars

Quince, which can be frustratingly hard to find, is a fruit worth the hunt. Found in nearly every colonial American garden, quince was once a household staple, prized for its high pectin content and used to make preserves. Quince fell out of favor once commercial pectin and gelatin were introduced in the late 1800s; the effort to prepare them likely discouraged use after grocers began consistently carrying apples and pears. With their irregular shape and fuzzy exterior, quince have never had the look that fits the commercial mold. Though inedible when raw and even a challenge to cut into (use a sharp knife!), the fruit transforms when cooked. It becomes aromatic and complex, turning the gorgeous hue of a peachy rose. Originally from the Caucasus, quince spread across Europe and the Levant before its relatives, the apple and pear. Aphrodite held the fruit sacred, and many believe it was the quince, not the apple, that grew in Eden. The Romans called quince "*melimelum*" and, as the pectin-rich quince were made into preserves long before other fruits, they are believed to have been the basis of the original marmalade. Normally, I favor unrefined sugar, but after doing a side-by-side comparison with white sugar, I have to recommend using white sugar if you're after the clearest, most vibrant color. Serve a spoonful of Quince Jelly with thick yogurt and pistachios, or take inspiration from the Spanish Manchego and membrillo and pair it with fresh ricotta or aged sheep's milk cheese. And whatever you do, don't discard the fruit itself after making the jelly—it too must be preserved! (See Preserved Quince, page 42.)

📖 Quince ripens in the fall and is available in specialty groceries through early winter. If you can't find any, ask around. Because it is a fruit that many households once grew, and the self-pollinating trees are known to last for decades, your neighbor might have an old, lonely tree waiting to be picked.

📖 Quince are like pears in that they ripen from the inside out. Selecting ripe fruit can be tricky, especially later in the season, when quince that may appear perfectly fine on the outside can have soft spots inside. If this is the case, cut out any of the mushy interior and proceed with the recipe. Let the quince's fragrance be your guide: choose firm fruit that is more yellow in color than green and that gives off an ethereal fragrance.

5 lb/2.3kg quince

10 cups/2.3L water

Trim the quince by cutting off the stems and blossom ends and any bruises or dark spots. Cut each quince into quarters and then into 1-inch/2.5cm pieces. In a large pot, cook the quince in the water at a low simmer for $1\frac{1}{2}$ hours. Add more water to the pot as needed to keep the quince covered.

To sterilize the jars and lids, preheat the oven to 350°F/180°C. Wash the jars and lids with hot, soapy water and set them on a rimmed baking sheet. Place in the oven for at least 10 minutes and up to 1 hour.

Set a colander over a large bowl and line the colander with several layers of dampened cheesecloth. Strain the quince mixture for 1 hour. Don't compress to push the liquid through or the juice will become cloudy. Save the strained fruit to make Preserved Quince (page 42).

3 cups/600g granulated sugar

2 Tbsp lemon juice

There should be about 1 qt/960ml of juice. (If there is more or less, measure $\frac{3}{4}$ cup/150g of sugar and $1\frac{1}{2}$ tsp of lemon juice for every 1 cup/240ml of juice collected.) Transfer the juice to a preserving pan or a large, heavy-bottomed saucepan and add the appropriate amount of sugar and lemon juice. Cook over medium heat, stirring with a wooden spoon, until the sugar dissolves. Cook at a simmer until the liquid reaches 221°F/105°C, 15 to 20 minutes on an instant-read thermometer. If you do not have a thermometer, use the plate test (page 51).

When the jelly is ready, carefully pour into the hot, sterilized jars, leaving $\frac{1}{4}$-inch/6mm headspace. Wipe the jar rims with a clean, dampened towel and close the jars with the sterilized lids. Place the jars upright in a large stockpot of water, adding more water as needed to cover the jars by at least 2 inches/5cm. Bring the water to a boil. Leave the jars in the boiling water to process for 10 minutes. Lift the jars out of the water and set them to cool in a protected spot, where they will not be moved or bumped for 12 hours. →

Check the seal of each jar by tapping on the lid; if you hear a hollow sound the jar did not seal. Any that did not seal should be transferred to the refrigerator, and the jelly should be eaten within 2 weeks. Label those jars that did seal and store in a cool, dark place for up to 1 year. Once opened, store in the refrigerator and eat within 2 weeks.

APPLE BUTTER

Makes 4 (4-oz/110g) jars

Apple butter is like the honey of cooked apples. It takes many, many apples, cooked slowly all day, to condense into a dark, thick spread. I often make mine in the slow cooker, filling the crock with as many apple pieces as will fit and cooking them until they get to the applesauce stage. I then add more raw chopped apples and repeat, until all have been added, and let the whole amount cook through the night in the slow cooker. Come morning, the mixture has reduced to the desired consistency, and the apple flavor has become more complex and condensed, revealing an intensity achievable only with time. If you don't have a slow cooker, a Dutch oven can be used in its place at 200°F/95°C in the oven. (I wouldn't recommend trying this on the stovetop, as it can easily scorch.) Most of the work is not active, so do this on a day when you'll be around the house. Given its depth (made more pronounced by warm spices), apple butter is as much a condiment as it is a jam. I love it on dark bread with cream cheese, with whole-grain pancakes, or as a side with pork. It is also immensely satisfying on the Flax-Coconut Muffins (page 71).

5 lb/2.3kg apples (about 12 large), peeled, cored, cut into eighths

1½ cups/360ml apple cider

¼ cup/60ml apple cider vinegar

1½ cups/300g granulated sugar

2 tsp ground cinnamon

½ tsp ground cloves

½ tsp freshly grated nutmeg

To make the apple butter in the oven: In a Dutch oven or other large, heavy-bottomed pot, combine the apples, apple cider, apple cider vinegar, sugar, cinnamon, cloves, and nutmeg. Cover and cook over medium-low heat on the stovetop, stirring occasionally, until the apples are very soft, 30 to 45 minutes. Use an immersion blender to puree the mixture until very smooth, or transfer to a countertop blender and puree in 2 or 3 batches, filling the blender no more than halfway and taking care not to burn yourself, as the apples will be extremely hot. Preheat the oven to 300°F/150°C. Return the pureed apples to the Dutch oven, or transfer to a casserole or other low-sided baking dish. Cook, uncovered, in the oven, stirring from time to time, about every 30 minutes, until the apple butter has a concentrated flavor and a beautiful, dark amber color, about 5 hours in total.

To make the apple butter in a slow cooker: In the slow cooker insert, combine the apples (as many as will fit), apple cider, apple cider vinegar, sugar, cinnamon, cloves, and nutmeg. Cover and cook on the low setting, stirring from time to time, about every 60 minutes, until the apples are very soft, about 1 hour. Use an immersion blender to puree the mixture until very smooth, or transfer to a countertop blender and puree in 2 or 3 batches, filling the blender no more than halfway and taking care not to burn yourself, as the apples will be extremely hot. Return the pureed apples to the slow cooker insert, add any remaining raw apples, and cook on the low setting overnight. By the next day, most of the moisture will have evaporated and the apple butter will have a concentrated flavor and a beautiful, dark amber color.

To sterilize the jars and lids, preheat the oven to 350°F/180°C. Wash the jars and lids with hot, soapy water and set them on a rimmed baking sheet. Place in the oven for at least 10 minutes and up to 1 hour. →

When the apple butter is ready, carefully ladle it into the hot, sterilized jars, leaving $\frac{1}{4}$-inch/6mm headspace. Wipe the jar rims with a clean, dampened kitchen towel and close the jars with the sterilized lids. Place the jars upright in a large stockpot of water, adding more water as needed to cover the jars by at least 2 inches/5cm. Bring the water to a boil. Leave the jars in the water to process for 10 minutes. Using canning tongs or cooking tongs, lift the jars out of the water and allow them to cool in a protected spot.

Check the seal of each jar by tapping on the lid; if you hear a hollow sound, the jar did not seal. Any that did not seal should be transferred to the refrigerator, and the apple butter should be eaten within 4 weeks. Label the jars that did seal properly and store in a cool, dark place for up to 1 year. Once opened, store in the refrigerator. Because this is not a high-sugar jam, it keeps for up to 1 month in the refrigerator.

CORN TORTILLAS

Makes 9 (5-inch/12cm) tortillas

In my ideal world, I'd make tortillas from fresh masa every time. Luckily, masa harina flour is a good alternative and makes any homemade tortilla a vast improvement over most store-bought ones. Masa (wet) and masa harina flour (dry) differ from the cornmeal used in cornbread because they have undergone a centuries-old process called nixtamalization. This means that when the corn is just harvested, it's dried and then soaked and cooked in an alkaline solution. This helps soften the corn while making it considerably more nutritious. You can make a small investment in a tortilla press, which will produce perfectly uniform rounds, or do what I do and press the tortilla dough between sheets of plastic wrap or wax paper underneath a frying pan. Traditionally, a *comal* (a flat griddle) is used to cook the formed tortillas, but a cast-iron pan works just as well. Try to resist tampering with the cooking tortilla. Tortilla makers pride themselves on turning the tortillas only once. To encourage an air bubble, which →

is the sign of a properly made tortilla, they tickle or poke the center, often with the end of a dry, clean towel. Whether or not your tortillas inflate on the griddle, they will certainly improve any meal, even a simple bowl of black beans (see page 167) with Tomatillo Salsa (page 18). Once you get this recipe down, as long as you have masa harina on hand you will be able to make tortillas anytime.

📖 To store the finished tortillas while making more, I wrap them in a clean kitchen towel. They steam slightly and become even softer before serving. The tortillas can be made a few hours in advance, but wrap them in foil instead of a kitchen towel until ready to serve. Before serving, warm them in an oven (or toaster oven) set at 300°F/150°C for 10 minutes, or until warmed through.

$1\frac{1}{4}$ cups/145g masa harina

1 cup/240ml hot water

$\frac{1}{4}$ tsp sea salt

Combine the masa harina, water, and salt in a medium bowl and knead into a smooth ball. Cover the bowl with plastic wrap and let sit for 30 minutes to allow the masa to completely absorb the water.

Break off golf ball-size pieces of dough, about 40g each. (Use larger pieces if you want to make bigger tortillas.) Roll each piece into a smooth ball. If using a tortilla press, place one piece of plastic wrap on the bottom of the press, set the dough ball on it, and then place another piece of plastic wrap on top of the dough before pressing. Alternatively, choose a plate that has a high enough ridge on its underside to make the tortilla the thickness you like when a dough ball is placed directly under the plate and the plate is pressed down to rest on the work surface. Or you can simply press tortillas with the bottom of a pan or even a book. Stack the pressed tortillas on a plate until you're ready to cook them.

$\frac{1}{2}$ to 1 tsp vegetable oil

Heat the oil in a cast-iron skillet over medium-high heat and cook the tortillas, one or two at a time, on each side until browned in a few spots and cooked through, 3 to 4 minutes total, depending on the thickness of the tortillas.

To store cooked tortillas, wrap in aluminum foil and set aside until completely cool. Place the foil packet in a resealable plastic bag and refrigerate for up to 3 days.

BREAK
FAST
AND
BRUNCH

GRANOLA

Makes about 12 cups/1.2kg

Granola lives a double life, considered health food by some and glorified oatmeal cookies by others. For this recipe, I've tried to retain its indulgent and crunchy characteristics, because that's much of its appeal, while using healthy oils (a combination of coconut and olive oils), natural sweeteners, and plenty of nuts and seeds. I've also taken to lightening up the texture by adding crisped rice to the mixture. For me, granola is most successful when it has sizable chunks amidst smaller crisped oats. My favorite way to enjoy this is on top of plain, whole-milk yogurt with a handful of berries, though it also makes a great impromptu fruit crisp topping—just top the assembled fruit filling with the uncooked granola and bake as called for. You could also use the finished granola as a topping for baked fruit.

📖 This is a flexible recipe. Feel free to use only one kind of oil or a combination of whatever you have in place of the specified combination. The combination of maple syrup and honey creates a quintessential "granola" flavor, but if you only have one sweetener on hand, the result will be just as good. Brown rice syrup will also work, with slightly less sweet results.

$\frac{1}{2}$ cup/120ml honey

$\frac{1}{2}$ cup/120ml maple syrup or brown rice syrup

$\frac{1}{4}$ cup/55g coconut oil

$\frac{1}{4}$ cup/60ml olive oil or unsalted butter

Combine the honey, maple syrup or brown rice syrup, coconut oil, and olive oil or butter in a small pot over medium-low heat. Stir until the coconut oil and butter have melted, and then remove from the heat.

Preheat the oven to 350°F/180°C. Line a baking sheet with parchment paper or a silicone mat. →

4 cups/400g rolled oats

2 cups/280g almonds,
coarsely chopped

1 cup/25g whole-grain
crisped rice cereal

$\frac{1}{3}$ cup/55g ground
flax seeds or 2 $\frac{1}{2}$ Tbsp
ground flax seeds and
2 $\frac{1}{2}$ Tbsp ground chia
seeds

$\frac{1}{4}$ cup/15g unsweetened
shredded coconut

$\frac{1}{4}$ cup/30g oat flour

$\frac{1}{4}$ cup/35g sesame seeds

1 $\frac{1}{2}$ tsp ground cinnamon

$\frac{3}{4}$ tsp sea salt

Combine the oats, almonds, rice cereal, flax seeds or flax-chia mixture, coconut, oat flour, sesame seeds, cinnamon, and salt in a large bowl. Add the honey-oil mixture and stir well.

Transfer the mixture to the prepared baking sheet, spreading the granola in an even $\frac{1}{2}$-inch/12mm layer. Bake, stirring every 10 to 15 minutes, until toasted and golden brown, about 30 minutes. Set the baking sheet on a cooling rack until completely cool and then break the granola into smaller pieces.

Store in an airtight container at room temperature for up to 3 weeks.

Mixed Nuts and Seeds Granola: In place of the almonds, use any combination of hazelnuts, walnuts, pecans, or other nuts you like. Instead of white sesame seeds, try an equal amount of black sesame seeds, hempseeds, pepitas, or a mixture of seeds.

FLAX-COCONUT MUFFINS

Makes 12

I've made these muffins with all sorts of flour, from almond to coconut to a mixture of my own making. I've found that oat flour is foolproof, and nearly everyone who tastes this muffin can't believe they're gluten-free because they are moist and delicious, two characteristics that are difficult to achieve in gluten-free baking. The flax seeds give the muffins a subtle nuttiness and the coconut sugar lightly sweetens them. Perhaps the best thing about these muffins is that they keep for several days and only get better. When I have a busy week ahead or foresee a houseful of company, I double the recipe and am never sorry. These freeze well and can be reheated for tea, snacks, or a quick breakfast.

📖 Coconut sugar, an unrefined sweetener, has a much lower glycemic index than white sugar and contains more flavor. High in omega-3 and lignans (a kind of antioxidant), flax seeds' nutritional assets stand up to high heat in the oven. If you don't eat flax seeds often, I recommend keeping them in the freezer or refrigerator and grinding them in a coffee mill (wiped clean with a damp cloth) as needed.

Unsalted butter, for the pan (optional)	Lightly grease a 12-well muffin tin or line with paper liners. Preheat the oven to 350°F/180°C.
$\frac{3}{4}$ cup/115g coconut sugar 2 Tbsp molasses 3 large eggs	In a large bowl, whisk together the coconut sugar, molasses, and eggs until the molasses is completely incorporated.
$1\frac{1}{4}$ cups/300ml coconut water $\frac{1}{3}$ cup plus 1 Tbsp/95ml olive oil $1\frac{1}{2}$ cups/225g ground flax seeds	Add the coconut water and oil to the egg mixture, whisking to blend, and then mix in the flax. Set aside for 5 minutes to let the flax soften.
$1\frac{1}{3}$ cups/160g oat flour 2 tsp baking soda $\frac{1}{2}$ tsp ground cinnamon $\frac{1}{2}$ tsp sea salt	In another large bowl, combine the oat flour, baking soda, cinnamon, and salt and mix well. Slowly add the flax mixture to the dry ingredients, stirring until completely blended. →

1 cup/115g peeled and grated apple (about 2 small apples)

1 cup/140g raisins

12 small apple slices (optional)

2 Tbsp raw sugar (optional)

Gently fold in the apple and raisins. Using an ice cream scoop or large spoon, portion the batter into the greased muffin tin or paper liners, filling each one all the way full.

Place an apple slice on top of each muffin. Sprinkle the tops of the muffins with the raw sugar.

Bake for 35 to 40 minutes, until the muffins are golden brown around the edges and a toothpick inserted in the center of the largest muffin comes out clean.

Set the pan on a cooling rack for 5 minutes. Lift out the muffins and place them on the rack to cool completely.

The muffins will keep, well wrapped, in the refrigerator for up to 5 days or in the freezer for up to 2 months. To defrost the muffins, let sit at room temperature for 15 minutes and then warm in a toaster oven or conventional oven at 350°F/180°C for 10 minutes.

Flax-Coconut-Carrot Muffins: In place of all or some of the grated apple, use peeled and grated carrot.

Flax-Coconut-Zucchini Muffins: Grated zucchini works well, instead of the apple but be sure to rid it of its excess water, or the muffins won't bake properly. Squeeze the grated zucchini, as if you were squeezing a washcloth of its water, until little water is released.

Flax-Coconut-Honey Muffins: Though not everyone's favorite, molasses does something magical here to round out the flavors. If you don't have it on hand, an equal quantity of honey works.

BANANA BREAD WITH STREUSEL TOPPING

Makes 1 (8½ by 4½-inch/22 by 11cm) loaf

When our household has a surplus of bananas quickly ripening on the counter, I am secretly pleased to have an excuse to make banana bread, which I prefer any day over a plain banana. For this recipe, I've updated the classic, using whole grain flours and making it extra moist with chia seeds. The streusel topping provides a welcome crunch in contrast with the soft bread.

📖 Chia seeds are not only rich in omega fatty acids, but are also hygroscopic, which means that when exposed to water, the seeds immediately hydrate, absorbing many times their volume and turning gelatinous. Because of this property, they're often used as a replacement for eggs in vegan recipes. To grind chia seeds, use a coffee grinder (wiped clean with a damp cloth). Because they contain high amounts of fat, process for only a few seconds so that the seeds do not become a paste.

1 Tbsp ground chia seeds 3 Tbsp water	In a small bowl, mix the chia seeds and water. Let sit for 10 minutes for the chia seeds to soften.
	Preheat the oven to 350°F/180°C. Lightly butter and flour an 8½ by 4½-inch/22 by 11cm loaf pan, knocking out the excess flour.
3 Tbsp/25g almond flour 3 Tbsp/25g oat flour 2 Tbsp granulated sugar ¼ tsp ground cinnamon Pinch of sea salt 2 Tbsp unsalted butter, at room temperature	Meanwhile, to make the streusel topping, combine the almond flour, oat flour, sugar, cinnamon, and salt in a bowl. Using your fingers, incorporate the butter, letting the mixture clump.
6 Tbsp/85g unsalted butter, at room temperature ¾ cup/150g granulated sugar	This recipe is easily mixed by a stand mixer fitted with the paddle attachment on medium speed or by hand with a spoon. In a bowl, cream the butter

until light and creamy, about 2 minutes with a mixer. Slowly add the sugar and beat until fluffy, about 2 minutes with a mixer.

2 large eggs

2 medium/170g very ripe bananas, peeled and well mashed

$\frac{1}{3}$ cup/80g sour cream

1 tsp vanilla extract

2 tsp lemon juice

Add the eggs, one at a time, mixing well after each addition. Add the mashed bananas and beat until the mixture is smooth. Scrape down the sides of the bowl with a rubber spatula. Mix in the sour cream, vanilla, lemon juice, and chia-water mixture.

$\frac{1}{3}$ cup/40g almond flour

$\frac{1}{3}$ cup/45g brown rice flour

$\frac{3}{4}$ cup/90g oat flour

$\frac{3}{4}$ tsp baking soda

$\frac{1}{2}$ tsp sea salt

1 cup/120g walnuts, coarsely chopped

$\frac{1}{2}$ tsp ground cinnamon

In another large bowl, stir together the almond flour, brown rice flour, oat flour, baking soda, salt, walnuts, and cinnamon. Add to the banana mixture, beating just until combined. Transfer the mixture to the prepared loaf pan and top evenly with the streusel.

Bake until a cake tester inserted in the center comes out clean, about 1 hour. Set the pan on a cooling rack until cool enough to handle, about 20 minutes, and then invert the loaf onto the rack, turn right-side up, and let cool completely. Serve the banana bread at room temperature.

Banana bread will keep, well wrapped, at room temperature for 4 days or in the refrigerator for about 1 week.

Banana Muffins: Line 18 wells of a muffin tin with paper liners. Using an ice cream scoop or large spoon, portion the batter into the wells, filling each three-quarters full. Top evenly with the streusel. Bake for 18 to 22 minutes, until a toothpick inserted in the center of the largest muffin comes out clean. Set the pan on a cooling rack for 5 minutes. Lift out the muffins and place them on the rack to cool completely.

SOUR CREAM COFFEE CAKE

Makes 1 (9-inch/23cm) cake

It may seem old-fashioned, but a good streusel on a coffee cake (its distinguishing characteristic) provides such a satisfying contrast to the cake itself that it's a classic worth revisiting. This cake has a toothsomeness that comes from both the almond flour and the sour cream. It is simple to put together and a back-pocket recipe for a morning of coffee and family.

Unsalted butter, for the pan	Preheat the oven to 350°F/180°C. Butter the bottom and sides of a 9-inch/23cm round cake pan.
$\frac{1}{4}$ cup/35g brown rice flour $1\frac{1}{2}$ Tbsp sweet rice flour 2 Tbsp plus 1 tsp potato starch $\frac{1}{4}$ cup/50g granulated sugar 1 tsp ground cinnamon 4 Tbsp/55g unsalted butter, at room temperature $\frac{1}{4}$ tsp baking powder $\frac{2}{3}$ cup/80g chopped walnuts, pecans, or almonds	To make the streusel, in the bowl of a standing mixer, mix the brown rice flour, sweet rice flour, potato starch, sugar, cinnamon, butter, baking powder, and walnuts, pecans, or almonds on medium-low speed just until it comes together. Alternatively, mix by hand in a medium bowl. The streusel should be a bit clumpy. If it isn't, squeeze it together in your hands and let it break into smaller pea-size lumps. Set aside at room temperature while you make the cake batter.
2 cups/240g almond flour 2 Tbsp sweet rice flour 2 Tbsp tapioca flour/starch $\frac{1}{2}$ tsp sea salt $\frac{3}{4}$ tsp baking powder	In a large bowl, whisk together the almond flour, sweet rice flour, tapioca flour/starch, salt, and baking powder.

2 large eggs

6 Tbsp/90g granulated sugar

$\frac{3}{4}$ cup/180g sour cream

Using a handheld mixer or a stand mixer fitted with the whisk attachment, beat the eggs and sugar on high speed until very thick and lightened in color, about 3 minutes. When you lift up the whisk, a ribbon of beaten eggs should trail back into the bowl. Add the sour cream and beat to incorporate.

Pour the egg mixture into the flour mixture and mix together just until smooth and blended. Transfer the batter to the prepared pan, spreading evenly. Scatter the streusel across the top. Using your fingertips, very gently push the streusel into the batter here and there.

Bake for about 25 minutes, until golden brown around the edges and a cake tester inserted in the center comes out clean. Place the pan on a wire rack to cool for at least 15 minutes before serving.

When completely cool, the coffee cake will keep, tightly wrapped, for up to 3 days at room temperature or about 1 week in the refrigerator.

BUCKWHEAT CRÊPES

Makes 2 cups/480ml crêpe batter, enough for 10 to 12 crêpes

Few foods are more reflective of place than buckwheat crêpes—properly called galettes—from Brittany, France. Chad and I spent a part of a summer there while visiting a friend's bakery in the area. A galette filled with ham and cheese, topped with an egg, along with a cup of hard cider is just what you wanted during a typically windy, bright, and often cool coastal day there. For the longest time, hearty buckwheat, a plant that is neither wheat nor a true grain but a relative to rhubarb and sorrel, thrived there while wheat could not. The earthy tones of buckwheat, which are bracingly straightforward and a little bitter, seem to me an exact mirror of its environment. Any self-respecting Breton will make the distinction between crêpes, which are →

made with white flour and served for dessert, and buckwheat galettes, which are crêpes in method but are wheat-free and accompanied only by savory or salty flavors. Because we are no longer in Brittany, I am calling this recipe Buckwheat Crêpes, and I hope that you will pair it not only with cheese and ham or sautéed mushrooms and an egg but also with sweet fillings, such as melted chocolate, sautéed apples, or pastry cream (see page 323) with raspberries and figs. Buckwheat pairs wonderfully with many flavors, bringing attention to an ingredient's hidden strengths. And don't think that a filling is even necessary—melted butter and hard cider are company enough.

📖 Why must this batter sit when it seems ready upon mixing? I always seek the quickest method for doing things, but after testing it, I recommend letting the batter rest for at least 2 hours if not overnight (the classic way to prepare it). The reason has to do with the starch in the flour, which over time, absorbs the liquid and swells. The batter will become more viscous, the texture of the crêpes will be more uniform and tender, and the cooked buckwheat will lose its bitter edge. If the batter has become too viscous, whisk in a splash of water or milk. Ultimately, the batter should be able to spread readily in the pan—thinner than a pancake batter and similar to heavy cream.

$\frac{3}{4}$ cup/105 g buckwheat flour 2 large eggs 1 cup/240ml whole milk 1 Tbsp olive oil $\frac{1}{2}$ tsp sea salt	In a blender, combine the flour, eggs, milk, oil, and salt and blend until very smooth. Place in the refrigerator to chill for at least 2 hours. The crêpe batter will keep, covered, in the refrigerator for up to 5 days.
Splash of water or milk Unsalted butter, for the pan	To make crêpes, whisk the batter and thin it with the water or milk if needed. It should be the thickness of heavy cream. Heat a small (6- to 7- inch/15 to 18cm) nonstick pan over medium heat and swirl in enough butter to coat the bottom of the pan. Ladle in about 3 Tbsp/45ml of batter, tilting the pan in all directions to spread evenly. Cook for about 1 minute, until the underside of the crêpe is lightly browned. Flip, then cook the second side for about 30 seconds. Transfer to a plate and let cool. Continue cooking the crêpes, adding butter to the pan as needed, until you've used up all the batter. Cooked crêpes can be cooled, stacked, and stored, tightly sealed, in the refrigerator for up to 3 days.

ANY DAY PANCAKES

Makes about 12 (4-inch/10cm) pancakes

Fluffy, moist, and higher in protein than average pancakes, these are made with whole grain flours. The tapioca flour/starch is key, ensuring that the pancakes remain light despite nutritional heft. Archer is so fond of these that I assemble large batches of a make-ahead mix. With the mix on hand, on any given morning I can make breakfast in just a few minutes.

📖 For the make-ahead mix, assemble a quadruple batch of the dry ingredients and store in an airtight jar at room temperature for up 3 months. When you are ready to cook the pancakes, measure out 1 heaping cup/130g of the mix and place in a large bowl. Proceed with the recipe, adding the egg, butter, and milk in the amounts given.

3 Tbsp/25g almond flour 2 Tbsp tapioca flour/starch $\frac{1}{3}$ cup plus 1 Tbsp/50g oat flour $\frac{1}{4}$ cup plus 1 heaping Tbsp/50g brown rice flour 1$\frac{1}{4}$ tsp baking powder 2 tsp granulated sugar $\frac{1}{4}$ tsp sea salt	Combine the almond flour, tapioca flour/starch, oat flour, rice flour, baking powder, sugar, and salt in a large bowl and mix well.
1 large egg 2 Tbsp unsalted butter, melted, or olive oil $\frac{3}{4}$ cup plus 2 Tbsp/210ml whole milk	Stir the egg, butter or olive oil, and milk together in a small bowl, add to the flour mixture, and mix with as few stirs as you need to get it all combined.
Unsalted butter, for the pan	Melt the butter in a large pan over medium heat. Spoon the batter into the pan, cooking a single pancake first to check if the pan is the correct temperature. Cook until the underside of the pancake is golden brown and air bubbles appear on top, about 1 minute. Flip and cook the second side until done. Repeat with the rest of the batter and serve immediately.

BUCKWHEAT DUTCH BABY WITH SAUTÉED APPLES

Makes 2 or 3 servings (one 12-inch/30cm pancake)

This golden puffed pancake never fails to stir up a fleeting moment of thrill for me, as if I were still a child at our dining room table in New York, watching my mother quickly place it on a trivet before it would begin to deflate. Food writer Craig Claiborne first wrote about it in *The New York Times* in 1966, and my family has been making it ever since. Claiborne named the pancake after the man who introduced him to it—David Eyre—but the recipe was an old one. Eyre presumably based it on the German recipe called Dutch Baby Pancake, and I've always loved the recommendation to serve it simply with a dusting of confectioners' sugar and freshly squeezed lemon juice. In this updated version, buckwheat flour gives it a nutty complexity and is a natural flavor partner for the sautéed apples. Of course, lemon and confectioners' sugar will do just as well, as would maple syrup or a fruit syrup, particularly one with a little tartness, such as blueberry or blackberry.

📖 Sweet rice flour is used to make Japanese mochi, a glutinous rice cake. I've found that by judiciously adding it to this recipe, the batter gains a necessary elasticity and behaves as if it had gluten.

2 large eggs $\frac{1}{2}$ cup/120ml whole milk Large pinch of sea salt	In a medium bowl, whisk the eggs, milk, and salt until well blended.
	Preheat the oven to 450°F/230°C. Place a 12-inch/30cm cast-iron skillet or heavy-bottomed, oven-safe pan in the oven to heat while you complete the batter.
Scant $\frac{1}{4}$ cup/28g oat flour 2 Tbsp buckwheat flour 2 Tbsp sweet rice flour	Add the oat flour, buckwheat flour, and sweet rice flour to the egg mixture. Whisk until mostly smooth; a few lumps are okay.
3 Tbsp unsalted butter	Carefully remove the hot pan from the oven and add the butter. Return the pan to the oven and leave it there just until the butter has melted. →

Carefully remove the hot pan from the oven once again and, if necessary, tilt the pan to evenly coat the bottom and sides with the melted butter. Pour the batter into the pan and return to the oven. Immediately reduce the oven temperature to 425°F/220°C and bake until puffed around the edges and golden brown, about 15 minutes.

2 cups/380g Sautéed Apples (page 28) (optional)

Serve the pancake in the pan straight out of the oven, topped with the sautéed apples.

David Eyre's Dutch Baby: As soon as you remove the pancake from the oven, instead of topping with the apples squeeze lemon juice all over and sift 2 Tbsp confectioners' sugar over the top. Serve immediately.

Half-Size Dutch Baby: Halving this recipe requires care when choosing the pan size. If the pan is too large for the amount of batter, the pancake won't rise properly. To make a generous single serving, use an 8-inch/20cm pan and reduce the ingredient amounts by half.

CRISPY WAFFLES

Makes 4 to 6

These waffles are made from a similar batter as the pancakes, however, they also have whipped egg whites, which give them the crispness and lightness you want in waffles. As for all of the recipes in this book that would typically contain wheat flour, I've devised a way to make these waffles with alternative flours, not only because I'm gluten-intolerant but also because there are so many interesting flours available that produce different flavors and textures in baked foods. In addition to the egg whites, the cornmeal adds crispness. Try substituting sorghum flour for the oat flour or masa harina for a more "corny" flavor. →

3 Tbsp/25g almond flour	Preheat the waffle iron. In a large bowl, combine the almond flour, tapioca flour/starch, oat flour, cornmeal, rice flour, baking powder, and salt and mix well.
2 Tbsp tapioca flour/starch	
$\frac{1}{2}$ cup /60g oat flour	
$\frac{1}{4}$ cup/35g cornmeal	
$\frac{1}{4}$ cup plus 1 heaping Tbsp/50g brown rice flour	
$1\frac{1}{4}$ tsp baking powder	
$\frac{1}{4}$ tsp sea salt	
2 large eggs, separated (2 egg yolks reserved)	Whisk the egg whites and sugar to soft peaks.
4 tsp granulated sugar	
2 Tbsp unsalted butter, melted, or olive oil	In a small bowl, stir together 1 of the reserved egg yolks (refrigerating the other egg yolk for another use), the butter or olive oil, and milk. Add to the flour mixture ingredients and mix with as few stirs as possible to get the batter combined. Gently fold in the whipped egg whites and use immediately.
$\frac{3}{4}$ cup plus 2 Tbsp/210ml whole milk	
Unsalted butter, melted, for the waffle iron	Brush the waffle iron with the butter. Spoon the batter into the preheated waffle iron. Cook until the waffle is golden brown on both sides, usually about 3 minutes per waffle. Repeat with the rest of the batter and serve immediately.

POPOVERS

Makes 12

Popovers are meant to be eaten right out of the oven when they're inflated like balloons and smell buttery rich. Good popovers never fail to bring you entirely into the moment, because they're so sensorial. Crispy and golden on the outside, they are warm to the touch, delicate, and airy, and steam profusely upon opening. Popovers are very similar to the Dutch Baby (page 83) in that their hallmark puffiness is a result of the eggy, wet batter, which creates enough steam during baking to leaven the bread and make a hollow interior. My challenge in using gluten-free flours was to engineer enough elasticity to enable a stable popover to form. Once again, just like with the Dutch Baby recipe, a small amount of sweet rice flour lends the necessary binding power. Served with butter and fruit jam, popovers are also wonderful for brunches because they look special and make the kitchen smell so good while baking. While popovers are distinctly American, they're quite similar to Yorkshire puddings, and the Anglophile in me can't help wanting to serve popovers with a Sunday roast beef. Popovers can also be flavored with aromatics for a savory accompaniment to a meal.

📖 While a popover pan creates the tallest popovers, a muffin pan can be used in its place with slightly more diminutive results.

Unsalted butter, for the pan	Lightly grease the wells of a 12-well popover tin or muffin tin. Preheat the oven to 400°F/200°C and place the tin in the oven.
3 Tbsp sweet rice flour 5 Tbsp/40g tapioca flour/starch 5 Tbsp/40g oat flour $\frac{1}{4}$ tsp sea salt	In a medium bowl, whisk together the rice flour, tapioca flour/starch, oat flour, and salt.
3 large eggs $\frac{3}{4}$ cup/180ml whole milk	In another medium bowl, whisk together the eggs and milk until frothy. Stir half of the egg mixture into the flour mixture, whisking just until well combined. Add the rest of the egg mixture and whisk to combine. Carefully remove the tin from the oven and pour the batter into the wells, filling each one three-quarters full (or about one-third full if using a muffin tin). Bake for 15 minutes without opening the oven door, until the popovers stand tall in their wells and are golden brown. Reduce the heat to 350°F/180°C and continue baking for 5 to 7 minutes longer. Set the pan on a rack to cool briefly and then lift the popovers out and transfer to a serving basket. Serve immediately.
	Savory Popovers: Stir 2 Tbsp minced mixed herbs, 2 tsp smoked Spanish paprika (pimentón), or 3 Tbsp finely grated hard cheese into the flour mixture.

KUKU SABZI (PERSIAN VEGETABLE AND HERB OMELET)

Makes 6 to 12 servings (one 10-inch/25cm omelet)

A few years back, we hosted a series of dinners called Tartine Afterhours, where our friend and cookbook author Samin Nosrat would take over the closed bakery and serve a multicourse dinner to about forty guests. It became immensely popular. Her menus would vary, but everyone always loved her Persian dishes, particularly the *kuku sabzi*, an omelet filled with herbs and greens. Samin told me that her mother's was greener than most, with the minimum number of eggs holding together the maximum amount of vegetables. This is a flexible, changeable recipe. I altered it slightly from Samin's, in part because of what was available in my own herb garden and refrigerator. Samin's often has copious amounts of dill and cilantro, while this recipe tends toward parsley, mint, and less cilantro. Make this with what greenery you have on hand. And I should add that if you are a parent with veggie-phobic kids, our daughter, who has recently declared herself a vegetarian yet seems to like no actual vegetable, devoured this in seconds. Serve it with lemony Aioli (page 10), Romesco Sauce (page 29), Tzatziki (page 17), or hot sauce. (Greek yogurt would be so good, too.)

📖 A word of caution: wash your greens really well. There's nothing worse than biting down on a grain of sand (leeks harbor the most). The best method is one I've used in restaurant kitchens, and it's the most thorough: fill a large container with plenty of cool water and add your greens. Swish them around really well, agitating with your fingers, and lift the greens out of the bath, shaking off the excess water. You can use the same water for many batches if they don't all fit at once. All of the dirt and sand will drift to the bottom.

2 large bunches (about $1\frac{1}{4}$ lb/570g) Swiss chard, collard greens, or spinach, washed

Cut or pull the chard or collard leaves off the stems. Chop the chard, collards, or spinach and set the chopped pieces aside. Thinly slice the chard or collard stems, discarding any tough parts at the base of each stem. →

3 Tbsp olive oil	Heat a 10-inch/25cm or 12-inch/30cm nonstick or well-seasoned cast-iron skillet over medium heat and add the olive oil. Add the leeks. Cook, stirring often, until they are soft, 6 to 8 minutes. Transfer to a large bowl.
1 large/110g leek, white and light green parts sliced in half lengthwise and then in $\frac{1}{2}$-inch/12mm pieces	
2 Tbsp olive oil	In a large stockpot with a lid over low heat, add the oil and water. Bring to a simmer and then add the greens and stems, cover, and cook until wilted, 3 to 4 minutes. Transfer the greens to a colander and let drain. Once cool enough to handle, squeeze out the excess liquid. Add to the bowl of leeks.
$\frac{1}{2}$ cup/120ml water	
4 cups/80g tender fresh herbs (such as flat-leaf parsley, cilantro, dill, and mint), chopped	Mix the herbs into the cooked greens and leeks. Season with salt and pepper to taste. Start by mixing in 1 tsp salt, then taste and adjust. It should taste just on the edge of too salty.
Sea salt	
Ground black pepper	
6 to 9 large eggs	Crack the eggs into the greens and herbs, one at a time, stirring after each addition. Add only as many eggs as needed to barely bind the mixture.
4 Tbsp/55g unsalted butter	Clean out the pan the leeks were cooked in to ensure the kuku sabzi will not stick. Return to medium heat and add the butter and olive oil. Once the butter is hot, add the greens and eggs mixture, packing it all into the pan. For the first 2 minutes of cooking, use a spatula or wooden spoon to gently pull the uncooked edges of the kuku sabzi into the middle.
2 Tbsp olive oil, plus more as needed	

Lower the heat to medium-low and continue cooking, without stirring, for about 10 minutes, until the underside is dark golden brown. If your stove is uneven, rotate the pan for even browning. To cook the other side, place a plate over the pan, invert the pan to turn the omelet out onto the plate, and then slide it back into the pan. Cook for 5 to 10 minutes, until set and golden brown on the bottom. Slide the omelet onto a serving plate. Slice into wedges and serve warm, at room temperature, or chilled.

Store, covered, in the refrigerator for up to 3 days.

MOLLET EGGS WITH AVOCADO AND ROE

Makes 4 servings

Mollet, the French term for "soft," yields firm whites and liquid yolks that are delicious on salads and toast. Mollet eggs are cooked at a gentle boil (as opposed to in the residual heat of the cooking water, as for other types of eggs that are cooked in their shells) and then immediatcly immersed in a bowl of ice water, which makes the eggs firm enough to easily peel even though the yolks encased in the whites remaining liquid. These eggs may be made ahead of time and then added to salads for days after (try one on the Bacon, Lettuce, and Tomato Panzanella, page 161, for example).

📖 For all other soft-cooked to firm eggs: Fill a pot with water so that the eggs will be covered by 1 inch/2.5cm. Bring the water to a boil, add the eggs, cover, remove the pot from the heat, and continue to cook in the hot water for the specified times (see below), followed by a brief chill (1 to 2 minutes for all but the 15-minute eggs) in a bowl of ice water. Cooking times are for large eggs stored at room temperature. If you are cooking eggs that have been stored in the refrigerator, add 1 minute to the times given. If the pot you are using is thin-walled, add 1 minute to the cooking time or keep the burner on low heat for the first minute. Once cooked, eggs will last for up to 5 days in the refrigerator.

📖 Cook 4 minutes for very soft-cooked eggs with liquid yolks that are barely warm and whites that are still a little translucent. This makes a saucy egg that is good for on a bowl of grains or greens, or in a soup or salad.

📖 Cook 5 minutes for eggs with just-set whites and liquid yolks that are warm. This is the perfect soft-cooked breakfast egg.

📖 Cook 6 minutes for eggs with firm whites and yolks that are just beginning to set.

📖 Cook 7 minutes for eggs with firm whites and yolks that are set around the outside but still soft in the center.

📖 Cook 8 minutes for eggs with firm whites and half-set yolks.

📖 Cook 9 minutes for eggs with firm whites and yolks that are three-quarters set.

📖 Cook 10 minutes for what I would call a perfect hard-cooked egg to be eaten as such (as opposed to a hard-cooked egg to be used for deviled eggs or egg salad), with only a dot of barely set yolk in the center. →

📖 Cook 15 minutes for hard-cooked eggs that will be used for deviled eggs and egg salad (that is, when you want a cold egg with a fully cooked yolk and no green, sulfurous rings around the yolks). After 15 minutes in the hot water, transfer the eggs to a bowl of ice water and let chill for another 15 minutes, circulating the eggs from time to time.

4 large eggs, in their shells

Prepare a bowl of ice water. Fill a small pot with enough water to cover the eggs. Bring the water to a boil. Gently lower the eggs into the water, keeping the water at a slight simmer. Cook for 5 minutes (or 6 minutes if using eggs from the refrigerator), drain, and gently roll the eggs around in the clean, empty pot to lightly crack their shells. Immerse eggs in the ice water to cool for 10 minutes. Carefully peel, or store in the refrigerator until ready to serve, up to 5 days. To warm before serving, gently immerse the eggs in simmering water and heat for 30 seconds.

2 ripe avocados, halved, pitted, and peeled

1 cup/140g Quick Vegetable Pickles (page 49)

2 to 3 Tbsp salmon or trout roe

Slice the avocados and divide among 4 small plates. Divide the vegetable pickles among the plates. Place 1 egg in the center of one of the plates and cut it open, letting the liquid yolk spill out. Repeat with the remaining 3 eggs and plates. Garnish the plates with the salmon or trout roe and serve.

Poached Eggs: Bring a pot of salted water to a boil. Lower the heat so that the water is just below simmering. (You should not see any bubbles, but the water should still be very hot to the touch.) Break an egg into a small bowl, and then tip the bowl into a fine-mesh strainer, letting the liquid part of the egg white pass through. Gently tip the egg into the water from the strainer, turning the egg onto itself with a wooden spoon to help keep its shape. Completely turn over the egg in the water once. Repeat with the remaining eggs. Cook the eggs for a total of 3 to 4 minutes. Using a slotted spoon, remove the eggs one at a time and briefly drain over paper towels. Transfer to individual serving bowls. If not serving right away, cool the eggs in a bowl of ice water, and then store in the refrigerator for up to 1 day. Reheat by slipping the eggs into a bowl of very hot water for 20 seconds; drain briefly and serve.

APPE
TIZERS
AND
SNACKS

GOAT CHEESE–GARLIC SPREAD

Makes about 1 cup/260g

My sister, Caitlin, makes this herby goat cheese spread that takes minutes to prepare and is unapologetically garlicky. She owns a distillery and has seen firsthand how it pairs well with her cocktails. My sister's recipe uses more garlic and is affectionately known in the family as Garlic Bomb. I use a little less (which is still plenty strong), so as not to entirely overpower a good goat cheese and to make it less "bomblike," but feel free to use as much garlic as you like. Archer often requests it for supper, and I'm wont to give in every time. Well-seasoned chèvre on a piece of rustic bread along with a generous salad . . . how can I turn her down? This can easily be scaled up for a large party (serve with vegetables, crackers, or toasted bread slices) or made for a hearty snack.

📖 Ricotta Cheese (page 33) is a good stand-in if you don't have goat cheese, but decrease the garlic to 2 cloves to match ricotta's milder character.

8 oz/230g soft, fresh goat cheese 3 cloves garlic, minced $\frac{1}{2}$ tsp ground black pepper 2 Tbsp olive oil $\frac{1}{4}$ cup/5g chopped mixed fresh herbs (such as flat-leaf parsley, rosemary, and chives)	In a small bowl, mix together the goat cheese, garlic, pepper, olive oil, and herbs. Transfer to a serving bowl or dish.
1 Tbsp olive oil	Drizzle the olive oil over the cheese mixture and serve.
	If not using immediately, store in a jar with a tight-fitting lid in the refrigerator for up to 1 week.

FIG-PLUM COMPOTE

Makes about 2 cups/500g

Choose plums that have good flavor and acidity to balance the sweetness of the figs. This recipe makes a small quantity, however, the compote keeps for months in the refrigerator if you make a double batch. Serve it with cheese and/or charcuterie.

8 figs, very ripe, stemmed and quartered

1 large plum, very ripe, cut into eighths

2 Tbsp honey

2 Tbsp red wine vinegar

Large pinch of ground black pepper

Pinch of sea salt

In a small saucepan, combine the figs, plum, honey, vinegar, pepper, and salt. Cook over low heat for 5 to 7 minutes, until the mixture thickens. Set aside to cool completely. Serve the compote at room temperature.

Store, covered, in the refrigerator for up to 3 months.

STUFFED DATES

Makes 12

This recipe for stuffed dates is more a guideline than an exact blueprint, riffing off of the idea that dates paired with most anything are delicious starters, perfect to begin a meal. Dates' dense sweetness and soft texture contrast well with rich, salty, or acidic foods. Slivers of aged cheese, dabs of creamy cheese, strips of anchovies, tiny slices of smoked or Canadian bacon and kumquat, or even tiny lamb patties (see the variation) stuffed into split dates create complex small bites that are easily assembled and will stave off hunger pangs. Play around with combinations—most cheeses, from a blue to a Brie to a Pecorino, work. Any sausage works as well, particularly chorizo or the spreadable 'nduja, and try warming the stuffed dates, too, as they become softer and more luscious when gently heated. →

📖 Take care to select dates that are plump and not too dried out. Medjool is a wonderful variety and probably the most available kind throughout the country. Other good varieties include Deglet Noor, Zahidi, and amber dates, but any semi-dry date that looks fresh will be good.

12 Medjool, Deglet Noor, Zahidi, or amber dates (or a combination), pitted

Split the dates lengthwise without cutting them all the way through.

1 slice Canadian bacon, cut into 1-inch-/2.5cm-long strips

2 kumquats, shaved crosswise into slices

2 white anchovies, rinsed and patted dry

4 walnut halves, toasted

2 Tbsp goat cheese

4 leaves arugula

Stuff each of 4 dates with a slice of Canadian bacon and 2 slices of kumquat. Stuff each of 4 more dates with half of an anchovy and 1 walnut half. Stuff the remaining 4 dates with 1½ tsp goat cheese and 1 leaf of arugula. Transfer the dates to a serving plate and serve at room temperature.

Lamb Sausage–Stuffed Dates: When you have time for a little more planning and preparation, try this variation for filling 12 dates: In a small bowl, gently mix 6 oz/170g ground lamb with ½ tsp sea salt, ½ tsp ground black pepper, ½ tsp chili powder, ½ tsp smoked Spanish paprika (pimentón), and a pinch of ground cumin. Form 1 petite patty, approximately 1-inch/2.5cm in diameter. Heat 1 Tbsp olive oil in a skillet over medium-high heat and pan-fry the test patty, turning it after about 30 seconds on the first side, until cooked through and browned at the edges. Taste and adjust the seasoning for the remaining lamb mixture. Repeat for the rest of the mixture. While still hot, stuff the tiny patties into the dates and serve warm.

CECI CACIO E PEPE (ROASTED CHICKPEAS WITH CHEESE AND PEPPER)

Makes about 1⅔ cups/250g

Just a while ago, it seemed I was seeing cacio e pepe in every food publication and at every restaurant. It was as if this classic Roman pasta dish of Pecorino cheese and black pepper had just been invented. In fact, the dish is the essence of *cucina povera*, which literally translates to "poor kitchen," and evokes the ability of Italian cuisine to make sumptuous food out of the simplest ingredients. Not much of a pasta eater myself, the marriage of the acidic sheep's milk cheese and the heat of the black pepper seemed too good to not try in other ways. So I came up with this: roasted chickpeas, or ceci, with the flavors of cacio e pepe. If roasting chickpeas is new to you, they turn surprisingly crisp on the outside. Between their texture and saltiness, this recipe ensures that they are the perfect snack with drinks or just before dinner. The fact that they are not fried and are a healthy legume is almost beside the point. The black pepper, a default spice for most cooks, will reassert its distinctive character, which has an earthier heat than red chiles. I prefer to use chickpeas I've cooked from scratch, but canned chickpeas work just as well and make this an even quicker-to-make snack.

1¾ cups/280g cooked chickpeas, or 1 (15-oz/420g) can chickpeas, rinsed and drained

½ tsp sea salt

10 grinds black peppercorns

1 Tbsp olive oil

Preheat the oven to 400°F/200°C. Toss the chickpeas, salt, pepper, and olive oil together on a rimmed baking sheet. Roast until the chickpeas are crisp on the outside, 8 to 10 minutes. →

6 Tbsp/35g finely grated Pecorino cheese

Sea salt

While the chickpeas are still hot, sprinkle the cheese over them and toss to coat. Taste and season with a bit more salt, if needed. Serve warm or at room temperature.

Store, covered, in the refrigerator for up to 3 days. Recrisp the chickpeas in a 400°F/200°C oven for about 5 minutes before serving.

Pimentón de la Vera Ceci Cacio: Chickpeas take to so many different flavors. If you want to branch out from the cacio e pepe combination, try smoked Spanish paprika (pimentón), substituting 1 Tbsp of the paprika for the pepper. And substitute a Spanish cheese like Manchego or Mahón for the Pecorino cheese.

Cumin and Garlic Ceci Cacio: Substitute 1 Tbsp ground cumin for the pepper. Add 4 cloves finely chopped garlic to the baking sheet with the chickpeas in the final minute of the roasting time (if added earlier, the garlic will burn).

GRANOLA BARK

Makes about 16 servings (one 13 by 18-inch/33 by 46cm sheet)

I have been auditioning granola bars for Archer, and I finally decided to make something in between the snack and the cereal: granola bark, a granola that forms a thin bar, and then easily broken into smaller pieces. Two recipes come to mind as those that shock home cooks the first time they make them: mashed potatoes, for how much cream and butter is used, and granola, which also has a surprising amount of fat and much more sugar than expected in a healthful snack or breakfast. So I've cut back, opting for the lower-glycemic sweeteners like maple syrup and coconut sugar. I use olive oil, but other healthful fats, like coconut oil, would do just as well, and of course, butter is a delicious option. The egg white and plumped flax seeds help bind the granola →

and make it extra crispy, doing the job that additional sweetener often does. I enjoy this bark over yogurt with fruit for breakfast, and I include it in Archer's lunchbox as a snack bar.

📖 The recipe works without the egg white, but the bark is slightly more crisp with the egg white.

1$\frac{1}{2}$ tsp ground cinnamon

3 cups/300g rolled oats (not quick-cooking)

1$\frac{1}{4}$ cups/175g almonds, chopped

1$\frac{1}{4}$ cups/60g unsweetened shredded coconut

$\frac{1}{2}$ cup/80g flax seeds or chia seeds, whole or ground

$\frac{1}{4}$ cup/35g sesame seeds

$\frac{1}{2}$ cup/60g almond flour or hazelnut flour

Combine the cinnamon, oats, almonds, coconut, flax or chia seeds, sesame seeds, and almond flour or hazelnut flour in a large bowl.

Preheat the oven to 325°F/165°C. Line a 13 by 18 inch/33 by 46cm rimmed baking sheet with parchment paper or a silicone mat.

$\frac{1}{2}$ cup/120ml maple syrup or honey, or $\frac{1}{4}$ cup/60ml of each

$\frac{1}{2}$ cup/75g coconut sugar

$\frac{1}{4}$ cup/60ml water

1 tsp vanilla extract

$\frac{1}{2}$ tsp sea salt

Combine the maple syrup or honey or a mix of both, coconut sugar, water, vanilla, and salt in a small saucepan and bring to a boil, stirring to dissolve the sugar and salt. Remove from the heat and let cool to warm room temperature.

$\frac{1}{3}$ cup/80ml olive oil or vegetable oil

1 large egg white, whisked until frothy

Add the olive oil and egg white to the cooled syrup mixture and whisk to incorporate. Pour over the oats mixture and mix well.

Spread the mixture evenly across the prepared baking sheet. Using another same-size baking sheet or the bottom of a pot, press the mixture down firmly to compact it before baking. Bake for 45 minutes or longer, until dark golden brown, rotating the sheet after about 15 minutes to promote even browning. While the granola bakes, open the oven door a couple of times to release steam.

Set the baking sheet on a cooling rack until the surface of the granola is crisp. Leave the oven on. If the surface it is still tacky to the touch once it has cooled, return the pan to the oven and continue baking for another 10 to 15 minutes, checking every 5 minutes. Don't let the bark get too dark, or it'll taste bitter.

Once cool, break the bark into pieces and store in an airtight container at room temperature for up to 2 weeks, or in the refrigerator for up to 1 month.

CHEESE-AND-PEPPER CRACKERS

Makes about 60 (1-inch/2.5cm) round crackers

I love the tradition of serving homemade crackers with a glass of wine. In a time when endless store-bought options are available though, it has to be a special recipe to convince anyone to forgo convenience. These crackers—conceived one evening when I had good cheese, a glass of wine, and nothing crispy in sight—are exactly what a cracker should be. The rice flour, which lends a fine texture, and the flavor of whatever aged cheese you have on hand, enhanced with a little mustard and hot pepper, make for a perfectly savory bite. These simple crackers are addictive and well worth taking out the rolling pin. Sometimes the smallest gestures are the most pleasing.

1 Tbsp ground chia seeds 3 Tbsp water	In a small bowl, mix the chia seeds and water. Let sit for 10 minutes for the chia seeds soften.
$\frac{1}{4}$ cup/35g brown rice flour $\frac{1}{4}$ cup/45g potato starch $\frac{1}{4}$ cup/30g oat flour $\frac{1}{2}$ tsp baking powder $\frac{1}{4}$ tsp sea salt	Combine the rice flour, potato starch, oat flour, baking powder, and salt in a medium bowl and whisk to thoroughly combine. →

1 cup/100g grated cheddar, Gruyère, or other firm cheese

$\frac{1}{4}$ cup/55g unsalted butter, at room temperature

2 tsp whole-grain or Dijon mustard

Pinch of ground red chile

In a large bowl, use a wooden spoon to mix the cheese, butter, mustard, and chile powder well. Stir in the chia-water mixture and then add the flour mixture and mix until a soft dough forms.

Shape the dough into a disk, wrap in plastic wrap, and refrigerate until firm, about 1 hour. (The dough can be kept in the refrigerator for up to 10 days or in the freezer, wrapped in additional plastic wrap, for several months. If you freeze the dough, let it thaw at room temperature for 20 minutes until still firm, but not brittle, before rolling it out.)

Preheat the oven to 350°F/180°C. Line a baking sheet with parchment paper.

2 Tbsp minced flat-leaf parsley

Unwrap the dough and roll it out into a circle that is $\frac{1}{4}$-inch/6mm thick. Gently transfer the dough to the baking sheet. Bake for 15 to 18 minutes, until fragrant, light golden brown, and crisp. Set the baking sheet on a cooling rack and let cool completely. Carefully transfer the cracker round to a cutting board and cut in a crosshatch pattern to create 1-inch/2.5cm squares. Sprinkle the parsley over the top and serve.

Store in an airtight container at room temperature for up to 2 weeks.

GOUGÈRES

Makes about 32 (2½-inch/6cm) gougères

These savory, eggy, and hollow pastries are said to originate in Burgundy, where they are served while tasting wine in cavernous cellars. Indeed, their casual elegance makes them a go-to when small bites are called for. Like potatoes, gougères take on just about any flavor with appealing clarity. When the dough is mixed with cheese, the unique notes of an aged cheddar, Jarlsberg, or hard goat cheese come through beautifully. Spices like saffron or cumin are delicious, too, though I am partial to our bakery's standard: gougères with black pepper, thyme, and Gruyère. I often look to particular cuisines for inspiration, pairing smoked Spanish paprika (pimentón) with Idiazabal cheese, or herbes de Provence and a classic French cheese. Gougères are my favorite when made petite and served fresh from the oven. When larger, between the size of a biscuit and a popover, they can accompany soup or be split open to make a sandwich. Either way, this is a recipe I recommend making your own.

📖 These gougères successfully rise when the oven is very hot. To ensure a surge of heat, start them on a bottom rack. Or, if you have a baking stone, position it at the very bottom of the oven and place the baking sheet on top of it. Once the gougères have risen and the crust is set, move the baking sheet to the center rack. Be sure not to open the oven while the gougères are midrise or they may fall.

½ cup/120ml whole milk ½ cup/120ml water ½ cup/110g unsalted butter ½ tsp sea salt 1 tsp granulated sugar	Combine the milk, water, butter, salt, and sugar in a medium saucepan. Bring to a boil over medium heat, stirring occasionally, to melt the butter.
⅓ cup plus 1 Tbsp/55g white rice flour ⅓ cup plus 1 Tbsp/50g oat flour ⅓ cup plus 1 Tbsp/50g tapioca flour/starch	Mix the rice flour, oat flour, and tapioca flour/starch together in a small bowl. Remove the milk mixture from the heat and add the flour mixture all at once. Stir with a wooden spoon until smooth. Return the saucepan to medium heat and cook, stirring constantly, over medium heat for 1 minute.

6 large eggs, plus 1 more,
as needed

Remove the saucepan with the milk-flour mixture from the heat and add the eggs one at a time, stirring immediately and vigorously after each addition. The dough should be thick and glossy and somewhat stretchy—if you lift the spoon up, the dough should drop back into the saucepan in a continuous trail as opposed to a single blob. If the dough is too thick, crack 1 additional egg into a small bowl, beat well with a fork, and stir in 1 tsp at a time, until the dough, or pâte à choux, is the proper consistency.

$\frac{3}{4}$ cup/70g grated
Gruyère or other firm
cheese such as cheddar
or Tomme de Savoie

1 tsp ground
black pepper

1 Tbsp fresh thyme
leaves, finely chopped

Mix the cheese, black pepper, and thyme into the pâte à choux.

Preheat the oven to 400°F/200°C. Line 2 baking sheets with parchment paper or silicone mats. Fit a large pastry bag with a plain $\frac{1}{2}$-inch/12mm tip, or cut a $\frac{1}{2}$-inch/12mm opening in the corner of a large plastic bag.

Transfer the dough to the prepared pastry bag. Holding the bag at an angle with the tip barely resting on the prepared baking sheet, gently squeeze the dough out to form a 2-inch/5cm-wide mound. (If you are using parchment paper and would like to be very accurate, you can draw 2-inch/5cm circles on the back of the paper.) Repeat to form approximately 32 mounds, spaced at least 2 inches/5cm apart from each other, on the 2 baking sheets.

1 large egg

Pinch of sea salt

Whisk the egg and salt together in a small bowl. Gently brush the tops and sides of the dough mounds with the egg wash. →

¾ cup/70g grated
Gruyère or other firm
cheese, such as cheddar
or Tomme de Savoie

Sprinkle the cheese evenly over the egg wash.
Bake on the lowest rack of the oven until deep golden
brown all over and hollow-sounding when tapped,
about 20 minutes. Resist the urge to open the oven
door while the gougères are baking; doing so may
cause them to fall. Serve hot or warm.

To store gougères, set the baking sheet on a
cooling rack, let cool completely, and then place in
an airtight container in the refrigerator for up to
3 days. Recrisp the gougères in a 350°F/180°C oven
for about 5 minutes before serving.

PISSALADIERE

Makes 8 to 10 servings (one 10-inch/25cm pie)

When Chad and I worked in France, bakers would warmly invite
us to their homes and, without fail, offer up pissaladiere soon after
our arrival. Each made this popular homemade pastry, topped with
caramelized onions, anchovies, and oil-cured olives, in their own way,
and none failed to satisfy. A proper pissaladiere from Nice, along
France's Mediterranean coast, is most often made with a yeasted
dough, but these days it's quite common for pissaladiere to be made
with a short flaky pastry, too. In my first book, my recipe used a
leavened brioche, but now I use the Cream Cheese Dough (page 36)
to make a gluten-free version. The tangy and crisp crust pairs well
with the sweet onions. Serve the pissaladiere as an appetizer or with
drinks, cut it into bite-size pieces, or pair it with a salad for a light lunch
or a first course. And, because it holds up well and is eaten at room
temperature, this pissaladiere also makes the loveliest picnic fare.

2 Tbsp olive oil

2 large yellow onions, thinly sliced

Pinch of sea salt

Pinch of ground black pepper

Heat the olive oil in a large skillet over medium-high heat. Add the onions, salt, and pepper and cook, stirring until lightly browned, about 10 minutes. Decrease the heat to low and continue to cook, stirring often to promote even browning, until caramelized, about 15 minutes longer. Season with the salt and pepper. Set aside to cool at room temperature.

Place a baking stone, if you have one, on the floor of the oven. Preheat the oven to 425°F/220°C.

$\frac{1}{2}$ batch Cream Cheese Dough (page 36), rolled out to a 10-inch/25cm circle approximately $\frac{1}{8}$-inch/3mm thick

Line a baking sheet with parchment paper. Place the dough circle on the prepared baking sheet, cover, and chill in the refrigerator until firm, about 10 minutes.

10 to 12 olive oil– or salt-packed anchovies, rinsed

20 oil-cured olives, pitted

Remove the dough from the refrigerator and spread the caramelized onions over the dough circle, leaving a $\frac{1}{4}$-inch/6mm border. Evenly distribute the anchovies and olives over the top. Return to the refrigerator and chill for 10 minutes.

1 large egg

Pinch of sea salt

Whisk the egg and salt together in a small bowl. Brush the egg wash over the edges of the dough circle. Place the baking sheet on the baking stone or on the lowest rack of the oven and bake for 20 minutes. Lower the oven temperature to 375°F/190°C, move the baking sheet to the center rack of the oven, and continue baking until the pastry has a dark golden brown color, 15 to 20 minutes. Remove the pissaladiere from the oven and place on a wire rack to cool for 10 minutes. Slice into wedges and serve warm or at room temperature.

When completely cool, wrap the pissaladiere in aluminum foil and store at room temperature for up to 2 days.

AGUACHILE WITH SHRIMP AND SCALLOPS

Makes 8 servings as an appetizer or 4 as a main course

Aguachile is Mexico's version of ceviche, the bright and assertive Peruvian method of "cooking" raw fish in lime or bitter orange juice. On a sweltering day, there's nothing better than a cold dish of avocado and tortilla chips with aguachile. Like many time-tested dishes, this recipe should be taken more as a guideline than a precise dictum. Use whatever fish or shellfish is exceptionally fresh and vary the herbs if cilantro isn't to your liking.

📖 This is meant to be eaten soon after it is made, but it will still be delicious, though its texture will be more "cooked," one day later.

12 oz/340g shrimp, peeled and deveined, cut in half from tip to tail

12 oz/340g scallops, cut in half horizontally

$1\frac{1}{2}$ cups/360ml freshly squeezed lime juice (about 9 limes)

$1\frac{1}{2}$ tsp sea salt

Place the shrimp and scallops in a shallow dish, pour in the lime juice, and mix in the salt. Cover and let marinate in the refrigerator for 30 minutes.

16 Corn Tortillas (page 62, or store-bought), cut into wedges

1 qt/960ml vegetable oil, for frying

Meanwhile, make the fried corn tortillas: Pour the oil to a depth of $\frac{1}{2}$ inch/12mm in a pan and heat over medium-high heat. Line a plate with paper towels and set nearby. Test the temperature by cutting a strip from one of the tortillas and carefully lowering it into the hot oil. If the tortilla sizzles right away, the oil is ready. Fry the wedges, a few at a time, flipping once or twice with tongs, until slightly puffed and crisp, about 1 to 2 minutes per tortilla. Transfer to the prepared plate and let cool. (Fried tortillas can be made a few hours ahead and recrisped as needed in a 400°F/200°C oven for 3 to 5 minutes.) →

2 or 3 serrano chiles, stemmed, seeded, and sliced	In a medium bowl, mix together the chiles, cucumber, and cilantro.
2 or 3 jalapeños, stemmed, seeded, and sliced	
1 cucumber, peeled, seeded, and cut into $\frac{1}{2}$-inch/12mm- thick slices	
1 bunch cilantro, coarsely chopped	
3 Tbsp water	Once the seafood has marinated, pour about half of the marinating liquid into a blender and add the water and a ladleful of the chile mixture. Blend to combine, then pour over the marinated seafood. Scatter the remaining chile mixture over the top and mix gently. (If not serving immediately, chill in the refrigerator for no more than 3 hours so that the seafood doesn't "cook" too much in the liquid.)
1 large or 2 small ripe avocados, halved, pitted, peeled, and sliced	Add the avocado to the seafood and chile mixture and serve the whole fried tortilla wedges on the side.

CHICKEN LIVER MOUSSE

Makes about 2 cups/380g

I've always loved a textured pâté, but this is like eating an Armagnac-scented cloud of butter and cream. In a few extra steps, it goes far beyond the usual treatment of liver sautéed with shallots and deglazed with wine and becomes a melt-in-your-mouth showstopper for any chicken liver fan. (I'd also consider this a conversion food for those who thought they could never like the stuff.) No matter how liver is prepared, an eye toward balance is essential. The key is a technique that goes against my better instincts: cook the livers until the outsides are a drab shade of gray. Richard Olney, the authority on French cooking, recommended this very technique because the diminutive size of livers make them easy to overcook, which will unpleasantly accentuate their iron flavors. This rich mousse, which builds flavor with shallots, flambéed Armagnac or Cognac, and ample butter and cream, can afford the loss of richness from the browned exterior. Because the interior of the liver remains beautifully pink, the mousse turns a gorgeous rosy tint. This mousse is incredible as is, but with quick-pickled currants and thyme, the sweet and herbaceous contrast makes this recipe addictive. Spread on lightly toasted baguette or walnut levain, there's nothing better.

8 oz/225g chicken livers Sea salt Ground black pepper	Generously season the chicken livers with salt and pepper on all sides and set aside.
2 Tbsp unsalted butter 2 shallots, thinly sliced	In a large pan, melt the butter over medium heat. Add the shallots and sauté in the butter until soft but not at all browned.
	Increase the heat to medium-high. Add the seasoned chicken livers to the pan of sautéed shallots and cook, turning once or twice, until gray on the outsides but still pink and rare in the centers when you cut one open to check, 3 to 4 minutes.
$\frac{1}{4}$ cup/60ml Armagnac or Cognac	Pour the Armagnac or Cognac into the pan with the livers and shallots and then carefully set aflame with a lit match. Once the flames in the pan go out, transfer the livers and their cooking juices to the bowl of a food processor or blender.
$\frac{1}{2}$ cup/110g unsalted butter, cut into pieces, chilled	Add the butter to the blended liver mixture and blend until very smooth.
	Pass the liver-butter mixture through a fine-mesh strainer into a large bowl, pressing and scraping with a rubber spatula. If the mixture is still warm, place the bowl in the refrigerator to chill for a few minutes. →

½ cup/120ml heavy cream	Whip the cream until soft peaks form when the whisk is lifted out of the bowl. Fold the whipped cream into the pressed liver mixture until thoroughly combined. Pack into small crocks or ramekins, cover, and chill in the refrigerator for about 2 hours or until set.
¼ cup/60ml sherry vinegar ¼ cup/60ml water ½ cup/70g fresh currants 3 sprigs fresh thyme	Meanwhile, make the quick-pickled currants by warming the sherry vinegar and water in a small saucepan. Remove from the heat and add the currants and thyme. Let pickle until plumped and cooled to room temperature, about 30 minutes.
1 baguette, cut into ¼-inch/6mm-thick slices, and lightly toasted	To serve, spread the chicken liver mousse on toasted bread and top with a few pickled currants.
	Store the liver mousse, tightly covered, in the refrigerator for up to 5 days.

SOCCA
(CHICKPEA CRISPS)

Makes 4 servings (about 8-inch/20cm pancakes)

There are countless names for a batter of chickpea flour and water that is cooked over a wood fire or fried: *socca, panisse, torta di ceci,* or *kalinti,* just to name a few. Regions from the southern coast of France to Italy have variations of this traditional street food, and Morocco and Algeria have versions that are more flanlike, with the addition of an egg. This is the kind of food for which a written recipe was only a recent necessity; street vendors selling the hot chickpea flatbread relied more on visual and tactile cues than on exact quantities. Socca are originally from Nice, France, where the batter is poured into large copper plates and cooked quickly in a wood-fired oven. The earthy chickpea flour crisps at the edges and blisters, becoming infused with the flavor of the fire. They are served piping hot with a good amount of fresh black pepper. I've run with tradition, making this a recipe suitable for the stovetop, taking the advice of my friend and author David Lebovitz to add a pinch of cumin to imitate the smoky effect. These fry up more like crêpes and can be made crispy, or kept a little chewy (as I prefer) in the center. I use a cast-iron or crêpe pan and make the socca much smaller. I've topped them with a sprinkling of rosemary, a flavor that can be pungent when fresh but is just right with the socca. Socca make a wonderful starter for an afternoon or evening gathering, as a sort of flatbread alongside grilled vegetables or fish, and I've even used a more sizable socca as a delicious base for a lemony arugula salad. The preserved lemon is my own addition; it pairs well with the chickpea and rosemary and adds a nice tartness.

📖 The batter can be made well ahead of time because these are flat cakes that use no leavening agent or egg and therefore do not require quick assembly in order to achieve a rise.

1 cup/120g chickpea flour $\frac{1}{4}$ tsp sea salt $\frac{1}{4}$ tsp ground black pepper Pinch of ground cumin (optional)	Combine the flour, salt, pepper, and cumin in a bowl.
1 cup/240ml water	While whisking the flour mixture, gradually pour in the water. Continue to whisk until smooth.
2 Tbsp olive oil $\frac{1}{4}$ Preserved Lemon (page 39), finely chopped	Whisk the olive oil into the batter. Mix in the lemon. Let rest, covered, at room temperature for at least 1 hour or up to 12 hours.
Water, as needed	After resting, the batter should have the same consistency as heavy cream. If it is too thick, whisk in additional water, 1 Tbsp at a time. →

2 Tbsp olive oil, plus more as needed	Heat the oil in an 8-inch/20 cm cast-iron skillet over high heat. Swirl the pan to evenly coat the bottom with oil. Ladle in some batter, tilting the pan to create a pancake no thicker than $\frac{1}{4}$ inch/6mm. Cook until golden brown around the edges, about 2 minutes, and then flip and cook the second side for about 1 minute, until golden and crisp. Transfer to a plate. Continue cooking the pancakes, adding oil to the pan as needed to prevent burning.
Coarse sea salt 1 Tbsp minced rosemary or thyme	Garnish with salt and rosemary or thyme and serve piping hot.
	To store socca, let cool completely, and then place in an airtight container in the refrigerator for up to 3 days. Recrisp the socca in a 400°F/200°C oven for 2 minutes before serving.

GRAVLAX

Makes about $1\frac{1}{2}$ lb/680g

In 1982, when I was a year out of high school, I worked in a seasonal salmon "camp" on the Kenai Peninsula, which juts out from the southern coast of Alaska. Boatloads of fish arrived there daily to be cleaned and broken down with the roe separated out. My job was to identify each fish's species (of the five species of salmon) and sort them accordingly for the Japanese market. I learned a lot that summer, as each fish came through a shoot to the assembly line, more than just the differences in tail shape and color, and worked harder than ever—before or since. Despite the inundation of fresh salmon for fourteen hours each day, my taste for it never dampened. I've always liked to cure my own fish, as the difference between store-bought and homemade is undeniable. The silky tenderness possible with home curing is lost in store-bought options. Through the years, I've homed in on the details—gauging the salt and sugar ratio and the curing time in relation to the thickness of the fish—that ensure an →

ethereal gravlax. For the most tender texture, I rinse the salmon of its herbs and salt once it has cured and refrigerate it for one more day, allowing the seasoning to evenly distribute. If you're too impatient to wait the entire curing time, don't hesitate to slice off a piece and sauté it in butter. A little heat does wonders to the highly flavored fish.

📖 If you do not have juniper berries, a splash of gin will do just as well in its place.

1 large bunch/40g dill, coarsely chopped

$\frac{1}{4}$ cup/40g sea salt

$\frac{1}{4}$ cup/50g granulated sugar

1 Tbsp ground white pepper or a combination of 1 $\frac{1}{2}$ tsp ground white, black, pink, or green pepper and 1 $\frac{1}{2}$ tsp ground allspice

6 (or more, if you like) juniper berries, crushed (optional)

Combine the dill, salt, sugar, pepper or pepper-allspice mixture, and juniper berries in a bowl and mix well.

Choose a glass or earthenware container large enough to accommodate the salmon. Lay a piece of cheesecloth across the bottom of the container, leaving at least 6 inches/15cm of cheesecloth hanging over two sides.

2 lb/910g salmon fillet, skin on

Check the salmon for pin bones (the tiny bones that aren't attached to the fish's skeleton) by running your fingers over the fillet. If you need to remove any, slide a hand under the fillet and lift the fillet slightly so it bends at the point where the pin bone is located. Grasp the protruding bone with tweezers or needle-nose pliers and gently pull the bone out. Repeat until all the pin bones are removed.

Spread about half of the dill mixture across the cheesecloth, place the fish on top, then spread the remaining dill mixture over the fish. Wrap the cheesecloth around the fish to cover completely. If you have a small rack that fits within the container, you can use it to elevate the cheesecloth-wrapped salmon, but it is not necessary. Cover the dish with plastic wrap, set a weight (such as a can of tomatoes) on top of the fish, and place in the refrigerator to cure for 5 to 7 days, depending on the thickness of the salmon. A thin fillet that's $1\frac{1}{2}$ inches/4cm thick requires only 5 days, whereas a thick 2-inch/5cm fillet will need 7 days to cure. After about 1 day of curing time, drain off any liquid that has accumulated in the container.

Remove the cured salmon from the cheesecloth and rinse under cool water, brushing off the dill mixture. Set the fish on a plate and return to the refrigerator, uncovered, for 24 hours.

After the final day in the refrigerator, thinly slice the unwrapped cured salmon on the diagonal, leaving the skin behind, and serve.

Sliced gravlax will keep, covered, in the refrigerator for up to 5 days. It can be tightly wrapped and stored in the freezer for up to 3 months.

SOUPS

ANCHO PEPPER SOUP

Makes 6 servings (about 7½ cups/1.7L)

I love a dinner table covered with small dishes of colorful garnishes that allow you to customize your own bowl. This soup lends itself well to this kind of improvisation. Typically, a good chicken stock makes the broth, but I wanted to shift emphasis to a smoky pepper flavor. The pureed ancho contributes a complexity usually found in a longer-simmering stew. Chicken still plays a role in the broth though. When the chicken thighs are browned in the soup pot, they leave caramelized, meaty bits (called fond) that contribute depth when mixed with sautéed onions. With the exception of a few items, the soup relies upon pantry ingredients and is itself quite straightforward.

📖 With this soup, I use ancho and pimentón dulce, but any mild and sweet dried peppers will do. Dulce rojo and guajillo work equally well. Adjust the number of peppers if using spicier ones.

📖 If you do not have Job's tears, consider using cooked hominy instead, which can be found canned in most grocery stores and Mexican markets, or skip this ingredient entirely.

1 Tbsp olive oil 1 lb/455g bone-in chicken thighs, skin on	Heat the oil in a large pot over medium-high heat. Add the chicken and cook, turning once or twice, until well browned and cooked through, 18 to 22 minutes, depending on the thickness of the meat. Transfer to a plate and pour off all but 1 to 2 Tbsp of oil left behind in the pot.
1 small yellow onion, chopped	Return the pot with oil and chicken fat to the stove over medium heat. Add the onion and cook, stirring with a wooden spoon and scraping along the bottom of the pot to release the browned bits, until the onion is translucent, 3 to 5 minutes.
2 cloves garlic, chopped 1 tsp ground cumin 1 bay leaf 4 tsp sweet Spanish paprika (pimentón dulce)	Add the garlic, cumin, bay leaf, and paprika to the sautéed onion and cook, stirring often, for 1 minute. →

4 dried ancho chiles, stemmed and seeded	Using tongs, quickly toast each chile over a flame or under the broiler, turning to toast all sides evenly, for a few seconds. Add to the pot with the onion mixture.
1 (14$\frac{1}{2}$-oz/411ml) can crushed or diced tomatoes 6 cups/1.4L water or Chicken Stock (page 32, or store-bought) 1 small dried hot chile (such as pequin or Calabrian), stemmed 2 tsp sea salt	Add the tomatoes and their juices, water or stock, dried chile, and salt to the onion-chile mixture and bring to a gentle simmer, and then cover the pot and cook for 30 minutes.
Sea salt, as needed	Discard the bay leaf. Blend the soup with an immersion blender, or transfer to a blender and blend until smooth. If transferring to a blender, use caution as the soup will be very hot; work in batches, filling the blender no more than halfway full. Taste and season with additional salt, if needed.
	While the soup simmers, finish preparing the chicken. Preheat the oven to 400°F/200°C. Remove the skin (set the meat aside) and roast the skin on a baking sheet in the oven until crispy, 6 to 8 minutes. Transfer the crispy skin to a paper towel to absorb excess oil. Shred the meat.
1 qt/960ml vegetable oil, for frying 8 to 10 corn tortillas (page 62, store-bought), cut into $\frac{1}{4}$-inch/6mm strips	Pour the oil to a depth of $\frac{1}{2}$ inch/12mm in a pan and heat over medium-high heat. Test the temperature by carefully lowering in a single strip of tortilla. The oil is ready when the tortilla sizzles right away. Fry the remaining strips in batches (don't crowd), about one tortilla's worth at a time, depending on the size of your pan. When the strips are golden brown, 1 to 2 minutes, transfer them to a paper towel and let cool.

2 ripe avocados, halved, pitted, peeled, and sliced

$\frac{1}{2}$ cup/120g crema, or sour cream thinned with a small amount of water

1 bunch cilantro, marjoram, or oregano, coarsely chopped

$1\frac{1}{4}$ cups/175g cooked Job's tears (page 169, Job's Tears Salad)

$\frac{1}{4}$ head white cabbage, cored and shaved as thinly as possible

2 limes, cut into wedges

Ladle the hot soup into bowls and serve the chicken meat; crisped skin; fried tortillas; avocados; crema or sour cream; cilantro, marjoram, or oregano; Job's tears; cabbage; and lime wedges alongside.

Store the soup, covered, in the refrigerator, for up to 5 days.

CAULIFLOWER-GARLIC SOUP WITH WATERCRESS PESTO

Makes 6 servings (about 7 cups/1.6L)

It never fails to amaze me that such a humble vegetable can make this beautiful soup—especially when that very vegetable was found in the back of the produce drawer long past its due. The delicacy of cauliflower is the key to its versatility. Steamed, roasted, or pureed, simply dressed with butter or added spice, cauliflower's mild, earthy sweetness somehow always comes through. In this soup, cauliflower becomes the backdrop for a generous amount of garlic, which in the company of good chicken stock gives backbone and depth. I've always gravitated toward soups that have an interplay of texture and flavor, and find that this creamy one does well with pungent toppings, like sautéed hedgehog mushrooms (or any kind of mushrooms for that matter). The watercress pesto is an ideal partner, for the cress's pepperiness and the mouthfeel of the pounded pine nuts are the perfect foil. Peppercress or arugula are good replacements for the watercress. →

2 Tbsp olive oil ½ yellow onion, sliced	Heat a large pot over medium heat and add the oil. When the oil is shimmering, add the onion and sauté until translucent, about 5 minutes.
6 cloves garlic, sliced	Add the garlic to the onion and cook until softened but not yet browned, 30 seconds to 1 minute.
1 qt/960ml Chicken Stock (page 32, or store-bought) or water 1 head/600g cauliflower, leaves trimmed, cored, and coarsely chopped	Add the stock and cauliflower to the sautéed onion and garlic. Bring to a boil, and then lower the heat so that the soup simmers. Cook until the cauliflower is tender, 10 to 15 minutes.
1 clove garlic ¼ tsp sea salt	Meanwhile, make the watercress pesto: Using a large mortar and pestle, pound the garlic and salt to a paste. Alternatively, use the back of a large knife to smash the garlic and salt to a paste.
Large handful/10g basil leaves Large handful/10g watercress leaves	Add the basil and watercress to the mortar and pound to a smooth puree. If working without a mortar and pestle, finely chop the herbs and place them in a medium bowl.
2 Tbsp pine nuts, lightly toasted and cooled	Add the pine nuts and pound to incorporate them but don't let the mixture become too smooth. Alternatively, use a large knife to coarsely chop and pound the pine nuts, and then mix them into the chopped herbs. Transfer the pesto to a small bowl.
2 Tbsp olive oil, plus more as needed	Drizzle in the oil, stirring until combined. If the pesto seems too thick, stir in a little more oil.
1½ tsp sea salt ¼ cup/60ml heavy cream Juice of 1 lemon	Puree the cauliflower mixture in a blender until completely smooth. Add the salt, cream, and lemon juice to the soup, and then taste and adjust the seasoning. To serve, ladle hot soup into bowls and top each with a spoonful of watercress pesto.
	Store the soup and pesto, separately and covered, in the refrigerator for up to 5 days.

BILLI BI SOUP WITH SAFFRON

Makes 6 servings as a first course or 4 as a main dish

I first tried Billi Bi (pronounced billy bee) when I was a bus girl at the Bird and Bottle Inn, a lovely place in upstate New York that my friend's parents owned. At that point, the creamy, wine-enriched soup of mussels was the fanciest I had ever tasted. The velvety consistency, achieved with the addition of egg yolks, marked a leap in sophistication for my palate. Now when I have Billi Bi, the Oyster Bar at Grand Central Station comes to mind, where there are tiers of giant stewpots simmering with a little seafood and a lot of cream. I've updated this recipe (the soup reached its apex of popularity in the 1970s) so that it is more balanced, adding saffron for its color and slight bitterness, along with parsley and lemon juice. Even with these additions, it remains a very French soup, fit for a special occasion, whether as a small first course or a beautiful main dish for a lunch or dinner. The delightful, slightly nonsensical name supposedly comes from an American scientist and gastronome, William Beebe, for whom the soup was invented at the turn of twentieth century. Serve with good crusty bread.

2 cups/480ml white wine	Bring the wine, water, shallots, bay leaf, black pepper, and cayenne to a boil in a large pot. Lower the heat so the liquid simmers and cook for 5 minutes.
1 cup/240ml water	
2 shallots, coarsely chopped	
1 bay leaf	
Pinch of ground black pepper	
Pinch of cayenne pepper	
2 lb/910g mussels, scrubbed and beards removed	Line a heatproof colander with cheesecloth and set inside the pot with the wine mixture. Add the mussels, cover the pot, and cook over medium-high heat until opened, 5 to 7 minutes, depending on their size. Using a slotted spoon, transfer the mussels to a bowl and discard any that have not opened. Slowly strain the mussel liquid that remains in the pot through the cheesecloth-lined colander into a bowl, taking care that any sand is left behind. Rinse the →

pot out, pour the mussel liquid back into the pot, and bring to a simmer.

1 cup/240ml heavy cream 2 large egg yolks 1 tsp lemon juice Large pinch of saffron Sea salt	In a bowl, whisk together the cream, egg yolks, lemon juice, and saffron. While whisking, add one ladleful of the hot mussel liquid to the cream mixture. Continue whisking and adding 1 ladleful at a time, until two-thirds of the hot stock has been added. Transfer all of it back to the pot. Cook over medium-low heat, whisking constantly, until the liquid has thickened, 3 to 5 minutes. Take care not to let it boil, or the yolks will curdle. Taste for seasoning, adding salt if necessary.
1 to 2 Tbsp chopped flat-leaf parsley, for garnish	The soup can be served with the mussels in the shell or out of the shell. Either way, ladle the hot soup into bowls and evenly distribute the mussels, garnish with parsley, and serve.

SIMPLE CRAB BISQUE

Makes 4 to 6 servings (about 5 cups/1.2L)

Over the holidays, I often visit my parents in Oregon, who years ago left upstate New York to move west. For us, wintertime on the Oregon Coast has turned into an occasion for crab feasts. After an evening of cracking Dungeness legs to dip in aioli, we collect the leftover bodies in a soup pot for the next day's bisque. My dad's always in charge of this, and his take is far less complicated than traditional bisques, which tend to call for making shellfish stock and thickening it with egg yolks or roux. His version is a soup that feels closer to the sea. While some bisques make use of the whole crab (or lobster or shrimp), this one uses just the bodies, making it a wonderful second meal and leaving nothing to waste. He starts after breakfast and the soup is ready by lunch. The dry sherry and cream lend it the classic bisque flavors, and the butter added at the end gives it the richness you might expect without the weight of flour. A toasted baguette and salad are all that's needed when you want indulgence with minimal effort.

📖 I prefer this bisque a little brothier, but if you long for a thicker consistency that's more in line with traditional bisques, make a little slurry with either 1 tsp of tapioca flour/starch or cornstarch dissolved in 2 Tbsp of water and add in the final minutes of cooking.

2 cooked Dungeness crab bodies, legs and "knuckles" removed, guts intact

$\frac{1}{2}$ lemon, sliced

2 small stalks celery, sliced

1 small onion, sliced

2 cloves garlic, crushed

4 sprigs thyme

1 bay leaf

1 cup/240ml white wine

1 qt/960ml fish stock, shellfish stock, or water, plus more as needed

Combine the crab, lemon, celery, onion, garlic, thyme, bay leaf, wine, and stock or water in a large stockpot. Add additional stock or water as needed to cover the crab bodies. Bring to a simmer and cook for 1 hour.

Strain the crab mixture through a fine-mesh strainer into a large bowl. Rinse out the pot and then return the strained liquid to the clean pot. Discard the crab, vegetables, and herbs.

$\frac{3}{4}$ cup/180ml heavy cream

6 Tbsp/85g unsalted butter

$\frac{1}{4}$ cup/60ml dry sherry

Sea salt

Ground black pepper

Add the cream, butter, and sherry to the stockpot of crab broth and cook over medium heat, stirring until the butter has melted completely. Season with salt and pepper to taste. Ladle into bowls and serve hot.

BLACK BEAN AND HAM HOCK SOUP

Makes 8 to 10 servings (about 2 ½ qt/2.4L)

I make this hearty soup when I anticipate a houseful of company. The ham hock gives such a savory richness to the cooking liquid that no other stock is necessary. I recommend finding a substantial hock, so that both marrow and meat contribute to the soup. Make this ahead of time, in great quantity, confident that it needs barely anything else to make the meal whole. Add a salad or cornbread, and you're set. If you have leftovers, this soup freezes well and reheats as if it were just made.

📖 It used to be that only a few kinds of beans were available at the grocery store: split peas, kidneys, and black beans, often looking worn-out in their fading plastic bags. Now, with so many beautiful heirloom beans available, I urge you to use any kind in this recipe. The result will be different, and wonderful, with each variety. If you're near a vibrant farmers' market, there may well be farmers growing and drying their own shell beans. While the price might be higher, the difference that freshness and variety can make is well worth it. If you can't find a local source, one of my favorite sources is Rancho Gordo, which sells such interesting, high-quality beans, and they ship everywhere. Their Ayocote Blanco, Yellow Indian Woman, or flageolet beans would all be terrific in this soup.

1 lb/455g dried black beans	Rinse the beans and place them in a large bowl. Pour in enough water to cover the beans by at least 3 inches/7.5cm and let them soak for several hours or overnight.
1 large/175g smoked ham hock 3 qt/2.8L water	In a large pot, simmer the ham hock in the water for 1 hour to create a flavorful broth.
2 Tbsp olive oil 1 large onion, finely chopped 2 carrots, finely chopped 2 stalks celery, finely chopped	Swirl the olive oil in a skillet set over medium heat. Add the onion, carrots, and celery, and cook, stirring occasionally, until the vegetables have softened and the onions are translucent, about 5 minutes. →

2 tsp ground cumin	Stir the cumin and garlic into the onion mixture and sauté for a few minutes. Add to the ham broth. Drain the beans and add them as well. Bring to a simmer and cook until the beans soften slightly but are not yet done, about 30 minutes.
4 cloves garlic, sliced	
1 (14½-oz/411g) can tomato sauce or crushed tomatoes	Add the tomato sauce or crushed tomatoes along with their juices, bay leaves, chile, salt, and oregano or marjoram to the soup and cook for another 45 to 60 minutes, until the beans are completely tender.
2 bay leaves	
1 dried poblano or ancho chile	
2 tsp sea salt	
1 tsp minced fresh oregano or marjoram	
	Remove the ham hock from the soup, pull all the meat off the bone, and return the meat to the soup. If the bone has marrow in it, make sure to scrape out the marrow as well and incorporate it into the soup. Discard the bay leaves.
Salt	Taste the soup and adjust the seasoning by adding salt, pepper, and a splash of red wine vinegar, lemon juice, or lime juice. Ladle into bowls and serve hot with a spoonful of the Chimichurri and sour cream on top.
Ground black pepper	
Red wine vinegar, lemon juice, or lime juice	
Chimichurri Sauce (page 14)	
½ cup/120g sour cream	Store, covered, in the refrigerator for up to 5 days or for up to 3 months in the freezer. Reheat over low heat.

STRACCIATELLA
(ITALIAN EGG DROP SOUP)

Makes 4 servings (about 1 qt/960ml)

Stracciatella means "little shreds or rags" and refers to the appearance of the cooked egg in this Roman egg drop soup. →

Eggs are whisked briskly, along with seasonings, and added to hot chicken broth while stirring. This is a soup to make when you have homemade broth, as it plays a central role. Nothing is more appetizing when you're under the weather or in need of a comforting meal on a cold, windy night. The recipe is easily scaled up or down, and it is a soup I find myself making often when I just need a quick dose of sustenance.

1 qt/960ml Chicken Stock (page 32, or store-bought)

Bring the stock to a simmer in a medium saucepan.

2 large eggs

2 Tbsp grated Parmesan cheese, plus more as needed

2 Tbsp chopped flat-leaf parsley, plus more as needed

1 tsp finely grated lemon zest

A few generous gratings of nutmeg

Sea salt

Ground black pepper

In a large measuring cup or bowl, whisk together the eggs, cheese, parsley, zest, and nutmeg. Season lightly with salt and pepper.

When you are ready to serve, stir the stock in a slow whirlpool over low heat and then slowly pour in the egg mixture, making sure not to let the stock boil. Continue to cook while stirring for about 1 minute, until the egg pieces are opaque and cooked. Remove from the heat. Taste and adjust the seasoning, adding a little more salt and pepper if needed. Garnish with additional Parmesan and parsley. Ladle the soup into bowls and serve.

Store, covered, in the refrigerator for up to 2 days. Reheat very gently over low heat so as not to overcook the egg.

Green Stracciatella: If there's spinach on hand, add a few handfuls toward the end of cooking. Likewise, a couple handfuls of tender shelled peas or favas, or nettle greens make delicious additions.

AVGOLEMONO (GREEK LEMON SOUP)

Makes 6 to 8 servings (about 2 qt/2L)

The Greek word, *avgolemono*, translates to "egg lemon," and it is this duo that's whisked together and added to warm chicken broth, thickening the soup until it becomes smooth and creamy. Avgolemono's ingredients resemble those in Stracciatella (page 138), but the effect is entirely different—an example of how regions may take the same foods and, through subtle shifts in technique, transform the outcome. Like stracciatella, avgolemono is best made with homemade chicken stock. It's the perfect soup to which to add any kind of cooked rice or grains. Avgolemono is traditionally made with white rice, but you may use barley, Job's tears, quinoa, brown rice, or farro instead. The soup makes a fine, simple supper all by itself. If it's springtime, fresh peas or fava beans make sweet additions, though don't feel obliged to add too many embellishments. The very simplicity of avgolemono, a harmonious trio of just three main ingredients, is what the soup is about.

📖 Because the eggs are whisked into the broth to make a smooth soup, take care not to boil the soup when adding the eggs or reheating, or the eggs will curdle.

1 whole (about 3 lb/1.4kg) chicken

1 small carrot, cut into 1-inch/2.5cm lengths

1 small onion, quartered

1 stalk celery, cut into 1-inch/2.5cm lengths

1 bay leaf

1 small sprig oregano or marjoram

Place the chicken, carrot, onion, celery, bay leaf, and oregano or marjoram in a stockpot and add water to cover by 1 inch/2.5cm. Simmer on low for 1 hour. Remove the chicken, which will be very tender, and place in a colander set over a bowl. Pull the meat from the bones (leaving it in long strips of 2 to 3 inches/5 to 7.5 cm) and remove the skin. →

Discard the skin and bones, vegetables, and herbs, but reserve the chicken meat. Return the stock that has collected in the bowl to the stockpot and bring to a simmer over low heat. You should have about 6 cups/1.4L of stock. Add more water, if needed, to total that amount.

1 cup/100g orzo or $\frac{3}{4}$ cup/150g white or brown rice	Add the orzo or rice to the stock and simmer, uncovered, until tender, about 6 minutes for orzo, 18 minutes for white rice, or 45 minutes for brown rice (or according to the directions on the packages).
4 large eggs $\frac{1}{4}$ cup/60ml lemon juice	In a small bowl, whisk together the eggs and lemon juice, stirring until completely blended.
1 tsp sea salt, plus more to taste (depending on how seasoned your stock is) Pinch of white pepper (optional)	When you are ready to serve, stir the stock in a slow whirlpool over low heat and then slowly pour in the egg-lemon mixture, making sure not to let the stock boil. Continue to cook while stirring for about 1 minute, until the egg pieces are opaque and cooked. Season lightly with the salt and white pepper. Remove from the heat. Taste and adjust the seasoning, adding a little more salt, white pepper, and lemon juice if needed.

Add the cooked chicken to the soup and stir until warmed through, about 1 minute. Ladle the soup into bowls and serve immediately.

Quick Avgolemono Soup: The soup can be made more quickly if you have chicken stock and store-bought roasted chicken on hand. To make the soup this way, start with 6 cups/1.4L stock and skip to the step when you add the orzo or rice and proceed, adding a couple handfuls of shredded roasted chicken in place of the simmered chicken meat. This quick and delicious soup is still worth making if you only have chicken stock and no cooked chicken on hand; simply skip the step of adding the meat.

KAPUSNIAK
(POLISH CABBAGE AND
SOUR CREAM SOUP)

Makes 6 to 8 servings (about 8½ cups/2L)

I first had this Polish sauerkraut soup, known as *kapusniak*, in a grand but fading hotel on the Baltic Sea, just outside the city of Gdansk. It was a windy, bone-chilling day, not unlike the gray San Francisco afternoon years later that sparked the memory of this satisfyingly tart soup. I had asked to try a traditional Polish specialty, and this is what was served—a soup with a wonderful balance of rich and sour flavors. It was a welcome salve, as hours earlier I had tried unsuccessfully to trace my family's Polish heritage at the historic city hall. Navigating a country without a handle on the language calls for a comforting bowl of soup at the end of the day. Kapusniak, made from humble ingredients, turns into something greater than the sum of its parts. The tang of the sauerkraut and sour cream pairs beautifully with the earthiness of mushrooms. The Job's tears are not traditional; kasha, barley, or rice would be good substitutes or skip the grain entirely.

📖 Slices of cooked kielbasa or sausage are often added to this soup just before serving, transforming it into a hearty and filling meal.

1 cup/170g Job's tears, barley, or other grain of choice 1 qt/960ml water Pinch of sea salt	Combine the Job's tears, water, and salt in a medium saucepan and bring to a low simmer. Cook for about 45 minutes, until tender. Remove from the heat and set aside. (Do not drain the water.)
1 yellow onion, sliced 1 Tbsp olive oil	In a large saucepan, sauté the onion in the oil over medium heat until translucent but not at all browned, 3 to 4 minutes. →

½ small head/340g green cabbage, cored and thinly sliced

2 cloves garlic, finely chopped

6 oz/170g mushrooms of any variety or a combination, sliced ¼ inch/6mm thick

1 bay leaf

1 qt/960ml chicken stock

Cooked Job's tears and liquid (from the first step)

Add the cabbage, garlic, and mushrooms to the sautéed onion and cook, stirring constantly, until the cabbage has softened slightly, about 2 minutes. Add the bay leaf and chicken stock, along with the cooked Job's tears and any remaining cooking water, to the cabbage mixture. Simmer gently over low heat for 10 minutes.

½ cup/120g sour cream or crème fraîche

8 oz/230g drained 5-Day Sauerkraut (page 44, or store-bought)

Juice of 1 lemon

Pinch of ground white or black pepper

1½ tsp sea salt, plus more as needed

Remove the soup from the heat and stir in the sour cream or crème fraîche and sauerkraut. Season to taste with the lemon juice, pepper, and salt, adding another ½ tsp or more salt to taste. Ladle the soup into bowls and serve hot. If making ahead, add everything except for the sour cream; it will curdle if it is in the soup when reheated.

Reheat the soup slowly over gentle heat. Store, covered, in the refrigerator for up to 2 days.

SUMMER GREENS SOUP

Makes 4 servings (about 1 qt/960ml)

This is a virtuous soup that doesn't feel especially so when you are eating it due to its silky texture. Whenever I take the time to make it, I wonder why I don't do so more often, considering the health benefits of eating so many raw green foods plus garlic and sauerkraut juice and yogurt. A couple of ingredients elevate this soup above other healthful soups: the addition of sauerkraut, which lends a tanginess and depth of flavor that you can only get with a fermented vegetable, and the greater than usual amount of herbs, which give it a beautiful color and much more flavor than cucumbers could ever add on their own.

2 ripe avocados, halved, pitted, peeled, and flesh scooped out

1 large stalk celery, including leaves, coarsely chopped

1 green bell pepper, coarsely chopped

1 bunch mixed herbs, such as cilantro, chives, tarragon, or chervil, leaves pulled from stems

1 bunch flat-leaf parsley, leaves pulled from stems

$\frac{1}{4}$ to $\frac{1}{2}$ jalapeño (depending on spiciness), stemmed and seeded

1 small clove garlic, coarsely chopped

1 large cucumber, peeled if necessary, coarsely chopped

$\frac{1}{2}$ cup/100g sauerkraut with liquid

2 cups/480ml cold water

1 Tbsp olive oil

2 Tbsp lemon juice

$\frac{1}{2}$ tsp sea salt

Ground black pepper

Combine the avocados, celery, bell pepper, mixed herbs, parsley, jalapeño, garlic, cucumber, sauerkraut and liquid, water, olive oil, lemon juice, salt, and pepper in a blender. Blend until smooth. Set aside at room temperature until ready to serve.

1 to 2 tsp water, for thinning

$\frac{1}{4}$ cup/60g yogurt

Pinch of sea salt

Blended soup, at room temperature (from the first step)

Olive oil, for garnish (optional)

Whisk 1 tsp of water at a time into the yogurt until it is slightly runny. Stir in the salt. When ready to serve, ladle the soup into bowls, drizzle a spoonful of the yogurt mixture over each bowl, and then drizzle with the olive oil. Serve immediately.

Store, covered, in the refrigerator for up to 2 days. Reheat over low heat.

SALADS, VEGETABLES, AND SIDES

VEGETABLE SLAW

Makes 4 to 6 servings

This recipe is from our chef friend Corbin Evans, with whom Chad worked in the early '90s. I like it for its simplicity and common sense. Use any white sauces or dairy that you have in the refrigerator, but only a little more than half of the total should be mayonnaise. This is how I cook and bake; I find a good ratio and then improvise. Use Greek yogurt, regular yogurt, kefir, crème fraîche, buttermilk, or sour cream. Use a light hand with the sugar, but do add it; it's one of those ingredients that can make or break the dish. This dressing goes with vegetables that have the bite that cabbage has so make sure to include some, or any Treviso or endive.

$\frac{1}{2}$ head green cabbage, cut into thirds and very thinly sliced

1 small bulb fennel, halved and very thinly sliced

1 endive, cut into very thin slices

6 stalks raw white or green asparagus, halved lengthwise and cut into 3-inch/7.5cm pieces

2 scallions, very thinly sliced on the bias with up to 2 inches/5cm of green

Combine the cabbage, fennel, endive, asparagus, and scallions in a large bowl.

6 Tbsp/90g mayonnaise or Aioli (page 10)

1 tsp granulated sugar

$\frac{1}{2}$ cup/115g (4oz) Greek yogurt

4 tsp apple cider vinegar

$\frac{1}{4}$ tsp sea salt

$\frac{1}{2}$ to 1 tsp hot sauce

Pinch of ground black pepper

1 clove garlic, minced

$\frac{1}{4}$ cup/35g Marcona almonds, halved

1 frond dill

Make the dressing in a small bowl by mixing the mayonnaise or Aioli, sugar, yogurt, vinegar, salt, hot sauce, black pepper, and garlic. Add the dressing and almonds to the vegetable mixture and toss. Garnish with the dill. Chill until ready to serve.

Store, covered, in the refrigerator for up to 5 days.

FATTOUSH WITH COUNTRY BREAD

Makes 6 servings

Fattoush is a Middle Eastern salad usually made with toasted pita, a variety of vegetables, and finished with the garnet-colored and tangy spice, sumac. Most cuisines have methods to reuse cooked staple grains, whether frying up tortillas into chips or sautéing day-old rice, vegetables, and eggs to make fried rice. The Italian version is panzanella (page 161), and both of these bread salads make substantive sides, or can stand on their own as a meal. This fattoush, made with country-style bread instead of day-old pita, would make an exceptional vegetarian meal when paired with the Roasted Baby Eggplant (page 182). As for many recipes, feel free to add or omit certain vegetables, depending on your preferences and what you have on hand.

3 slices country-style bread 2 Tbsp olive oil	Preheat the oven to 350°F/180°C. To make the croutons, pull the bread apart into large, irregular pieces, about 1-inch/2.5 cm square. Toss the bread in a bowl with the olive oil, spread out in one layer on a baking sheet, and toast in the oven until golden, about 10 minutes. Set the croutons aside to cool.
1 Tbsp sumac 2 Tbsp warm water	Mix the sumac and water and set aside for 10 minutes.
2 Tbsp red wine vinegar $\frac{1}{4}$ cup/60ml olive oil $\frac{1}{2}$ tsp sea salt, plus more as needed Ground black pepper	Whisk together the red wine vinegar, olive oil, sea salt, pepper, and sumac water and set aside. →

2 red or yellow bell peppers, cut into $\frac{1}{2}$-inch/12mm pieces

$\frac{1}{2}$ red onion (or $\frac{1}{4}$ if large), cut into $\frac{1}{2}$-inch/12mm slices

3 tomatoes, cut into $\frac{1}{2}$-inch/12mm cubes

4 or 5 small Persian cucumbers, cut into $\frac{1}{2}$-inch/12mm cubes

5 radishes, very thinly sliced

1 bunch mint, coarsely chopped

Toss the bell peppers, red onion, tomatoes, cucumbers, radishes, and mint together with the croutons. Dress with three-quarters of the dressing, adding more as needed and serve. If making the salad ahead, dress the vegetables without the croutons and keep refrigerated, adding the bread 10 minutes before serving.

Fattoush with Pita Bread: Substitute 4 rounds of day-old pita bread, also torn into irregular pieces, for the country-style bread. Proceed as directed for the country-style bread.

TREVISO SALAD

Makes 4 servings

Treviso, when seared just slightly, transforms into a more complex vegetable and is the foundation of this versatile salad. If you haven't yet had Treviso, it's recognizable by its oblong shape and deep magenta color ribbed with white. It is often found in grocery stores next to its rounder cousin, the standard radicchio. Most vegetables in the chicory family, including Treviso, are at least slightly bitter and have sturdy, lettucelike leaves. When cooked, these chicories develop an unexpected sweetness. In this recipe, Treviso retains its crunch where untouched by heat and becomes softer, with a different flavor, where cooked. Treviso's texture and bitterness stand up well to the assertive garlic sauce with anchovies. This salad can be made ahead and served at room temperature and goes nicely with the Dry-Rubbed Tri-Tip (page 249) or Spatchcocked Roasted Chicken (page 228).

1 Tbsp olive oil

2 heads Treviso, halved lengthwise

Sea salt

Ground black pepper

$\frac{1}{2}$ batch Bagna Cauda (page 12)

Heat a frying pan over high heat for 1 minute. Add the oil and let it heat for 1 minute, and then place each Treviso half flat-side down in the pan. Cook 3 to 5 minutes, until browned. Arrange the Treviso fried-side up on a serving platter and season to taste with the salt and pepper. Toss with the Bagna Cauda and serve.

KALE AND CUCUMBER SALAD WITH TAHINI-LEMON DRESSING

Makes 4 servings (about 5 cups/560g)

The nutty, rich flavor of tahini inspired this lemony dressing, which pairs well with the strong flavor and texture of kale. I recommend adding sumac, a spice made from ground sumac flowers, for an additional tangy pop. Its crimson color adds variation and enlivens the earthier qualities of this salad. You'll find that it is hearty enough for a light meal and that it can be made hours ahead. Have a wedge of lemon on hand to brighten the salad right before serving.

📖 If you've never made a tahini dressing before, there will come a point when you'll think you're doing something wrong. Mixing tahini with oil or any liquid will cause the tahini to seize up and look quite oily. Don't fret. Just keep on whisking, adding a few drops of water, and the ingredients will eventually blend.

3 Tbsp/45g tahini

2 Tbsp lemon juice

$\frac{1}{4}$ cup/60ml olive oil

2 tsp water, plus more as needed

$\frac{1}{4}$ tsp sea salt

$\frac{1}{2}$ small clove garlic, minced (optional, but very good)

$\frac{1}{4}$ tsp ground cumin (optional)

Make the dressing in a small bowl by whisking together the tahini, lemon juice, olive oil, water, salt, garlic, and cumin until smooth and creamy. If the dressing isn't readily emulsifying, add a little more water, $\frac{1}{4}$ tsp at a time, whisking to incorporate. →

1 large bunch/370g kale, stems and tough ribs removed, and leaves cut into $\frac{1}{4}$-inch-/6mm-wide ribbons	Combine the kale, cucumber, pepper flakes, and lemon in a large bowl. Pour in the dressing and toss well.
1 large/350g cucumber, (peeled and seeded, if over 1 $\frac{1}{2}$ inches/4cm in diameter), cut into $\frac{1}{2}$-inch/12mm-thick slices	
$\frac{1}{4}$ tsp red pepper flakes, plus more to taste	
$\frac{1}{8}$ lemon, shaved as thinly as possible	
1 tsp ground sumac, plus more to taste (optional)	Transfer the salad to a serving bowl, garnish with the sumac, and serve.

ENGLISH PEA, PEA SHOOT, FENNEL, AND GOAT CHEESE SALAD

Makes 4 to 6 servings

Tender spring vegetables are always welcome after winter's heartier greens and roots. The key to this springtime salad is a light, quick hand in cooking. Everything should look and taste vibrant and crisp. Although difficult to find, fiddlehead ferns (available in spring and early summer) would be a very nice addition. Goat cheese makes this substantial enough for a light lunch or brunch. If you don't have goat cheese, then ricotta, homemade (page 33, or store-bought), works just as well. If I wanted a more filling meal, steamed new potatoes would fit right in.

📖 Chiffonade is a method of cutting fine leaves of herbs or greens into thin ribbons. Stack a pile of leaves (like mint or basil), roll them compactly, and slice with a sharp knife in thin strips across the roll.

📖 To shave the lemon into paper-thin slices, use a sharp vegetable peeler or a mandoline. You may at times have to use the peeler like a knife, sawing it back and forth gently as you peel off a thin layer of lemon.

6 spears/100g raw asparagus, tough bottoms trimmed

1 cup/150g freshly shelled English peas

1 large bunch/170g arugula

1 large bunch/100g pea shoots

1 bulb/260g fennel, sliced as thinly as possible

½ lemon, shaved

1 small bunch mint, leaves cut into chiffonade

4 to 6 oz/115 to 170g goat cheese

Prepare a bowl of ice water. Bring a stockpot of water to a boil. Add the asparagus and cook for 1 minute (unless the asparagus spears are pencil thin, in which case cook the peas and asparagus together for a total of 2 minutes). Add the peas and cook for 2 more minutes. Using a slotted spoon, transfer the asparagus and peas to the bowl of ice water and let cool, about 5 minutes. When cool, drain and pat dry.

Arrange the cooked asparagus and peas, arugula, pea shoots, fennel, and lemon on a serving platter. Scatter the mint over evenly. Dot the goat cheese around the platter.

⅓ cup/80ml olive oil

2 Tbsp lemon juice

Sea salt

Ground black pepper

Make the dressing by whisking together the olive oil and lemon juice. Season with salt and pepper to taste.

Drizzle the dressing over the salad, toss gently, and serve.

PURPLE SALAD

Makes 4 to 6 servings

There is a point in the early summer when purple fruit and vegetables are ripe at the same time. They all happen to taste delicious together and have a variety of textures and shades of color that create a crisp, refreshing, and beautiful chopped salad. Dressed with a red wine vinaigrette, the salad is a great accompaniment to pork or lamb roasts, chicken, or grilled steak.

2 purple bell peppers, cut into 1-inch/2.5cm pieces

$\frac{1}{2}$ red onion, halved and thinly sliced

4 figs, quartered (optional)

$\frac{1}{2}$ cup/100g champagne grapes (or other purple variety, halved)

2 cups purslane, larger leaves pulled off stems with small bunches of leaves left on tender stems

4 to 6 small purple carrots, quartered lengthwise

4 small plums, pitted and cut into wedges

$\frac{1}{2}$ cup/75g purple cherry tomatoes, halved

1 small head radicchio, halved, cored, and thinly sliced

In a serving bowl, toss together the peppers, onion, figs, grapes, purslane, and radicchio.

1 Tbsp red wine vinegar, plus more as needed

2 Tbsp olive oil, plus more as needed

Sea salt

Ground black pepper

Make the vinaigrette in a small bowl by whisking together the vinegar and olive oil. Season with salt and pepper to taste. →

Drizzle the vinaigrette over the salad mixture in the bowl and toss to coat. Taste and adjust the seasoning, adding more vinegar or olive oil as needed, and serve.

If making more than 1 hour before serving, prepare and combine all of the vegetables and fruits and store in the refrigerator. Make the vinaigrette and dress the salad right before serving.

CELERY ROOT AND CITRUS SALAD

Makes 4 to 6 servings

This is really two salads on the same plate. They may seem an unlikely match, but I like to serve them as a duo because the flavors, colors, and textures work together so well, one creamy and crunchy and the other soft, bright, and spicy. Both celery root and citrus are harvested at their peak in winter months, a reminder that growth happens even in the coldest months of the year. Together they forge a lively bond that brightens even a blustery day. The citrus is a visually striking contrast to the dressed celery root, and the tang of grapefruit, with a touch of heat in the vinaigrette, punctuates the celery's creamy dressing. Try these salads alongside crab, lobster, or fish, all of which love citrus and creamy dressings. They would go equally well with roasted chicken or pork.

📖 Celery root salad is best served within 2 hours after making it because the celery root softens over time. If you would like to prepare it ahead, you can combine everything except the celery root and then mix it in just before serving.

📖 This salad is most interesting when the citrus is cut into various shapes and sizes.

½ small/140g celery
root, peeled and cut
into julienne

2 Tbsp mayonnaise

2 tsp lemon juice

2 tsp whole-grain
mustard

Pinch of sea salt

Pinch of granulated sugar

Pinch of white pepper
(optional)

Combine the celery root, mayonnaise, lemon juice, mustard, salt, sugar, and white pepper in a bowl and toss well to coat.

1 pink grapefruit

1 Oro Blanco or other
white grapefruit

2 blood oranges

1 Cara Cara or navel
orange

1 pomelo

Cut a thin slice off the top and bottom (the stem and blossom end) of the grapefruits and oranges. Stand each on one flat end on a cutting board. Using a very sharp paring knife, cut from top to bottom along the contour of the fruit, cutting away the peel and white pith, and rotating the fruit as you go.

Slice about half of the fruits crosswise into ¼-inch/6mm-thick rounds, discarding any seeds. Hold the remaining fruit in your hand one at a time and carefully slice between the membranes to release the segments. Reserve the web of membranes that's left behind to make the dressing.

Peel the pomelo, discarding all the cottony white pith and use your fingers to liberate the fruit segments from the papery membranes. Arrange all the citrus on one side of a serving platter.

Juice of ½ lemon

2 Tbsp olive oil

Pinch of red pepper
flakes

Sea salt

Ground black pepper

Squeeze the reserved citrus membranes and collect all the juice in a small bowl. Stir in the lemon juice, olive oil, and red pepper flakes. Taste and season with salt and black pepper. Pour the dressing over the citrus fruits.

Arrange the celery root salad on the platter with the dressed citrus on the other side and serve.

ROMANESCO SALAD

Makes 2 servings as a main course or 4 to 6 as a side course

Romanesco is an Italian heirloom cauliflower with bright green, fractal-like florets. It was previously found only at niche markets, but thankfully, more farmers are growing Romanesco across the country. If you cannot find Romanesco, any kind of cauliflower will do. When steamed or boiled, Romanesco is silky tender and goes well with crispy or salty embellishments and the richness of the eggs. If I had them in the pantry, chopped anchovies would be excellent with these flavors, as would a side of white beans fragrant with olive oil. Equally delicious warm or cold, this can be a quick supper or lunch made a day ahead.

📖 Walnuts can replace the pine nuts, and olive oil can substitute for the walnut oil, which is sometimes difficult to find.

📖 To make fresh breadcrumbs, it's preferable to use a loaf of bread that is at least a day old. Slice off the crusts and cut the bread in to large pieces. Using a food processor or blender, break the bread into large crumbs, taking care to not overcrowd the processor, which could cause the bread to clump instead of breaking down. Put the breadcrumbs on a baking sheet and toast in the oven at 350°F/180°C for about 12 minutes (depending on how fresh your bread is), until light golden brown.

1 large/680g Romanesco, cut into approximately 5 irregular pieces	In a large pot, fitted with a steamer basket and enough water to steam inside, or filled with water, add the Romanesco and steam or boil the pieces until just tender, 4 to 6 minutes.
3 large 10-minute eggs (see page 92), peeled and halved or quartered	Arrange the cooked Romanesco and eggs on a serving platter.

¾ cup/30g coarse breadcrumbs, toasted

¼ cup/30g pine nuts, lightly toasted

¼ cup/35g salt-packed capers, rinsed, chopped

2 Tbsp chopped flat-leaf parsley

½ tsp fresh thyme leaves

1 Tbsp walnut oil, plus more for garnish

1 Tbsp olive oil, plus more for garnish

1 Tbsp sherry vinegar, plus more for garnish

Sea salt

Ground black pepper

Combine the breadcrumbs, pine nuts, capers, parsley, thyme, walnut oil, olive oil, and vinegar in a medium bowl, season with salt and pepper, and mix well. Scatter over the Romanesco and eggs. Drizzle a little more walnut oil, olive oil, and/or vinegar over the top and serve.

BACON, LETTUCE, AND TOMATO PANZANELLA WITH BASIL SALSA VERDE

Makes 4 servings as a main course or 8 as a side course

I first made this as an accompaniment to Dry-Rubbed Tri-Tip (page 249), dressed with a salsa verde that is rich in basil and screams of summer. You can't find a more satisfying salad on a warm evening. Serve it as a main dish, with the tri-tip or with the Spatchcocked Roasted Chicken (page 228). Watercress or peppercress would be good, spicy substitutes for the butter lettuce or arugula.

3 large/570g tomatoes, cored and sliced into wedges

Sea salt

Ground black pepper

Place the tomatoes in a large, shallow bowl or on a serving platter and season with salt and pepper. The salt will draw out some of the tomato juices while you prepare the rest of the salad and then will become part of the dressing. →

4 strips/170g thick-cut bacon, cut into ½-inch/12mm pieces, cooked to your preference (slightly soft is best)

2 small heads/230g butter lettuce, torn into bite-size pieces

2 large handfuls/70g arugula or other small-leaf lettuce

Add the bacon, butter lettuce, and arugula or other small-leaf lettuce to the tomatoes.

3 thick slices country-style bread, ripped into 1- to 2-inch/2.5 to 5cm pieces

3 Tbsp olive oil, plus more as needed

Preheat the oven to 400°F/200°C. To make the croutons, in a medium bowl, toss the bread in the olive oil. The bread should be lightly coated; if not, add more oil and toss well. Transfer the coated bread pieces to a baking sheet and toast in the oven until golden, about 8 minutes. Set aside to cool.

1 large/190g very ripe tomato, halved

⅓ cup/80ml Basil Salsa Verde (see page 14), plus more as needed

Squeeze the tomato halves over the lettuces and tomatoes, letting the juice drip over the lettuces. Add the croutons. Dress with ⅓ cup of the Basil Salsa Verde to start, adding more as necessary to lightly dress the greens and, when combined with the tomato juices, to barely soak into the croutons. The croutons should still retain some of their crispness.

If making this salad in advance, assemble everything except the lettuces and croutons. Add them just before serving and toss well, adding more dressing if necessary.

CHICKEN–CELERY ROOT SALAD

Makes 6 to 8 servings ($3\frac{1}{2}$ qt/1.6kg)

I was inspired to make this after receiving a farmers' market box with more celery root than I could handle. After grabbing a cold roasted chicken from the refrigerator, I added the flavors and textures of remoulade, the classic French preparation of celery root, to a chicken salad. Apple and cabbage are natural partners and bright parsley is the right herb to match these fall flavors. Now, I often roast an extra chicken just to make this salad. Leftover holiday turkey would also be quite delicious.

📖 If preparing this a few hours ahead of time, make the entire salad, holding off on adding the parsley. Just before serving, add the chopped leaves, so that their brightness remains vivid.

$1\frac{3}{4}$ lb/800g roasted chicken meat from Spatchcocked Roasted Chicken (page 228, or store-bought)

Remove the meat from the roasted chicken, tear into bite-size pieces, and place in a large bowl.

1 medium/400g celery root, peeled and cut into julienne

Add the celery root, apples, walnuts, parsley, and cabbage to the chicken and mix well. →

3 apples (a mix of sweet and tart), cut into julienne

$1\frac{1}{2}$ cups/180g walnuts, toasted

1 bunch flat-leaf parsley, coarsely chopped

$\frac{1}{2}$ small/400g head green cabbage, cored and finely shredded

3 Tbsp/45ml coarse-grain mustard

1 $\frac{1}{2}$ tsp sea salt

Juice of 1 lemon

$\frac{1}{4}$ tsp ground black pepper

$\frac{3}{4}$ cup/180ml olive oil

$\frac{1}{4}$ cup/60ml white wine vinegar or champagne vinegar

Make the dressing by whisking together the mustard, salt, lemon juice, pepper, olive oil, and white wine vinegar or champagne vinegar in a small bowl. Pour the dressing over the salad, toss to coat, and serve.

TOMATO, SHELLING BEANS, AND CUCUMBER SALAD

Makes 4 to 6 servings

We opened Tartine Manufactory in the month of August, and our chef Sam put this salad on our first menu to highlight the most seasonal vegetables we had: tomatoes, cucumbers, and shelling beans. This is a really simple salad or side dish and would be hearty enough for a light dinner with the addition of poached eggs (see page 95).

📖 If you don't have shelling beans, use canned or dried beans. About 1 pound/455g of shelling beans yields 1 $\frac{1}{2}$ to 2 cups of beans. Because shelling beans haven't been dried, they don't swell as much during cooking, so your yield will be close to what you started out with.

1 lb/455g shelling beans (such as black-eyed peas, cranberry beans, or cannellini), shelled

Place the beans in a pot, cover with water, bring to a boil, and cook until tender, about 15 minutes for black-eyed peas, 20 minutes for cranberry beans, and 45 minutes for cannellini and other larger variety of beans. Let cool to room temperature. If not using right away, store cooked beans in their cooking broth.

1 Tbsp red wine vinegar

3 Tbsp olive oil

Sea salt

Ground black pepper

Make the dressing in a large bowl by whisking together the vinegar and olive oil. Season with salt and pepper to taste. →

1½ to 2 cups/240 to 325g cooked shelling beans (from first step), drained

2 cups/300g cherry tomatoes, halved

2 small cucumbers, halved lengthwise and cut into ½-inch/ 6mm pieces

1 small bunch Thai or Italian basil, leaves pulled from stems and thinly sliced

½ small shallot, halved and thinly sliced

3 oz /85g goat cheese

To the bowl with the dressing, add the beans, tomatoes, cucumbers, basil, shallot, and goat cheese. Gently toss, season with a bit more salt if needed, and then serve.

Store the salad, covered, in the refrigerator for up to 3 days.

MANY BEAN SALAD WITH PRESERVED LEMON AND HERBS

Makes 4 to 6 servings (about 6 cups/1.2kg)

This salad can be made with ease from the pantry and is exceptionally fresh and filling. The variation of beans make for an interesting bite every time, and the salsa verde and preserved lemon are a refreshing addition to the beans. If you have access to fresh shelling beans (available in the summer months), the difference between them and dried or canned is remarkable. They are smooth and creamy and don't turn to mush when fully cooked—very worth seeking out.

📖 Many small farmers are now growing a wider variety of shell beans. If you are lucky enough to find fresh shelling beans, use 12 oz/340g of fresh beans for each of the three types of beans in the recipe. The cooking times will vary according to size, however most will cook within 30 minutes. If you do not find varieties that you like at a grocer or farmers' market, my favorite source for heirloom beans is the purveyor Rancho Gordo, which has an online store. Select a few different beans that vary in color, size, and texture. When using canned beans, I pay extra attention to the acid and salt in the dressing because canned beans often require slightly more acid than usual to penetrate the beans. The salt, depending on how the beans are canned, should be adjusted accordingly.

📖 If the beans are so tender that they may break apart when tossed, you can first arrange them on the platter, and then spoon the Salsa Verde mixture over the top.

$\frac{3}{4}$ cup/125g dried or 1 (15-oz/425g) can Royal Corona or other large white bean, rinsed well and drained if canned

$\frac{3}{4}$ cup/150g dried or 1 (15-oz/425g) can Scarlet Runner or other red bean, rinsed well and drained if canned

$\frac{3}{4}$ cup/170g dried or 1 (15-oz/425g) can canario, black bean, flageolet, or other smaller bean, rinsed well and drained if canned

Soak and cook the dried beans separately, in three pots, as they will cook at varying speeds. It's fastest if you soak the beans the night before, but if you don't, do a quick hot-soak by bringing the pot of beans and water to a boil, turning off the heat for at least 1 hour, and then simmering over low heat until they are completely tender. Beans that are the same size can be cooked together. If using canned beans, set them aside until you're ready to assemble the salad.

Let the cooked beans cool in their liquid. (They can be made ahead and stored in their liquid, covered, in the refrigerator for up to 3 days.)

$\frac{1}{2}$ cup/120ml Salsa Verde (page 13)

1 clove garlic, thinly sliced

2 Tbsp red wine vinegar, lemon juice, or other vinegar, plus more as needed

$\frac{1}{4}$ red onion, very thinly sliced

$\frac{1}{4}$ Preserved Lemon, thinly sliced (page 39, or store-bought)

Sea salt

Ground black pepper

Combine the Salsa Verde, garlic, vinegar or lemon juice, onion, and Preserved Lemon in a large bowl. Using a slotted spoon, transfer the cooked beans to the bowl. Toss gently to coat and then taste and season with salt and pepper, plus more vinegar or lemon juice, if needed. Arrange on a platter and serve.

DARK LEAFY GREENS WITH LEMON-GARLIC-HERB DRESSING

Makes 4 servings

My dad grew up in Kentucky, where a pot of greens would always be on the table. Made of collards, mustard greens, or turnip tops, the long-stewed greens were often made with salt pork and could go with anything. This is more of a method than a recipe, valuable for its flexibility and always-good results. I don't cook my greens as long as my Kentucky relatives cook theirs, but I do often nod to the South with a splash of apple cider vinegar added at the end. My method is to start with a little water in the bottom of a pan, along with olive oil and a pinch of red pepper flakes. To this I add heaps of greens, putting the cut-up stems of more tender ones (like chard, young kale, or collards) on the bottom, topped by the leaves. Everything is cooked until tender and the liquid is reduced. For this recipe, I'm going beyond the vinegar and dressing it with a bright Lemon-Garlic-Herb Dressing (page 24). Serve this alongside a poached egg in the morning, on top of crusty bread spread with ricotta for lunch, or beside a roast for dinner.

1 lb/455g leafy greens (such as collards, mustard greens, turnip tops, kale, or a combination)

Strip the leaves from the stems of the greens. Rinse and dry the leaves and slice into wide ribbons. Chop the tender stems.

2 Tbsp olive oil

2 oz/55g salt pork or slab bacon, diced (optional)

Pinch of red pepper flakes

Sea salt

Ground black pepper

$\frac{1}{4}$ cup/60ml water

Heat the olive oil in a medium pot over medium-high heat. Add the salt pork or bacon and cook for 4 to 5 minutes, until crisp. Add the red pepper flakes and the stem pieces and then pile the greens on top. Season with salt and pepper and add the water. Cover the pot, reduce the heat to low, and let simmer for about 5 minutes. Remove the lid and check the greens, turning the leaves once and cooking for a few more minutes, if needed, until tender.

$\frac{1}{3}$ cup/80ml Lemon-Garlic-Herb Dressing

Transfer the greens to a serving dish and top with half of the dressing, tossing to evenly distribute. Add the remaining dressing, if necessary, to evenly coat the greens, and toss once more. Serve immediately.

Store in the refrigerator, tightly covered, for up to 2 days.

JOB'S TEARS SALAD

Makes 4 to 6 servings (about 8 cups/1.3kg)

Before this year, I had never tried Job's tears, a grain native to Southeast Asia, that when hulled, has the shape of a teardrop. I suspect, like quinoa, its use will become more widespread because it is both nutritionally rich and unexpectedly delicious. When cooked, Job's tears have a mild flavor along with a nice bite that remind me of both hominy and barley, though it is unrelated to either and is gluten-free. It goes by many names, including coix seed and tear grass, and is most popular in Asian cooking. The Japanese call it *hato mugi.* Chinese groceries often sell it as Chinese pearl barley. Acupuncturists hold the grain in high esteem, believing that it calms the nervous system. Once I started cooking Job's tears, I began to see endless possibilities. Each grain is substantial in size, takes well to vivid dressings, and holds its shape in soups. For this salad, I've borrowed from a classic tabbouleh recipe, substituting Job's tears for bulgur. The shift in the grain's size makes this dish surprisingly toothsome and filling enough for a gratifyingly simple supper.

$1\frac{1}{2}$ cups/260g Job's tears

6 cups/1.4L water

Pinch of sea salt

Combine the Job's tears, water, and salt in a medium saucepan and bring to a simmer. Cook for about 45 minutes, until tender. Drain and let cool. →

2 cups/300g cherry tomatoes, quartered, or 2 large/300g tomatoes, diced

½ large English cucumber, finely diced, or 2 small Persian cucumbers, finely diced

4 cups/80g flat-leaf parsley, finely chopped

1 shallot, finely chopped, or 3 scallions, white and light green parts only, finely chopped

1 bunch mint, finely chopped

3 Tbsp olive oil, plus more as needed

2 Tbsp lemon juice, plus more as needed

½ tsp sea salt

Ground black pepper

In a large bowl, toss together the tomatoes, cucumber, parsley, shallot or scallions, mint, olive oil, lemon juice, salt, and pepper. Mix in the cooked Job's tears. Taste and adjust the seasoning, adding more lemon juice and olive oil, if you like, and serve.

Store, covered, in the refrigerator for up to 4 days.

BLACK-EYED PEAS, HAM, AND COLLARDS

Makes 4 to 6 servings (about 1 qt/850g)

For this recipe, I looked to a trinity of Southern ingredients—black-eyed peas, ham, and collards—and rearranged their proportions for a modern approach. The ham, sizzled until crispy, is an accent of salt and crunch. The collards are not cooked as long as Southern tradition once called for, and the mustard vinaigrette, while not traditional except for the apple cider vinegar, goes well with the collards and cuts the richness. This is a side for summer, winter, fall, and spring because it goes well with so many things, perfectly accompanying roast meats, pork chops, sautéed trout, thick slices of August tomatoes, poached eggs—you get the idea. Personalize this as you see fit. The possibilities are endless and satisfying.

1 cup/180g dried or 1 (15-oz/425g) can black-eyed peas, rinsed and drained if canned

1 qt/960ml water

1 tsp sea salt

Combine the dried black-eyed peas, water, and salt in a large saucepan. Bring to a boil, decrease the heat to low, and simmer until the peas are completely soft, about $1\frac{1}{2}$ hours, adding water as needed to keep the peas submerged. Remove from the heat and drain. If using canned beans, set them aside until you're ready to serve.

1 Tbsp olive oil

6 oz/170g ham, cut into $\frac{1}{4}$ by $\frac{1}{2}$ inch/6 by 12mm pieces

Heat the oil in a skillet over medium heat. Cook the ham, stirring occasionally, until crisp and golden, 5 to 7 minutes. Transfer the ham to a plate, leaving any fat in the skillet for flavor.

14 collard greens, washed, ribs removed, and leaves coarsely chopped

2 Tbsp water

Add the collards and water to the skillet. Cover and cook until the collards are tender, 4 to 6 minutes, removing the cover and stirring once or twice. Transfer the collards to a large bowl.

$\frac{1}{4}$ cup/60ml olive oil

2 Tbsp Dijon mustard

1 shallot, thinly sliced

2 tsp apple cider vinegar

$\frac{1}{4}$ tsp sea salt

Ground black pepper

Make the dressing by gradually whisking the olive oil into the mustard in a small bowl until smooth. Whisk in the shallot, vinegar, salt, and pepper. Adjust the seasoning, adding more salt and pepper to taste.

Gently toss the cooked black-eyed peas, collards, and ham with the dressing, taking care not to break up the peas. (If making a few hours ahead, toss together everything except the ham; mix it in just before serving.) Taste and adjust the seasoning, and then serve.

ROYAL CORONA BEANS WITH CHIMICHURRI SAUCE AND SMELTS

Makes 4 to 6 servings (about 3½ cups/720g)

Corona beans are sumptuous runner beans with origins in Italy. Once cooked, they will plump to an astonishing size. Coronas, like all beans, benefit from an overnight soak, as the water absorbed prevents them from expanding too fast and falling apart during cooking. This is an extremely simple recipe that is deeply satisfying because of the combination of textures of the beans and fish, and the bright, herbaceous chimichurri. The fried smelts are crunchy and wonderful with the beans. You can substitute any other small fish, such as fresh sardines or anchovies. Made with or without the sardines, this dish is hearty enough to be an entrée, but you could also add a poached, fried, or soft-cooked egg.

📖 If you cannot find Royal Corona beans at your grocer, check out Rancho Gordo's heirloom beans. Their Royal Corona beans inspired this recipe.

1½ cups/250g dried Royal Corona beans	Soak the beans in plenty of water for 8 hours or overnight.
	Drain the soaked beans and then add them to a large saucepan. Add enough fresh water to cover by at least 1 inch/2.5cm. Bring to a boil over high heat. Lower the heat so that the liquid barely simmers and continue cooking until completely tender, 2 to 3 hours or more, depending on how fresh the beans are. While the beans cook, add hot water as needed to keep them submerged. Keeping these beans intact is what makes this recipe special. Make sure to watch the flame and lower to a simmer, so that the beans are cooked gently and remain whole. Too many times, I've left the kitchen and kept the pot at a rapid boil.

Sea salt	Season the beans with salt to taste. Let the beans cool in their liquid. (They can be stored in their liquid, covered, in the refrigerator for up to 3 days.)
$\frac{3}{4}$ cup/105g white rice flour $\frac{1}{4}$ tsp ground black pepper 1 Tbsp sea salt 8 oz/230g fresh smelts	In a shallow plate, combine the rice flour, pepper, and salt. Dredge the fish in the rice flour mixture.
1 cup/240ml vegetable oil, plus more as needed	Line a plate with paper towels. Heat the oil in a frying pan over medium-high heat, adding more, if needed, until it is $\frac{1}{4}$ inch/6mm deep. When the oil is hot and shimmering, add the fish and fry until golden, 2 to 3 minutes per side. Using a slotted spoon, remove the fish from the oil and place on the paper towels to drain.
$\frac{1}{2}$ cup/120ml Chimichurri Sauce (page 14)	Using a slotted spoon, transfer the cooked beans to a serving bowl and top with the fried smelts. Pour the Chimichurri Sauce over the top and serve.

SUCCOTASH

Makes 4 servings

Succotash is traditionally a two-ingredient dish—corn and lima beans—which are boiled and topped with a little butter. The recipe dates to the middle of the 1700s, having originated from the Narragansett Native Americans, whose word for it translates to "broken corn kernels." The name always sounded much more exciting than the frozen corn and lima beans from my childhood, although I hasten to add that we didn't grow our own lima beans, which I'm sure would have made a much more delicious combination. Adding a little bacon and cider vinegar adds crunch, salt, and flavor; the small amount of vinegar balances the bacon. →

1½ lb/680g fresh lima, fava, or shelling beans, shelled (about 2 cups/300g)	Bring a pot of salted water to a boil. Add the shelled beans and cook until tender, about 2 to 4 minutes for lima, 1 to 2 minutes for fava, and up to 20 minutes (depending on the size of the bean) for most shelling beans. Drain and set aside to cool. If using fava beans, when cool enough to handle, slip off the outer white skin of the beans.
4 oz/115g bacon, cut in ¼-inch/6mm strips	Cook the bacon in a skillet over medium-high heat until almost done. Pour off all but 1 Tbsp of the fat.
2 or 3 ears of corn, shucked and kernels cut off cob	Add the corn and cooked, drained beans to the pan with the bacon and quickly cook over medium heat until the corn, which cooks quickly, is cooked through, 2 to 3 minutes.
2 tsp apple cider vinegar Sea salt Ground black pepper	Remove the pan from the heat, stir in the vinegar and season with salt and pepper. Serve immediately.
	Store, covered, in the refrigerator for up to 2 days.

ROASTED FALL VEGETABLES AND APPLES

Makes 4 to 6 servings

I am always ready come fall, after a summer of eating tomatoes with salt and copious lettuces, for that moment when I suddenly crave the substance of roasted squash with thyme. Use whatever kinds of squashes and roots you have on hand. If you're lucky enough to find crab apples, use those, but apples of any kind will do just as well. There will be a fair amount of chopping, but I urge you to make it easy (and beautiful) for yourself: cut the vegetables large enough so that they're reminiscent of the original form. With the sweetness of the cooked onions and apples and substance of squash, you only need a simple roast of any kind—chicken, turkey, or pork—to go with it. →

1 delicata squash, cut into $\frac{1}{4}$-inch/6mm-thick slices, seeds scooped out

1 (2 to 3 lb/910g to 1.4kg) hubbard squash, cut into $\frac{1}{4}$-inch/6mm-thick slices, seeds scooped out

2 red bell peppers, cut into $\frac{1}{2}$-inch/12mm-wide strips

4 crab apples, cored and halved, or 2 apples, cored and cut into eighths

2 red or yellow onions, peeled and cut into 1-inch/2.5cm thick slices

8 cloves garlic, peeled and lightly crushed

6 sprigs thyme, leaves pulled from stems

3 Tbsp olive oil

Sea salt

Ground black pepper

Preheat the oven to 400°F/200°C. Toss the delicata and hubbard squash, bell peppers, crab apples or apples, onions, garlic, thyme, and olive oil together directly on a baking sheet that is large enough to accommodate the vegetables in a single layer. Season with salt and pepper. Roast, stirring once or twice, until the vegetables are nicely browned in a few places and the squash is tender all the way through, about 30 minutes.

Red wine, white wine, or apple cider vinegar or lemon juice

After removing the roasted vegetables from the oven, drizzle with vinegar or lemon juice and serve.

ZUCCHINI-HERB FRITTERS

Makes 4 to 6 servings (six 4-inch/10cm fritters)

Fritters are overlooked as a quick way to use vegetables. The crunch of pan-frying adds dimension, versatility, and heft. They are wonderful as is, with a squeeze of lemon and thick yogurt on the side, or beneath a poached egg. The only trick in these is to squeeze the zucchini of their excess moisture after salting. That way, you'll get the crispiness any good fritter deserves.

I prefer smaller zucchini for their sweetness and delicate texture. However, garden zucchini have the uncanny ability to become giant overnight; don't let the big ones go to waste. Just be sure to remove any large seeds, and once grated, let the salted zucchini sit for 30 minutes before proceeding with the recipe.

1 lb/455g grated zucchini 1 tsp sea salt	In a large bowl, toss together the zucchini and salt and let stand for 15 minutes. Gather the mixture in a tea towel and squeeze to wring out nearly all of the liquid. Return the squeezed zucchini to the bowl.
2 Tbsp chopped flat-leaf parsley $\frac{1}{2}$ tsp finely chopped fresh marjoram 1 large egg 7 Tbsp/80g potato starch Sea salt Ground black pepper	Add the parsley, marjoram, egg, and potato starch to the zucchini and mix well. Season with salt and pepper.
	Line a plate with paper towels or newspaper and place it near the stovetop.
Olive oil or peanut oil, for frying	Heat a skillet over medium-high heat. Add enough oil to coat the bottom of the skillet. Add about $\frac{1}{4}$ cup/65g of the zucchini mixture to the skillet, pressing down with a spatula to form a $\frac{1}{4}$-inch/6mm-thick fritter. Fry until golden brown on the first side, then flip and fry the second side until golden, about 5 minutes total. Transfer the fritter to the paper towel–lined plate. Repeat with the remaining zucchini batter, adding oil to the skillet around the fritters if the pan seems to be getting too dry. Serve hot or at room temperature.
	The fritters can be made several days ahead and stored, covered, in the refrigerator. Reheat them in a 350°F/180°C oven until hot and crisp before serving, about 10 minutes.

BEETS AND GREENS WITH HAZELNUTS AND HONEY-VINEGAR DRESSING

Makes 4 to 6 servings

I don't usually save beet greens since there aren't enough of them to make a whole dish, and I typically skip beets altogether when I'm looking for a vegetable because I generally find them too sweet. Combining them in one dish gives you a little of both, with a dressing that is a little *agrodolce*, or sweet-sour. The hazelnuts go perfectly with the beets' earthiness. This would pair as well with salmon as it would with pork or chicken.

4 gold, orange, or red beets, peeled, and tops trimmed and reserved	Cut the beets into $\frac{1}{2}$-inch/12mm squares. Bring a medium pot of salted water to a boil. Add the beets and cook until tender, about 10 minutes. Using a slotted spoon, transfer the beets to a serving plate. Cool to room temperature. Cut into bite-size pieces.
	Bring another medium pot of salted water to a boil and add the beet tops. Simmer for 3 minutes and then transfer to a colander to drain. Place the tops on the serving plate alongside the cooked beets.
1 Tbsp white wine vinegar Pinch of sea salt 2 tsp honey 2 Tbsp olive oil	Make the dressing by whisking together the vinegar, salt, honey, and oil. Pour the dressing over the beets and tops.
$\frac{1}{4}$ cup/30g hazelnuts, toasted, chopped $\frac{1}{2}$ cup/50g champagne grapes	Garnish the beets and tops with the chopped hazelnuts and grapes and serve.

PAN-ROASTED EGGPLANT

Makes 4 servings

This is more of a suggestion than a recipe, and one that I have to remind myself to do more often. Consider this just one example of what you can do with an eggplant when you see it at the market. For this, the eggplant is simply fried in olive oil, seasoned with salt and pepper, and cooked until soft and well browned. Finish it off with any type of seasoning you have—red pepper flakes, za'atar, gomashio—and a generous squeeze of lemon juice. Spread pan-roasted eggplant on bread, eat with rice, or fold it up and eat it out of the pan.

$\frac{1}{4}$ cup/60ml olive oil, plus more as needed	Heat the oil in a skillet over medium-high heat. Season the eggplant with the salt and pepper and carefully place in the pan, frying until golden brown and soft, about 5 minutes for each side, depending on the circumference of the eggplant. Add more oil to the skillet around the eggplant if the pan seems to be getting too dry.
$1\frac{1}{2}$ lb/680g eggplant (any type), cut crosswise into $\frac{1}{2}$-inch/12mm-thick slices	
Sea salt	
Ground black pepper	
1 lemon, halved	Sprinkle with the seasoning and generously squeeze lemon juice over the eggplant. Serve immediately.
2 tsp seasoning (such as red pepper flakes, za'atar, gomashio)	

ROASTED BABY EGGPLANT WITH YOGURT SAUCE

Makes 4 servings as a main course or 6 as a side course

This is a wonderful dish to serve warm or at room temperature, so it can be made well ahead of time and dressed with the Yogurt Sauce (page 16), which is spiked with minced garlic. It is also delicious dressed with the Chimichurri Sauce (page 14) instead of the yogurt dressing, as the acid in the chimichurri balances the richness of the eggplant. However you make it, perhaps the best thing about →

eggplant is how versatile it is. Because it has an inherent meatiness, it can be a wonderful main dish for a vegetarian dinner, but it also goes well with lamb, steak (see the Dry-Rubbed Tri-Tip on page 249), or Spatchcocked Roasted Chicken (page 228) and a big green salad.

📖 To ensure even cooking, use baby eggplants that are approximately the same thickness. Most will need to be cut in half, but some may need to be cut into thirds and others left whole.

📖 If the eggplants turn a nice brown color before they have cooked through, cover loosely with aluminum foil to prevent further coloring while they continue cooking.

$1\frac{1}{2}$ lb/680g baby eggplant, cut lengthwise in half or thirds to $\frac{3}{4}$ inch/2cm thick 3 to 4 Tbsp olive oil $\frac{1}{4}$ tsp sea salt	Preheat the oven to 425°F/220°C. Toss the eggplant in a medium bowl with the oil and salt to completely coat. Spread out on a roasting pan or in a baking dish and roast until golden brown on cut sides and soft when pierced with the tip of a paring knife, 15 to 20 minutes.
$\frac{1}{2}$ cup/120ml Yogurt Sauce (page 16)	Arrange the roasted eggplant on a serving platter, drizzle with the yogurt sauce, and serve.
	Any leftovers can be stored, well wrapped, in the refrigerator for up to 2 days and reheated in a 350°F/180°C oven for 10 to 15 minutes.

MASA HARINA AND MILLET CORNBREAD

Makes 1 (8-inch/20cm) square or 1 (8-inch/20cm) round

A gluten-free cornbread that is fluffy, rather than dense, can be hard to come by. After many trials, I came upon masa harina and considered its finer texture as a potential asset in this quest. Masa harina is the kind of cornmeal used in tortillas and tamales. It differs from the traditional cornmeal used in cornbread or polenta in that it has undergone a centuries-old process called nixtamalization, which makes the corn softer and more nutritious. On a whim, I added millet flour, because of its golden hue and good flavor; it is also mineral rich and nearly a complete protein. This cornbread bakes up light, beautifully golden, and balanced with a corn flavor that is just sweet enough. I love it griddled with a little butter and a dark honey, like a buckwheat honey, but it would also partner well with the Black Bean and Ham Hock Soup (page 136), the Dark Leafy Greens with Lemon-Garlic-Herb Dressing (page 168), or most any roast bird or pork.

📖 If you use a cast-iron skillet to bake the cornbread, melt the butter directly in the pan, and you will save a step in buttering it.

Unsalted butter, as needed	Preheat the oven to 400°F/200°C. Butter an 8-inch/20cm square baking dish. Alternatively, use an 8-inch/20cm cast-iron skillet, and melt the butter in the skillet.
1 cup/150g masa harina $\frac{1}{2}$ cup/70g millet flour $\frac{1}{4}$ cup/45g potato starch $\frac{1}{4}$ cup/30g tapioca flour/starch 2 tsp baking powder	In a large bowl, mix the masa harina, millet flour, potato starch, tapioca flour/starch, and baking powder. Make a well in the center.
6 Tbsp/85g unsalted butter, melted 2 large eggs $1\frac{1}{2}$ cups/360ml whole milk $\frac{3}{4}$ tsp sea salt 2 Tbsp granulated sugar	In a separate bowl, whisk together the butter, eggs, milk, salt, and sugar. Pour the egg mixture into the well of the flour mixture and mix just until blended.
	Transfer the batter to the buttered baking dish or cast-iron skillet. Bake for 25 minutes, or until the tip of a knife inserted in the center of the cornbread comes out clean. Set the pan on a cooling rack to cool, about 10 minutes. Cut the cornbread into squares or wedges and serve.
	Store, well wrapped, at room temperature for up to 3 days.

WHOLE-LOAF CHEESY GARLIC BREAD

Makes 4 to 8 servings

Make this delightful, hands-on version of garlic bread when you have a good rustic loaf and expect an enthusiastic crowd. This riff on the classic halved baguette slathered with butter and minced garlic is strikingly geometric in look. A good visual analogy for how it should look is when half a mango is sliced so that it forms diamonds and then the convex outside is pushed inward, forcing the cubes of fruit to arch and separate. You'll create this same effect by placing the loaf arched over a garlic bulb. The loaf balances on top of the garlic and opens as it bakes. Beyond its aesthetic appeal, it is exceptionally delicious, warm in the interior, and crisp on top with bits of cheese and flecks of garlic and butter flavoring both crumb and crust. I love this bread as a centerpiece for a barbecue or to accompany a roast or a supper of soup and salad.

📖 The bread can be prepared ahead of time, wrapped well, and kept in the refrigerator for several days before baking. I have no idea where this idea originated, but it is a classic in the making, inspiring eager diners to bump arms as they pull off pieces.

2 heads garlic	Preheat the oven to 375°F/190°C. Cut the top quarter off of the garlic heads and rub with the oil, making sure some seeps into the top of each. Season with the salt. Wrap in aluminum foil and bake for 30 minutes.
2 Tbsp olive oil	
2 pinches of sea salt	
1 oval or round loaf country-style bread	Lower the oven to 350°F/180°C. Slice the upper crust of the loaf in a crosshatch pattern, cutting down through the upper crust and the middle of the loaf but not cutting all the way through to the bottom crust. Place the roasted garlic heads, cut-side down, in the center of a baking dish and set the loaf on top of them, gently pressing the ends of bread so that it curves in a convex shape to reveal the interior cubes and crevices. →

$\frac{3}{4}$ cup/165g unsalted butter, plus more as needed

4 cloves garlic, finely chopped

1 tsp sea salt

$\frac{1}{4}$ tsp ground black pepper

2 Tbsp chopped flat-leaf parsley

1 tsp chopped fresh thyme

$\frac{1}{4}$ tsp chopped fresh rosemary

Melt the butter in a small saucepan over medium heat. Decrease the heat to low, add the chopped garlic, and swirl the pot to gently cook the garlic without letting it brown, about 1 minute. Add the salt, pepper, parsley, thyme, and rosemary, swirling to mix well.

Brush the flavored butter into all the crevices and on top of the bread. If you need more butter, melt a few more tablespoons and keep basting the bread until it's covered.

1 to 2 cups/100 to 200g semi-firm or firm cheese, such as Raclette, Fontina, Cheddar, or Gruyère, grated

Sprinkle the cheese over the loaf, making sure some settles between the cuts as well as on top. (The loaf can be made up to this point, then wrapped well, and placed in the refrigerator for up to 3 days.)

Bake for about 20 minutes, until the cheese has melted and is crisp on top. Serve straight out of the oven, along with the roasted garlic for scooping out and spreading on the bread.

CHEESE AND CORN SOUFFLÉ

Makes 4 to 6 servings (one 4-qt/3.75L baking dish)

I've always loved the comfort of spoon bread, a Southern dish that is more like a savory pudding than straightforward cornbread. This is practically a soufflé—it is very light and relies on only whipped egg whites for leavening. It doesn't have the customary béchamel →

sauce and has a generous amount of fresh corn that would weigh down a classic soufflé. I prefer this hybrid for flavor and texture. If you don't have the cheese I call for, any quality cheese that is in your refrigerator will do. I've served this with a roast and salad and felt a feast had effortlessly appeared. For a lighter supper, serve with a salad or Ancho Pepper Soup (page 126); either would be an ideal partner for this savory, cheese-laden spoon bread.

Unsalted butter, for the pan	Preheat the oven to 400°F/200°C. Butter the bottom and sides of a 4-qt/3.75L baking dish and dust the sides with the Parmesan.
3 Tbsp grated Parmesan cheese	
$\frac{1}{4}$ cup/55g unsalted butter	Melt the butter in a large saucepan set over medium heat. Add the onion and sauté, stirring often, until translucent but not browned, 3 to 4 minutes. Add the nutmeg.
$\frac{1}{2}$ cup/70g finely chopped onion	
Pinch of freshly grated nutmeg	
6 Tbsp/60g finely milled cornmeal	Whisk the cornmeal, cheddar or Gruyère, Parmesan, milk, salt, and egg yolks into the onion mixture and then remove from the heat.
2 cups/200g grated cheddar, Gruyère, or other firm cheese	
$\frac{1}{4}$ cup/25g grated Parmesan cheese	
2 cups/480ml whole milk	
$\frac{1}{4}$ tsp sea salt	
3 large eggs, separated	
	Whip the egg whites until stiff peaks form and remain when you lift the whisk out of the bowl. Using a rubber spatula, gently fold the whipped egg whites into the cheese mixture.
$\frac{1}{4}$ cup/25g grated Parmesan or Gruyère	Transfer the batter to the prepared dish, sprinkle the grated Parmesan or Gruyère on top, and bake until golden, well-puffed, and no longer liquid in the center, about 35 minutes. Serve straight from the oven.

CORN, GREEN BEANS, AND PARMESAN

Makes 4 to 6 servings

This is another salad that we made when we first opened Tartine Manufactory (see also the Tomato, Shelling Beans, and Cucumber Salad, page 164). Our chef, Sam, made this wonderful combination of two kinds of corn—fresh from the cob, and a corn called *quicos*, or *maiz gigante* (which also goes by the commercial name of corn nuts). The quicos are dry, crunchy, and salty and are balanced by the lime in the dressing and the sweetness from the fresh corn. Adding green beans and topping it with Parmesan cheese makes it a more substantial dish that could serve as one part of a two-item dinner, paired with a summer soup (such as the Summer Greens Soup, page 144), or a simple roasted chicken (see Spatchcocked Roasted Chicken, page 228). If you can get them, nasturtium leaves add a very nice peppery flavor.

3 ears of corn, shucked and kernels cut off cob	In a skillet over medium-high heat, cook the corn just until heated through, about 2 minutes. Set aside.
6 oz/170g green beans, yellow wax beans, or a combination trimmed	Prepare a bowl of ice water. Bring a saucepan of water to a boil. Add the beans and blanch until bright in color, about 1 minute. Using a slotted spoon, transfer the beans to the bowl of ice water and let cool, about 12 minutes. When cool, drain and pat dry. →

3 scallions, sliced thinly on bias

1 bunch cilantro, leaves pulled from stems

$\frac{2}{3}$ cup quicos (corn nuts), coarsely chopped

2 Tbsp lime juice, plus more as needed

1 Tbsp green or red hot sauce, plus more as needed

3 Tbsp olive oil

Sea salt

Ground black pepper

Nasturtium leaves for garnish (optional)

In a large mixing bowl, combine the cooked corn and green and/or yellow beans, scallions, cilantro, quicos, lime juice, hot sauce, olive oil, salt, and pepper. Taste and add more lime juice, hot sauce, salt, and pepper, if needed. Transfer to a serving dish and garnish with the nasturtiums.

2 oz/55g piece of Parmesan, for garnishing

Grate the Parmesan over the whole dish and serve.

Store in the refrigerator, covered, for up to 5 days. The quicos will lose some of their crunch after the first day.

SORGHUM AND CORN "RISOTTO"

Makes 4 servings (about 5 cups/1.2kg)

I wanted to make a risottolike dish using whole grains. I'd used sorghum flour in baking, but never the whole grain in cooking. It's always exciting to discover new ingredients, especially when it is a food of central importance in other parts of the world. Sorghum doesn't need a lot of water to grow, so it is a staple grain for arid regions in Africa and India. It's also grown in the United States in great quantity, but the variety grown is for livestock. Sorghum has →

a mild sweetness and texture that remains intact no matter how long it is cooked. It pairs well with corn, and I unify them in this dish by cooking the sorghum in a quick stock made of water and corncobs. The finished dish requires less attention than risotto but is similarly loose and creamy and is made slightly more toothsome by the sorghum, which keeps its integrity even after it is cooked. I would liken this recipe's versatility to grits or polenta. We first ate it alongside a ham steak, but it works with poached eggs and greens, or just as is, topped with sea salt and freshly ground black pepper. Try it with a dollop of crème fraîche, added just before serving.

📖 Sorghum takes awhile to cook. Unlike risotto, you don't have to stir the whole time; just make sure that the sorghum is always nearly submerged, adding more water to the pot when necessary. Feel free to cook the sorghum in advance, as far as a day ahead of time. It will not lose its toothsomeness even if it is cooked again, along with the rice and corn.

📖 Corncobs boiled in water infuse the broth with corn's sweetness. However, if you're pressed for time, it is not a necessary step.

4 ears corn, shucked 1 qt/960ml water	Cut the corn off of the cob and reserve the kernels. Bring the water to a boil in a pot. Snap the cobs in half and add them to the pot. Boil for about 20 minutes, until the cobs have infused the water with their flavor. Remove from the heat and reserve the cooking water. Discard the cobs.
2 Tbsp unsalted butter 1 small or $\frac{1}{2}$ large yellow onion, finely chopped	Melt the butter in a large saucepan over medium-low heat. Add the onion and sauté until tender but not at all browned, about 3 minutes. Lower the heat if necessary to prevent any browning.
$\frac{1}{2}$ cup/85g whole-grain sorghum	Add the sorghum to the onion and cook, stirring, for 2 minutes.
	Add 2 cups/480ml of the cob water to the sorghum, bring to a simmer, and cook until the sorghum is almost tender, about 1 hour 15 minutes. Make sure that the sorghum is always nearly submerged, adding more water to the pot when necessary.

½ cup/100g short-grain or long-grain rice

Once the sorghum is almost tender, add the rice and remaining 2 cups/480ml of cob water. (Don't worry if you don't have to time this perfectly, as the sorghum will not become mushy if cooked a little longer.) Cook at a simmer until the rice is tender, 20 to 30, minutes depending on the type of rice used. While the rice cooks, continue adding water as needed to keep the grains nearly submerged.

Fresh corn kernels (reserved from the first step)

¼ cup/60ml heavy cream, plus more as needed

Sea salt

Ground black pepper

Add the corn kernels and cream to the sorghum-rice mixture and cook for 2 to 3 minutes. The starch from the corn will thicken the liquid slightly. Season with salt and pepper. Use an immersion blender or transfer to a blender, to puree about one-quarter of the mixture. Stir to incorporate, taste for seasoning, adjust the consistency to your liking by adding more cream, and serve hot.

RESTAURANT MASHED POTATOES

Makes 6 servings

In one of my early restaurant jobs, I *was* the mashed potato station, peeling, cutting, boiling, and processing through a food mill every night. Russets are the best variety to mash because of their mealy texture. When forced through a ricer or food mill, their fine particle size absorbs water and fat easily. Mashed potatoes do have a lot of cream and butter in them. Just view them as an occasional splurge. If you have parsnips on hand, steam, process, and fold in a few when serving with game birds. And, for a celebration, a few drops of truffle oil, or shavings of a real truffle, transform this humble side.

📖 Potatoes possess incredible amounts of starch, which is both an asset and a curse. When making a gratin, the starch acts as a thickener, contributing to the velvety sauce. But in mashed potatoes, too much starch can cause them to become gummy or sticky. Russet potatoes work better than waxy potatoes because their cells separate more easily so they needn't be worked →

much in order to achieve a smooth consistency. This is what's behind the advice to never use an electric mixer or food processor to mix mash potatoes. If you were to do this, the potato's starch would release en masse, making for a gummy consistency. A ricer breaks apart the potato much more gently, allowing a higher proportion of the cells to remain intact.

📖 If you've ever made mashed potatoes ahead of time and found them to be impossibly stiff after sitting for a few hours, whisk in enough warm liquid, either milk or a mixture of milk and cream, until the right consistency is again achieved.

4 lb/1.8 kg russet potatoes	Bring a pot of salted water to a boil. Peel the potatoes, cut into 2-inch/5cm pieces, and drop them into the water. Boil until the potatoes are tender when pierced with the tip of a knife, about 20 minutes.
	Transfer the potatoes to a colander to drain. Process the potatoes using a ricer or food mill set over a serving bowl.
$\frac{3}{4}$ cup/180ml whole milk $\frac{3}{4}$ cup/180ml heavy cream $\frac{1}{4}$ cup/55g unsalted butter Sea salt Ground black pepper	In a small saucepan, bring the milk, cream, and butter to a simmer. Season with salt and pepper. Pour the warm mixture over the potatoes, stir until well mixed and creamy, and serve.

COTTAGE FRIES

Makes 4 to 6 servings

I will rarely go through the trouble of making french fries. However I will often make cottage fries, the tasty yet much more quickly made cousin of french fries. The trick is a very hot oven, a good amount of olive oil (they are essentially frying), and flipping them a couple of times to get them uniformly golden. If done right, you can achieve a proper fry—with a crunchy exterior, soft inside. Dip in Aioli (page 10), Buttermilk-Herb Dressing (page 21), or Romesco Sauce (page 29). →

3 lb/1.4kg russet potatoes (about 4 large)	Preheat the oven to 450°F/230°C. Wash and peel the potatoes or leave the peel on, if you like, and cut in half lengthwise. Cut each half lengthwise into 4 long wedges.
3 Tbsp olive oil 1½ tsp sea salt 1 tsp ground black pepper	In a large bowl, toss the potatoes with the olive oil, salt, and pepper. Transfer the potatoes to a baking sheet, spreading them out in one layer. Roast in the oven for 30 minutes, until golden brown, flipping the wedges after the first 10 minutes and again 10 minutes later while also periodically opening the oven door to let out steam. Let cool for 5 minutes and then serve.
	Store leftover potatoes in the refrigerator for up to 4 days. Recrisp them in a 300°F/150°C for 8 to 10 minutes.

CREAMED POTATOES WITH DILL

Makes 4 servings (about 5 cups/1.1kg)

My Swedish grandmother often made this comforting classic to accompany her own pickled herring. Waxy potatoes, such as fingerlings, are boiled and then dressed in a cream-enriched béchamel topped with copious amounts of fresh dill. Perhaps because the potatoes are just boiled and then dressed, this approach feels lighter than a gratin, and for this reason, makes a fine accompaniment to fish, like Hot-Smoked Salmon with Salsa Verde Cream Sauce (page 225), Gravlax (page 120), and sautéed trout or halibut. All-purpose wheat flour can be used to make the béchamel, but after several experiments, I find that the potato starch works just as well for a wheat-free version. When you're making the roux, just cook until it bubbles gently and then add the milk and cream. Though not commonly used in béchamel, cream gives depth to the sauce and does wonders for the potatoes.

1 $\frac{3}{4}$ lb/790g waxy potatoes (such as fingerlings or any new potato), peeled and cut into $\frac{1}{2}$-inch/12mm cubes	Boil the potatoes in plenty of salted water until tender, about 10 minutes. Drain.
1 cup/240ml whole milk, plus more as needed 1 cup/240ml heavy cream	In a small pot, warm the milk and cream to just under a simmer, then remove from the heat.
3 Tbsp unsalted butter 2 Tbsp potato starch or all-purpose wheat flour $\frac{1}{2}$ tsp sea salt Large pinch of ground white pepper A few gratings of whole or pinch of ground nutmeg (optional but traditional) Whole milk, as needed	Make the béchamel sauce by melting the butter in a medium saucepan over medium-high heat. Add the potato starch or all-purpose wheat flour and whisk to incorporate. While whisking, slowly pour in the hot milk and cream mixture. Whisk in the salt, white pepper, and nutmeg. Continue whisking until the mixture comes to a simmer. If it is too thick, thin with 1 tsp of additional milk at a time. If it's too thin, simmer for 1 to 2 minutes.
1 bunch dill, coarsely chopped	When ready to serve, gently mix the cooked potatoes and the dill and béchamel sauce, taking care not to break up the potatoes. Transfer to a bowl and serve immediately.

RÖSTI POTATOES

Makes 4 to 6 servings (one 10-inch/25cm rösti)

Crispy on the outside and steamed until soft in the inside, rösti potatoes are officially a Swiss dish, although their resemblance to latkes cannot be ignored. Whenever I have these, I'm brought back to my childhood in Brooklyn, when latkes were more common—and absolutely delicious with applesauce and sour cream. Rösti potatoes can be made in one large cake, to the diameter of whichever pan you use, so it can feed many people in just one batch. And, it beautifully accompanies Gravlax (page 120), Applesauce (page 27), or Crème Fraîche (page 37) spiked with finely grated horseradish. →

The key to a successful rösti that turns golden and doesn't stick to the pan is to make sure that the pan is very hot when the potatoes go in. By immediately lowering the heat and covering the pan, the potato simultaneously steams and browns.

Make sure to squeeze as much moisture from the potatoes as possible for the best texture when cooked. One way to do this is to grate the potatoes over a clean kitchen towel or cheesecloth, wrap them in the towel, and wring out every bit of moisture. If your rösti refuses to stick together, there's probably still too much moisture in the potatoes.

$1\frac{1}{2}$ lb/680g russet potatoes, peeled and grated with largest holes on box grater

$1\frac{1}{2}$ tsp sea salt

$\frac{1}{4}$ tsp ground black pepper

Mix the grated potato with the salt and pepper in a large bowl and let sit for 5 minutes to draw out the moisture. Working with one handful at a time, squeeze as much liquid out of the potatoes as possible.

$\frac{1}{4}$ cup/60ml olive oil, or enough to be to $\frac{1}{8}$ inch/3mm deep in a 10-inch/25cm skillet

Heat the oil in the skillet over high heat until very hot and shimmering.

Add the potato mixture to the oil in the hot skillet, pressing to form a flat cake about $\frac{1}{2}$ inch/12mm thick. Cover the skillet with a lid, lower the heat to medium-low, and cook for 7 to 10 minutes, shaking the pan to avoid sticking. If there is still a good amount of oil left in the pan, tip it out before inverting the rösti. When the rösti is deep golden brown on the bottom, set a large plate over the skillet, and carefully invert it onto the plate. Add a little more oil to the pan, let it heat for a moment, and then slide the rösti back in to cook on the second side for 5 to 10 minutes, until golden. Transfer to a warm plate and serve warm.

Rösti can be made a few hours ahead and reheated in a 350°F/180°C oven for 5 minutes or served right after cooking.

POTATO GRATIN

Makes 4 to 6 servings (one 3-qt/2.8L gratin dish)

I learned a trick from a chef in culinary school that never fails to make a well-seasoned, perfectly cooked, and beautifully golden gratin. Potato gratins are often baked entirely in the oven, but by first simmering the sliced potatoes on the stovetop in milk and cream, the starch is activated and this jump-starts the cooking process, ensuring an evenly baked gratin and offering you the opportunity to adjust the seasoning before it goes in the oven. I love to use any good-flavored cheese and urge you to use a high-quality Gruyère, Tomme de Savoie, or Comté. Because potatoes take on the flavors in the dish you are making, the cheese's unique flavor will come through. Leeks are a natural with potato, and the nutmeg adds just a hint of warmth. A potato gratin is fit for a crowd, as it can be made ahead and is impressive looking. If it's just for a family supper, leftovers are always relished. It's not possible to make too much.

📖 Because the texture and starchiness of the potato are key to the gratin's success, use russets.

📖 If making the gratin ahead, be aware that potatoes will soak up any residual liquid (the same holds for mashed potatoes). To make ahead, use $\frac{1}{2}$ cup/120ml more liquid than when you serve it straight out of the oven.

1 clove garlic, halved 1 Tbsp unsalted butter, for the pan	Preheat the oven to 350°F/180°C. Prepare a 3-qt/2.8L gratin dish by rubbing the inside surface first with the cut garlic and then coating with the butter.
1 Tbsp unsalted butter 1 leek, white and light green parts thinly sliced crosswise and rinsed well, or 1 small onion, diced	Melt the butter in a large pot over medium heat. Add the leek or onion and cook, stirring often, until tender but not yet browned, about 3 minutes. →

2 $\frac{1}{4}$ lb/1kg russet potatoes, peeled and very thinly sliced

2 cups/480ml whole milk

2 cups/480ml heavy cream

2 cloves garlic, finely sliced

A few gratings of whole or large pinch of ground nutmeg (optional but traditional)

1 tsp sea salt

2 cups/200g grated firm cow's milk cheese (such as Gruyère, Tomme de Savoie, or Comté)

1 cup/100g grated firm cow's milk cheese (such as Gruyère, Tomme de Savoie, or Comté)

Add the potatoes, milk, cream, garlic, nutmeg, and salt to the pot with the cooked leek or onion and bring to a boil over medium-high heat. Once at a boil, decrease the heat to medium and simmer for 5 minutes, stirring continuously. The starch in the potatoes will begin to thicken the milk and cream. Turn off the heat and stir in the cheese. Transfer the potato mixture to the gratin dish. Level the surface. Taste the liquid and season with more salt, if necessary (depending on the saltiness of the cheese).

Scatter the cheese evenly over the top of the gratin. (The unbaked, assembled gratin can be covered and refrigerated for up to 2 days or tightly wrapped and frozen for up to 3 months.)

Bake for 45 minutes to 1 hour, until the cheese on top is nicely browned and bubbling. If baking the gratin from the refrigerator or freezer, let it come to room temperature first and then bake. Let cool slightly before serving.

Root Vegetable Gratin: Substitute 8 oz/230g parsnips or celery root for 8 oz/230g of the potatoes, also thinly sliced, and proceed as directed in the recipe. These sweeter roots go nicely with turkey or duck.

FRIED POTATOES AND ROASTED OYSTER MUSHROOMS

Makes 6 servings

Beef Daube (page 256), the French-style stew, calls for an accompaniment worthy of its savory richness. These crisped potatoes and sautéed mushrooms are a welcome contrast to a daube's tender meat. The potatoes are classic in their preparation, undergoing two stages of cooking. Steam the potato rounds until slightly undercooked and then fry them until they are perfectly golden. The ideal is a crispy exterior with soft interior. Parboiling potatoes creates a cooked, irregular exterior that, when fried, crisps while the interior stays soft from steaming or boiling. Don't limit yourself to serving this with only the daube. This is a dish that goes with many things, from roasted chicken to pork chops.

4 large russet potatoes	Line a baking sheet with paper towels. Cut the potatoes crosswise into rounds, $\frac{1}{2}$ to $\frac{3}{4}$ inch/12mm to 2cm thick. Place a steaming basket in a stockpot, add water, and bring to a boil. Line the steaming basket with potato rounds, cover the pot, and steam until they can be pierced with the tip of a knife with some resistance. Transfer the potatoes to the baking sheet and pat dry with the paper towels.
12 oz/340g oyster mushrooms, gently wiped clean 2 Tbsp olive oil Sea salt Ground black pepper	Preheat the oven to 400°F/200°C. Place the mushrooms in a large baking dish. Drizzle with the oil and sprinkle with salt and pepper. Gently toss to coat. Roast in the oven until the mushrooms are softened and have golden brown ridges, about 15 minutes. Keep warm.
1 qt/960ml canola oil Sea salt	In a Dutch oven, over high heat bring the oil to 350°F/180°C. Add the potato rounds about 8 at a time (or as many as will fit in a single, uncrowded layer) and fry, turning gently with long-handled tongs, until golden brown, 6 to 8 minutes. Return

to the baking sheet to drain on the paper towels and repeat with the remaining potatoes. Sprinkle the rounds with salt.

Gremolata (page 10)

Transfer the mushrooms and potatoes to a serving dish. Spoon the Gremolata over the top, toss gently to coat, and serve.

CHRIS KRONNER'S ONION RINGS AND TEMPURA VEGETABLES

Makes 4 to 6 servings

Chris Kronner, our chef in the early days of Bar Tartine, has the ability to make old standards seem new again. That was certainly true when I first had his onion rings. They are crisp, light, and let the onion flavor come through more than most with their too-thick batters. The only drawback to a starch-based batter is that because of its lower protein content, it does not brown as well. The pinch of baking soda I've added is not for leavening, but rather for making the crust golden brown by changing the pH.

   📖 The trick to frying is to set up everything before you begin. Line a cooling rack with paper towels, have all of your vegetables cut and ready to go, and keep the oil at 350°F/180°C. I always have a thermometer nearby, but if you're without one, you can test the temperature using one onion ring. It should vigorously bubble, but not burn, when put into the hot oil. Start off slightly higher—at 360°F/182°C—to ensure that the heat will not dip too far below 350°F/180°C when all of the rings are added.

   📖 This recipe makes about 2 cups/480ml of batter, which is enough for 5 cups/600g sliced onions or other vegetables.

   📖 The onion rings can be made an hour or so ahead of serving and recrisped in an oven preheated to 375°F/190°C for 3 to 5 minutes. →

$1\frac{2}{3}$ cups/230g white rice flour or brown rice flour

3 Tbsp potato starch

3 Tbsp cornstarch, arrowroot starch, or tapioca flour/starch

1 tsp sea salt

Pinch of baking soda (optional)

1 cup/240ml sparkling water, plus more as needed

Mix the rice flour, potato starch, cornstarch or arrowroot starch or tapioca flour/starch, salt, and baking soda in a large bowl. Gradually whisk in the sparkling water, adding more water as needed until the batter has the consistency of thick buttermilk.

5 cups/600g red or yellow onions, sliced into $\frac{1}{4}$-inch/6mm-thick rings or half-moons or other vegetables (such as broccolini, cut into florets; fennel, cut into $\frac{1}{4}$-inch/6mm-thick half-moons; zucchini, sliced lengthwise into $\frac{1}{4}$-inch/6mm-thick strips; sweet potato, cut into $\frac{1}{8}$-inch/3mm discs; green beans; or cauliflower, cut into $\frac{1}{4}$-inch/6mm-thick pieces)

Rinse and prepare the vegetables. Thoroughly pat them dry.

1 qt/960ml vegetable oil (such as peanut, grapeseed, sunflower, or safflower)

Pour the oil into a heavy-bottomed pot over medium-high heat and heat to 360°F/182°C. Line a plate with paper towels and place it near the stovetop.

Dredge a single piece of vegetable in the batter and carefully drop into the hot oil as a test fry. The oil is the correct temperature if it immediately bubbles and the vegetable is cooked through after 3 to 5 minutes. Chopsticks work very well for both dredging the vegetables in the batter and turning them over in the oil.

Once the vegetable is cooked, use chopsticks or tongs to transfer it to the paper towel–lined plate. Continue cooking the vegetables in batches, adding only as many as will fit in a single layer in the oil. Serve hot or at room temperature.

BRANDADE

Makes 4 to 6 servings (one 1-qt/960ml baking dish)

Brandade, a puree of salt cod laden with olive oil or cream, proves that invention born out of necessity can be delicious. The recipe traces its origins to the French port cities of Nimes and Marseilles, and versions are now made throughout the Mediterranean. Salt cod itself has an even longer history as an ingenious way to preserve whole fish. As far back as medieval times, cod from Norwegian waters were skinned and salted whole and then sold to cities throughout Europe. Hours, even days, of soaking are required to remove the overbearing salinity, but for the fish lovers among us, the wait is worthwhile. Soaked cod pureed with potato, olive oil, and milk or cream is a heavenly combination of brine and richness, especially when spread upon toasted bread. Because salt cod can be hard to find and its quality is not always apparent, I have made a recipe that pays homage to the original but uses fresh fish instead. Rather than pureeing it smooth, the potatoes are coarsely mashed and flakes of fish are folded in. Perhaps a virtue of its more substantive texture, I see this as a side (or main course), even though traditional brandade is considered an appetizer. With a brightly dressed salad and crusty bread (and a glass of wine), this makes a fine supper.

📖 If cod is not available, any white fish will work. If it is especially delicate or thin, watch closely to prevent it from overcooking.

📖 A quick method for making breadcrumbs is to put 1-inch/2.5cm chunks of stale bread into a blender or food processor and pulse until broken down.

$1\frac{1}{2}$ cups/360ml whole milk

4 cloves garlic, lightly smashed

4 bay leaves

4 sprigs thyme

1 tsp sea salt

3 to 5 grinds black peppercorns

Combine the milk, garlic, bay leaves, thyme, salt, and pepper in a medium saucepan. Simmer over low heat for 10 minutes and then remove from the heat. Let sit for 1 hour to infuse the milk with the aromatics. →

1 lb/455g fresh cod fillets, skin and bones removed	Place the cod in the milk mixture and return the saucepan to the heat. Cook very gently at a bare simmer until the fish is almost cooked through, 4 to 7 minutes, depending on the thickness of the fillets. You can use the tip of a small knife to flake the fish apart and see if the center of the thickest part is nearly opaque. Remove from the heat and allow the fish to finish cooking in the milk for a few minutes. Transfer the fish to a cutting board and, using 2 forks, gently flake apart, and then set aside.

Preheat the oven to 400°F/200°C. Butter the bottom and sides of a 1-qt/960ml baking dish or several smaller ramekins.

1 lb/455g whole small potatoes, peeled and boiled	In a large bowl, coarsely mash the potatoes.

$\frac{1}{2}$ cup/120ml heavy cream $\frac{1}{4}$ cup/60ml olive oil Juice of 1 lemon Pinch of ground red chile or red pepper flakes Sea salt Ground black pepper	Add the $\frac{1}{2}$ cup/120 ml of the fish-cooking liquid, the cream, olive oil, lemon juice, and ground red chile or red pepper flakes, and salt and pepper to the bowl with the mashed potatoes and mix well. Add the flaked fish, gently folding it in, and then taste and adjust the seasoning. Transfer to the prepared dish and smooth the surface with a spatula.

3 slices country-style bread, ground into coarse breadcrumbs 3 Tbsp olive oil 2 sprigs thyme, leaves pulled from stems	Combine the breadcrumbs, olive oil, and thyme in a small bowl. Evenly distribute over the fish-and-potatoes mixture. Bake until the breadcrumbs are golden brown and the brandade is bubbling, about 20 minutes. Serve hot.

Brandade can be stored, covered, in the refrigerator for up to 5 days. To reheat, cover the baking dish with aluminum foil and place in a 325°F/165°C oven for 10 minutes. Remove the foil and continue heating for another 5 minutes, until the breadcrumb topping is crisp.

MAINS

RICOTTA DUMPLINGS

Makes 2 servings as a main dish or 4 as a side course

Every culture has a dumpling. Made from humble ingredients, dumplings become a canvas for simple sauces. These ricotta dumplings, which are fluffy and light, are most similar to gnocchi and incredibly versatile. They can be dressed with brown butter, a quick tomato sauce, or made herbaceous by adding 2 Tbsp of chopped basil or sage to the dough. Usually, I poach the dumplings and then add them directly to a sauce or pan-fry them in butter. But my most recent success was to bake them in a shallow pan of Rich Tomato Sauce (see page 32) and then dust with grated Parmesan cheese, enabling them to simultaneously brown on the top while cooking in the sauce. Nothing could be more straightforward in its flavors—the simple combination of tomato and cheese never fails.

📖 You may substitute another cheese for the Parmesan. If you use a cheese that has a higher moisture level than Parmesan, such as cheddar, add an additional 1 Tbsp of potato flour to the dough.

1 tsp olive oil

6 oz/170g mixed greens, such as chard leaves, tatsoi, arugula, and spinach

Heat the olive oil in a large skillet over medium-high heat, add the greens and sauté about 1 minute, until bright green and wilted. Transfer the cooked greens to a piece of cheesecloth or a clean kitchen towel and squeeze and wring to remove all excess moisture. The cooked and squeezed greens should weigh about 2 oz/55g.

6 oz/170g Ricotta Cheese (page 33, or store-bought)

1 large egg

¾ cup plus 2 Tbsp/85g grated Parmesan

Pinch of sea salt

Pinch of ground black pepper

Pinch of ground nutmeg

2 Tbsp sweet rice flour

3 Tbsp potato flour

In a medium bowl, combine the cooked greens, ricotta, egg, Parmesan, salt, pepper, nutmeg, rice flour, and potato flour just until the mixture comes together. Portion the mixture into 1 Tbsp log-shaped pieces. →

Bring a stockpot of salted water to a simmer. Drop the dumplings into the simmering water a few at a time and cook until they float, about 3 minutes. Using a slotted spoon, lift the dumplings out of the water and transfer to a colander to drain. Handle the dumplings gently, as they will be tender.

$\frac{1}{4}$ cup/55g
unsalted butter

Melt the butter in a skillet over medium-high heat. Add the dumplings and gently fry about 1 minute, until lightly browned. Serve hot.

Store, covered tightly, in the refrigerator for up to 2 days. To reheat, gently warm in a sauce over low heat.

Baked Ricotta Dumplings in Tomato Sauce: To bake in a tomato sauce, spoon a layer of the Rich Tomato Sauce (see page 32) in a low, wide casserole dish and top with spoonfuls of the freshly made dumpling dough (without boiling first). Grate a few tablespoons of Parmesan cheese on top and bake at 350°F/180°C for 35 minutes, until the top is lightly browned.

SPRING RISOTTO

Makes 4 to 6 servings

Delicate spring vegetables are well suited for a risotto, which is by its very nature a fairly neutral palette that can take on myriad flavors. Risotto achieves its creaminess because of the starchy and absorbent rice, usually Arborio or Carnaroli, that takes up well-seasoned stock and wine. It is not a dish to make ahead because even after you're done cooking, the rice continues to absorb the thick sauce you've worked so hard to create. I've spent a lot of time making risotto in restaurants and, while doing so, learned one secret that makes the outcome within your control: Partially cook the risotto ahead of time, and then finish it just before you're ready to serve. This way, the risotto only requires 10 or so minutes to finish, rather than its usual 20 to 30 minutes. This is especially useful for dinner guests and even family meals, when it can be difficult to estimate everyone's timing. With pesto mixed in at the last minute, the whole dish becomes perfumed with basil and a vernal green.

📖 To prepare the risotto ahead of time, cook the vegetables and the rice up until you add the wine and 1 cup/240ml of stock. Once the rice has absorbed the liquid, spread the rice and onion mixture on a baking sheet to hold until you're ready to finish cooking. Just before dinner, return the rice to the pot and resume cooking until done.

1 bunch asparagus, woody ends trimmed, cut into 2-inch/ 5cm lengths

8 oz/230g English peas, shelled

8 oz/230g sugar snap peas, stems and strings removed

6 oz/170g fiddlehead ferns (optional)

Bring a large pot of generously salted water to a boil. Prepare a bowl of ice water. Add the asparagus to the pot and blanch, just until bright green, about 1 minute. Using a slotted spoon, transfer to the ice water to stop the cooking, about 30 seconds. Transfer the asparagus to a colander to drain. Repeat with the English peas, sugar snap peas, and fiddleheads. →

1 Tbsp olive oil

2 cloves garlic, minced

$\frac{1}{2}$ yellow onion, minced

2 cups/400g Arborio or Carnaroli rice

Heat the oil in a large sauté pan over medium heat. Add the garlic and onion and sauté just until translucent, about 30 seconds. Add the rice and stir until opaque, about 1 minute.

1 cup/240ml dry white wine

1 cup/240ml Chicken Stock (page 32, or store-bought), hot

2 tsp sea salt

Stir the wine into the rice, bring to a simmer, and cook, stirring periodically, until the rice absorbs the wine, about 5 minutes. Stir in stock and salt, return to a simmer, and let cook until the liquid has been absorbed. Spread the rice mixture on a baking sheet and set aside until you are ready to finish the dish, or skip this step and keep cooking, continuing with adding the hot stock.

1 qt/960ml Chicken Stock (page 32, or store-bought), hot

Sea salt

Ground black pepper

$\frac{1}{2}$ cup/50g grated Parmesan cheese

$\frac{1}{3}$ cup/85g store-bought basil pesto

About 15 minutes before you're ready to serve, return the rice mixture to the sauté pan and cook over medium heat. Stir 1 cup/240ml of the hot stock into the rice mixture and cook until the moisture has been nearly absorbed. Season with salt and pepper. Repeat for the remaining 3 cups/720ml of stock, adding 1 cup/240ml at a time. When you still see liquid pooling here and there in the pan, remove from the heat and stir in the blanched vegetables and the Parmesan. Quickly stir in the pesto and serve.

Store risotto, covered, in the refrigerator for up to 2 days.

SEAFOOD SALAD WITH LEMON-GARLIC-HERB DRESSING

Makes 4 servings as a main course or 6 as an appetizer

This is very similar to the chilled seafood salads Chad and I had when working in the south of France, where all along the Côte d'Azur, every restaurant serves them chilled, lightly dressed, and with a glass of wine. The success of these salads lies in the contrasting textures of different fish, shellfish, and squid, and of course, a vivid vinaigrette. When you're at the fishmonger, and you spot beautiful seafood, this is a wonderful dish to make. A chilled glass of good white wine, often a Muscadet, is the classic accompaniment in France.

📖 I count on "carry-over" cooking (the cooking that results from the heat the food retains), to finish cooking seafood perfectly, rather than fully cooking it on the heat and then relying on a plunge in an ice water bath to stop the cooking. With fish and shellfish, I find that an ice water bath dilutes the flavor. With this in mind, I call for cooking the fish and shellfish in this recipe ever so briefly, knowing that they will finish cooking through after they come out of the poaching liquid.

---

3 cups/720ml water

2 bay leaves

3 sprigs thyme

$\frac{1}{2}$ lemon, sliced

$\frac{1}{2}$ shallot or $\frac{1}{4}$ onion, coarsely chopped

10 black peppercorns

1 tsp sea salt

Combine the water, bay leaves, thyme, lemon, shallot or onion, peppercorns, and salt in a large pot and bring to a boil over high heat. Lower the heat to low and simmer for 5 minutes.

---

12 oz/340g halibut or other firm white fish fillets, cut into 4 to 6 pieces, pin bones removed

12 oz/340g squid, cleaned

8 oz/225g shrimp, peeled and deveined

8 oz/225g scallops

Adjust the heat to bring the seasoned water to a very low simmer. Add the halibut to the pot and poach just until almost done, about 3 minutes. Using a spatula, gently transfer to a platter and let cool. Repeat, poaching the remaining seafood in batches, working with only one type of seafood at a time. →

Each batch will take approximately 2 to 4 minutes, depending on how cold your seafood is and how hot the poaching liquid is. When all the seafood has been poached, reserve the poaching liquid and keep it at a low simmer.

10 oz/280g small waxy potatoes, cut into 1-inch/2.5cm pieces

Add the potatoes to the poaching liquid and cook just until tender when pierced with the tip of a knife, about 10 minutes depending. Transfer the potatoes to a colander to drain and then place in the refrigerator to chill.

$\frac{1}{2}$ cup/120ml Lemon-Garlic-Herb Dressing (page 24), plus more as needed

8 oz/230g arugula

Pour 6 Tbsp/90ml of the dressing over the seafood and toss gently to coat. Reserve the remaining dressing. Place the dressed seafood in the refrigerator to chill for at least 30 minutes or until you are ready to serve. When you are ready to serve, place the arugula in a bowl, add the remaining 2 Tbsp of dressing and toss to coat. Add the potatoes to the platter with the seafood and pass the platter and arugula at the table.

CHOPPED SALAD OF SALMON AND VEGETABLES

Makes 4 to 6 servings

Chopped salads can be creatively composed with such a variety of ingredients and textures that it is often easy to build a meal simply from what you have at home. We just adjust our ingredients to use up our abundance of vegetables and sauerkraut or other pickles we have in the refrigerator. Cooked grains, chunky vegetables (raw and cooked), fish or meat, nuts or seeds, fruit (fresh or dried) are all possible additions, and can be endlessly combined. The main objective is to assemble a mixture of ingredients that retain their integrity when tossed together. Essential to making the salad exciting, rather than perfunctory, is a piquant addition that gives occasional bursts of intensity. Olives or capers do the job, or, as for this salad, chopped bread-and-butter pickles. If you have no salmon, another fish that is firm enough to flake (like tuna or halibut) could be used in its place, and chicken or steak would do just as well. Instead of asparagus, snap peas or green beans would give the requisite bite. Start with this as a template and then begin to improvise with boiled potatoes, cooked farro, or roasted carrots.

📖 This salad would also be delicious with the addition of fresh, lightly cooked peas, fava beans, soybeans (edamame), or corn.

6 spears/100g asparagus, woody ends trimmed

8 oz/230g marble potatoes or larger wax potatoes cut into 1-inch/2.5cm pieces

Prepare a bowl of ice water. Bring a pot of generously salted water to a boil. Add the asparagus and cook for 3 minutes. Using a slotted spoon, transfer the asparagus to the bowl of ice water and let cool, about 10 minutes. Add the potatoes to the pot and boil until they are tender when pierced with the tip of a knife. Transfer the potatoes to a colander to drain. When the asparagus and potatoes are cool enough to handle, pat them dry. Cut the asparagus into 1-inch/2.5cm pieces.

4 cups/80g mixed salad greens (any combination of romaine, arugula, frisée, butter lettuce, miner's lettuce, or oak leaf), chopped

½ bunch dill, coarsely chopped

1 or 2 ripe avocados, halved, pitted, peeled, and sliced

⅓ cup/45g sliced Bread-and-Butter Pickles (see Quick Vegetable Pickles, page 49, or store-bought), coarsely chopped, or other pickle, sauerkraut, or capers

½ cup/120ml Lemon-Garlic-Herb Dressing (page 24)

Sea salt

Ground black pepper

In a large bowl, toss the salad greens, dill, avocados, pickles, and cooked asparagus, and potatoes together with about half of the dressing. Season with salt and pepper to taste. Arrange the salad on a serving platter. →

2 (4-to-6 oz/115 to 170g) cooked salmon fillets (see One-Side Sautéed Salmon, page 223), cooled and coarsely flaked

Place the salmon on top or around the sides of the salad and serve with the remaining dressing on the side.

ONE-SIDE SAUTÉED SALMON WITH CHIVE BUTTER SAUCE

Makes 4 servings

I worked as a server in a Scandinavian restaurant in New York City in the late '80s, where I served a dish like this one; this is my affectionate replication. It's a recipe that has stayed in my memory for so long because of its striking flavors, simplicity, and visual appeal: salmon seared on the skin side only, with the top of the fillet rare, and then served with a vibrant, green chive sauce. It is definitely a dish for people like me who love medium-rare or rare salmon. I'm sure it was served with a potato side dish at that New York City restaurant. The Rösti Potatoes (page 201) or Fried Potatoes and Roasted Oyster Mushrooms (page 206) would be a nice crispy contrast to the delicate salmon and a foil for the butter sauce.

1 (1 lb/455g) salmon fillet, skin on

Check the salmon for pin bones (the tiny bones that aren't attached to the fish's skeleton) by running your fingers over the fillet. If you need to remove any, slide a hand under the fillet and lift the fillet slightly so it bends at the point where the pin bone is located. Grasp the protruding bone with tweezers or needle-nose pliers and gently pull the bone out. Repeat until all the pin bones are removed.

Sea salt

Ground black pepper

Season the skin side of the fish with salt and pepper. →

1 Tbsp olive oil

Heat the oil in a skillet over high heat. Place the salmon skin-side down, gently pressing on the top if it curls up on the bottom. Lower the heat to medium and cook until the fish turns opaque about three-quarters up from the bottom of the fillet, about 4 to 6 minutes for medium-rare, or to your preferred doneness. Transfer the salmon to a plate and let cool slightly while you make the sauce.

$\frac{1}{2}$ cup/110g unsalted butter

2 small or 1 large (1.5 oz/45g) bunch chives, chopped into $\frac{1}{4}$-inch/6mm pieces

2 Tbsp coarsely chopped flat-leaf parsley

$\frac{1}{4}$ tsp sea salt, plus more as needed

$\frac{1}{4}$ tsp lemon juice, plus more as needed

Melt the butter in a small saucepan over low heat. Add the chives, parsley, salt, and lemon juice to the melted butter, stirring often, for 2 minutes. Do not let the sauce boil.

Transfer the sauce to a container that will fit an immersion blender (such as a Mason jar). (Due to the small amount of sauce, using a regular blender may not work, unless you have one with a small capacity container.) Mix to blend the sauce. Season to taste and add more salt and lemon juice if needed.

Pour the sauce on the serving plate, place the salmon on top, and serve.

HOT-SMOKED SALMON WITH SALSA VERDE CREAM SAUCE

Makes 4 servings

Most salmon is cold-smoked, meaning that it is placed in a smoky, cool environment, which does not cook the fish but essentially cures it. Hot-smoking, on the other hand, involves placing the fish in a heated smoky container and infusing it with smoke while cooking it at the same time. When hot-smoking is done well, the result is savory, tender, and moist, and the amount of smoke flavor can be subtle to strong. To hot smoke fish, purchase a stovetop smoker or just create one yourself from a pan with a cover, a rack, and wood chips. Most kinds of woods are available in chip form at well-stocked cooking supply stores. The fish is cooked in batches, unless you are able to use a proper grill with a smoker, I recommend cooking no more than 2 to 4 servings at a time (depending on the size of your pan), which works out because it cooks quickly and isn't meant to be piping hot when served. The herb-laden cream accents the smokiness beautifully.

📖 Wood chips can be found at most kitchen and hardware stores. I use maple, but any food-friendly wood chip will work.

📖 When selecting the salmon, choose center-cut fillets rather than the tail end, as you want your fillets to be even in thickness. Try this technique with other meaty fish, like swordfish or halibut, keeping their footprint in the pan about the same and the thickness of each at 1 inch/2.5 cm.

📖 Choose a large pan with a lid or, in lieu of a lid, use a stainless-steel bowl that fits the pan so that the bowl acts as a dome for the pan. There should be a tight seal between bowl and pan, preventing any smoke from escaping.

1 cup/90g wood chips (such as maple, cherry, mesquite, applewood, hickory, or grapevine)	Soak the wood chips in water for a few minutes. →

4 (6-oz/170g) salmon fillets, skin on

Sea salt

Ground black pepper

Season the salmon with salt and pepper on both sides. Open your kitchen windows and doors and turn on your range hood. Choose a pan with a tight-fitting lid or, instead of a lid, use a bowl that fits snugly over the pan to make a tight seal. Heat the pan over high heat for 1 minute.

1 Tbsp olive oil

Add the oil to the hot pan, and then place 2 salmon fillets, skin-side down, in the pan. Alternatively, if you have a rack that fits inside your pan, position it in the pan first, and place the salmon on the rack. Toss in a handful of the soaked chips around the fillets and immediately cover the pan with the lid or bowl. Cook for 6 to 8 minutes, or until the fish is cooked to your preferred doneness. There's no need to flip the salmon over; it'll be evenly cooked and very moist. Transfer the cooked salmon to a plate and repeat with the remaining 2 fillets. If using a store-bought smoker, follow the manufacturer's instructions and cook all of the salmon at one time.

$\frac{1}{3}$ cup/80ml Salsa Verde (page 13)

$\frac{1}{3}$ cup/80g Crème Fraîche (page 37, or store-bought) or sour cream

Sea salt

Ground black pepper

2 Tbsp salmon or trout roe (optional)

Mix together the Salsa Verde and Crème Fraîche or sour cream and season with salt and pepper to taste. (The salsa verde–cream sauce can be made ahead and stored, covered, in the refrigerator for up to 4 days.) Gently fold in the salmon or trout roe just before serving.

Serve the salmon hot or at room temperature with the salsa verde–cream sauce on the side.

SEAFOOD STEW WITH AIOLI

Makes 4 to 6 servings

A good seafood stew with an aromatic broth is a luxury rarely made in a home kitchen. What sets apart a great seafood stew from a satisfactory one is how well the fish is cooked. So while I don't consider this a difficult recipe, it does require attention once the seafood is ready to cook. But I find there is no better recipe to take advantage of fresh, seasonal seafood of all kinds. This liberally borrows from both Italian- and French-style fish stews, aioli being the common finishing touch. Its rich mouthfeel and heady garlic flavor join the saffron-tomato broth and tender seafood, and it is delicious slathered on toasted bread. If you have a fennel- or anise-flavored liqueur, such as Pernod, sambuca, or pastis, a splash in the soup pot just before serving will highlight the fennel flavor.

📖 Timing is the most important aspect of this dish because the small pieces of fish and shellfish cook at different rates. It is easy to tell when mussels or clams are cooked through, as their shells open up. For fish, aim to slightly undercook the pieces, turning off the flame when there's still a touch of translucent, uncooked flesh in the center of each piece. By the time the stew is served, the fish will be perfectly done from the carry-over cooking.

2 Tbsp olive oil ½ yellow onion, sliced 1 bulb fennel, halved and sliced	Heat the oil in a Dutch oven or other heavy-bottomed pot with a lid over medium heat. Add the onion and fennel and cook, stirring often, until softened but not yet browned, about 4 minutes.
3 cloves garlic, sliced (1 by 4-inch/ 2.5 by 10cm) strip of orange peel 2 sprigs thyme, leaves pulled from stems 1 bay leaf Pinch of cayenne pepper 1 (6-inch/15cm) sprig tarragon	Add the garlic, orange peel, thyme, bay leaf, cayenne, and tarragon to the pot and sauté, stirring, for 2 minutes. →

2 ½ cups/600ml water

1 cup/240ml Quick Tomato Sauce (page 30, or store-bought) or crushed tomatoes

4 to 6 small/280g potatoes (such as fingerlings), halved lengthwise

2 pinches of saffron

Add the water, tomato sauce or crushed tomatoes, potatoes, and saffron to the pot. Bring to a boil over high heat and then lower to a simmer. Cook until the potatoes are almost done, 10 to 15 minutes. (The stew can be made up until this point and held at room temperature for a couple of hours or stored, covered, overnight in the refrigerator. When you are ready to serve, gently heat the stew to a simmer and then proceed with the recipe.)

1 lb/455g halibut or other firm white fish, cut into 4 pieces, pin bones removed

8 oz/225g shrimp, peeled and deveined

8 oz/225g clams, scrubbed

8 oz/225g squid, cleaned, cut into 1-inch/2.5cm rings

Add the halibut or other white fish, shrimp, clams, and squid to the tomato mixture, starting with the largest pieces of fish (so that they are closest to the hot liquid) and ending with the squid, which will cook the quickest. Cover the pot and gently simmer until the clams have opened and the fish is nearly cooked through, 5 to 7 minutes.

1 Tbsp Pernod, sambuca, or pastis (optional)

Sea salt

Remove the stew from the heat. Stir in the Pernod, sambuca, or pastis. Let sit, covered, for 2 to 4 minutes to allow the fish to gently finish cooking. Taste the broth and adjust the seasoning, adding salt as needed.

¾ cup/180g Aioli (page 10)

Small handful of fennel fronds

Ladle the stew into shallow bowls. Spoon some Aioli into each bowl, garnish with the fennel fronds, and serve.

SPATCHCOCKED ROASTED CHICKEN

Makes 4 to 6 servings

The dream of a roasted chicken is often better than the reality. The breast meat is either too dry while the skin is crisped and golden, the breast meat is succulent while the thigh remains chewy and the →

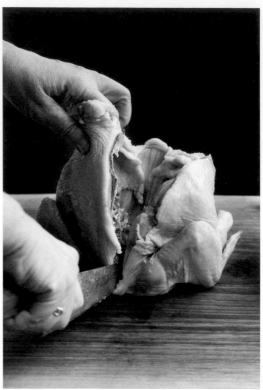

skin barely colors. Unsatisfied, I wanted to find a guaranteed method that would produce the ideal roasted bird. To my surprise, the old technique of spatchcocking—or butterflying—a chicken, where the backbone is removed and the entire bird can lay flat on the roasting pan, has become my absolute favorite method.

I was inspired by food writer J. Kenji López-Alt's thorough exploration of the *whys* and *hows* of spatchcocking fowl. He explains that a perfectly cooked bird, with moist breast meat and tender legs, is difficult to achieve because breast meat is done at 150°F/65°C degrees and leg meat needs to go up to 170°F/76°C degrees in order for the collagen to break down. Traditional ways of roasting a chicken, when the breast is thrust high into the oven's heat and exposed as much as the folded thigh is sheltered, exaggerate the differences between the two. When the chicken is spatchcocked, the thighs are more fully exposed to the oven heat, and because of how air circulates in an oven, the outer parts of the chicken cook more quickly than the interior. (Just think of how cookies crisp and brown at the edges first.) Finally, by laying the pan on the bottom of the oven, the thighs receive a blast of heat, while the breast, slightly elevated by the sternum lifting it, is buffered.

The practice of adding a dry rub is one I learned long ago from Zuni Café, a San Francisco restaurant renowned for its succulent, wood oven–roasted chickens that are still on the menu thirty-five years after opening. Here, the rub is as simple as salt and thyme, but a dry rub can be a more involved mixture of spices and herbs, such as the one on page 252. (If you use that rub, omit the amount of salt in that recipe and instead follow the amount used in this recipe, calculating how much you'll need based on your chicken's weight.) Use any left-overs for Chicken–Celery Root Salad (page 163) and use the bones to make a flavorful chicken stock.

📖 Moisture is the enemy of browning. To get the crispest and most golden chicken skin, leave the seasoned chicken uncovered in the refrigerator for at least a few hours or up to 1 or 2 days. The dry, cool air will evaporate the surface moisture on the chicken, and once roasted, the chicken will effortlessly turn golden. However, a roasted chicken cannot always be planned ahead. If you haven't the time to season the bird ahead of time and dry out its skin, pat it dry as thoroughly as possible with paper towels. →

📖 Always let any meat or poultry that you are cooking have a chance to come up to room temperature before exposing it to heat, whether on the stove or in the oven. Remove the chicken from the refrigerator at least 30 minutes before roasting. This ensures that the meat on the surface and the interior are at similar temperatures when the cooking process begins.

📖 If the chicken is smaller or larger than 3 lb/1.4kg, use the ratio of $\frac{1}{2}$ tsp of sea salt per 1 lb/455g of chicken. The bird is done when an instant-read thermometer inserted in the center of the thigh registers 170°F/76°C and 150°F/65°C when inserted in the breast. (The USDA recommends a temperature of 165°F/74°C for all poultry.)

---

1 whole chicken (about 3 lb/1.4kg)

To remove the backbone from the chicken, use a large, sharp knife or very sharp kitchen shears and work on a secure cutting board. The best way to do this is to place a dampened towel on top of your work surface and set the cutting board on top of it. Hold the chicken upright, so that its back faces you. The back will come out in a long strip about $1\frac{1}{4}$-inches/3cm wide, so place your knife a little more than $\frac{1}{2}$-inch/12mm to the right of the spine and cut down the length of the back. I find it easiest if you go down one side halfway, then the other side halfway, and so on, until the entire back is cut out. It generally takes a few cuts to do this. Discard the backbone.

$1\frac{1}{2}$ tsp sea salt

4 to 6 sprigs thyme, leaves pulled from stems (optional) or dry rub (page 252, with salt adjusted)

Lay the chicken flat, with the uncut side facing up. In some cases, the breastbone may need to be pushed on a bit to flatten it more. The legs should be pointing outward from the body rather than inward toward each other. Separate the breast meat from the skin and slip about half of the thyme leaves or dry rub under the skin on the surface of the meat. Repeat for the thighs with the remaining thyme or dry rub. Rub one-quarter of the salt over the underside of the bird and the rest on the skin side, making sure to get some under the wings and thighs. There should be a little less on the wings and a little more on the breast, legs, and thighs. Place the bird skin-side up on a platter and refrigerate, uncovered, or for at least 3 hours or up to 1 to 2 days.

When you are ready to roast the chicken, place a pizza stone on the floor of your oven and preheat the oven to 450°F/230°C for at least 30 minutes. Transfer the chicken to a baking sheet and let it come to room temperature while the oven and stone are preheating.

Set the baking sheet directly on the stone and roast the chicken for 25 to 30 minutes, rotating the baking sheet after about 15 minutes so that the chicken cooks evenly. Use an instant-read thermometer to check for doneness. The center of the thigh should reach 170°F/76°C and the center of the breast should reach 150°F/65°C. When it does, remove the pan from the oven.

Transfer the chicken to a cutting board and let cool for at least 10 minutes before slicing and serving.

FRIED CHICKEN

Serves 4

Chickpea flour makes a surprisingly good fried chicken crust. It's crispy and light, with a delicious savory flavor that takes well to the herbs and strong seasonings traditionally used in fried chicken coatings. If you have the time, give the chicken the overnight treatment in the buttermilk or kefir; even if you only have an hour, the fried chicken will benefit from this step.

📖 The soaking step is equivocal to giving the chicken a bath in salted lactic acid. You are brining the meat as well as letting the lactic acid break down and flavor the muscle. If you don't have buttermilk or kefir, water down some yogurt. Milk contains lactic acid as well; however, it doesn't hold onto the seasoned coating mix as nicely as a thicker liquid does.

📖 I find bean flours, such as chickpea and fava bean flour, not ideal for sweets. Even though some bakers like to use bean flours to increase the protein content in a flour mix, the bean flours can leave baked goods with a dry texture and even with a distinctly, unpleasantly acrid flavor if too much is used. →

4 bone-in chicken breasts	Combine the chicken, buttermilk or kefir, and salt in a large bowl. Cover and refrigerate overnight.
4 bone-in chicken thighs	
2 bone-in chicken drumsticks	
1 qt/960ml buttermilk or kefir	About 30 minutes before you're ready to fry, remove the chicken from the fridge and let rest in the buttermilk at room temperature.
1 Tbsp sea salt	
Vegetable oil, for frying	Pour at least $1\frac{1}{2}$ inches/4cm of vegetable oil into a heavy-bottomed pot or tall-sided pan and heat to 360°F/182°C. Line a baking sheet with paper towels.
2 cups/240g chickpea flour	Meanwhile, mix together the chickpea flour, potato starch, salt, and pepper. The chickpea mixture can be put in a paper or plastic bag or in a shallow bowl.
1 cup/180g potato starch	
$1\frac{1}{4}$ tsp sea salt	
$\frac{1}{2}$ tsp ground black pepper	

When the oil is ready, lift a piece of chicken out of the buttermilk, letting the excess drip off, and dredge the chicken in the chickpea mixture. Carefully place in the hot oil and fry, turning once, until golden brown and cooked through, 4 to 6 minutes on each side, depending on the size of the piece and the temperature of the chicken. Working in batches, fry as many pieces of chicken as will fit in a single, uncrowded layer at a time. Using tongs, transfer the fried chicken to a baking sheet lined with paper towels. Let cool slightly before serving.

SAVORY BREAD PUDDING WITH WILD MUSHROOMS AND BACON

Makes 4 servings (one 9-inch/23cm baking dish)

There was once a time at the bakery when we had leftover loaves of bread at the end of the day. Not wanting the loaves to go to waste, we turned them into bread pudding—the first savory dish we offered. The combination of wild mushrooms, bacon, and custard came together at the tail end of winter after a deluge of rain, when beautiful wild mushrooms were at the market. Together, the bacon and aged cow's milk cheese gives this dish quiche Lorraine–like flavors and the leeks add beautiful texture. If you have greens on hand, steam or lightly sauté them, as you would with spinach or kale, and then fold them in just before baking.

📖 Bread pudding is best when made with stale bread. If you have only a fresh loaf, purposely "stale" it the day before, so that it absorbs the custard better: Refrigerate the fresh bread, preferably already cut into cubes. The cold temperature hastens the redistribution of moisture from the protein to the starch in the bread, leading to the characteristic "stale" texture. If making it the day of, just cube the bread and place it on a baking sheet in a 350°F/180°C oven and lightly toast.

Unsalted butter, for the baking dish	Preheat the oven to 350°F/180°C. Butter the inside surfaces of a 9-inch/23cm square baking dish with at least 2-inch/5cm sides.
8 oz/225g country-style bread, preferably day-old	Cut the bread into 1-inch/2.5cm cubes. Spread them out on a baking sheet and place in the oven to toast for a few minutes, until lightly toasted. Set aside.
8 oz/225g thick-cut bacon, cut into $\frac{1}{4}$-inch/6mm pieces 2 small or 1 large/110g leek, white and light green parts sliced $\frac{1}{2}$ inch/12mm thick and rinsed	In a skillet over medium-high heat, cook the bacon until slightly crisped but not yet fully browned. Transfer to a large bowl and pour off all but 2 Tbsp of fat from the skillet. Add the leeks to the skillet and cook over medium-high heat, stirring often, until soft, 3 to 5 minutes. Transfer to the bowl with the bacon. →

2 Tbsp olive oil,
as needed

1 lb/455g mixed wild
mushrooms, sliced
$\frac{1}{4}$ inch/6mm thick

If the pan looks dry, swirl in 1 Tbsp of the olive oil. Add about half of the mushrooms and sauté, stirring occasionally, until crisp and lightly browned in a few places, 3 to 5 minutes. Transfer the mushrooms to the bowl and cook the remaining mushrooms, adding as much of the remaining 1 Tbsp of oil to the skillet as needed. Transfer to the bowl and let cool.

$\frac{1}{2}$ cup/50g grated
Parmesan cheese

$\frac{1}{3}$ cup/7g flat-leaf
parsley, chopped

2 tsp fresh thyme leaves

$\frac{1}{2}$ tsp sea salt

Add the cheese, parsley, thyme, and salt to the cooked mushroom mixture and mix well.

6 large eggs

2 cups/480ml whole milk

1 cup/240ml
heavy cream

In another bowl, whisk together the eggs, milk, and cream until well blended. Pour over the mushroom mixture and stir to combine. Gently mix in the toasted bread cubes.

$\frac{1}{4}$ cup/25g grated
Gruyère, Comté, or
other firm cheese

Ground black pepper

Carefully pour the bread mixture into the prepared baking dish. The custard should come right up to the top but not cover the highest cubes of bread. (If you have extra, fill a buttered ramekin and make an additional tiny bread pudding.) Scatter the cheese evenly over the pudding and grind a light dusting of pepper on top. Bake until the custard is no longer runny but still a bit wobbly in the center, 40 minutes to 1 hour (and about 25 minutes for a ramekin). It will continue to cook as it sits before serving. Serve the bread pudding hot or at room temperature.

Any leftovers can be stored, well wrapped, in the refrigerator for up to 3 days and reheated, covered with aluminum foil, in a 350°F/180°C oven.

CIDER CARAMEL PORK RIBS

Makes 4 to 6 servings

I based these ribs on a classic Vietnamese dish of chicken cooked in a clay pot with caramel sauce and aromatics. The clay pot (or any vessel with a tight-fitting lid) cooks the meat to melting doneness while infusing it with a caramel flavor, made by reducing apple cider and cooking it together with layers of salt, spice, and vinegar. The key to cooking meat with steam—which goes for any type of stew or braise—is finding the perfect level of heat at which the liquid is kept at a lazy bubble, like champagne in a glass. Meat cooked higher than this dries out, no matter how long it's left to cook. You will want to use up every drip of sauce, and rice is probably the best vehicle.

📖 Allow 4 or 5 ribs per person, depending on size of rib.

📖 The cider caramel marinade used for these ribs can also be used to marinate up to 4 lb/1.8kg of chicken.

1 qt/960ml apple cider

$\frac{1}{4}$ cup/60ml water

In a large saucepan over medium-high heat, reduce the apple cider until a little more than $\frac{1}{4}$-inch/6mm high, about 20 to 25 minutes at a rolling boil. Watch the cider closely as it reduces at this point because the last step goes very quickly, progressing from caramel to burnt. When it becomes a caramel, or is at least thickly coating the bottom of the pan and is a nice dark caramel color, add the water and swirl the pan so that the cider caramel doesn't burn.

4 cloves garlic, minced

1 tsp peeled, grated gingerroot, or $\frac{3}{4}$ tsp ground ginger

2 Tbsp tomato paste

1 Tbsp fish sauce

2 Tbsp soy sauce

1 Tbsp miso

Juice of 1 lime

1 Tbsp apple cider vinegar

$\frac{3}{4}$ tsp red pepper flakes

2 Tbsp plum jam or hoisin sauce

In a bowl, combine the garlic, ginger, tomato paste, fish sauce, soy sauce, miso, lime juice, vinegar, pepper flakes, plum jam or hoisin, and cider caramel. →

1 large onion	Cut the onion in half, trim the root end, peel away the outer layer. Cut the onion into $\frac{1}{4}$-inch/6mm pieces from root end to blossom end. Place in the bottom of a large Dutch oven.
2 to 4 lb/910g to 1.8kg baby back ribs, cut into sections of 2 or 3 ribs, depending on the size of the ribs	Preheat the oven to 275°F/135°C. Coat the ribs with the cider caramel sauce on both sides, place the ribs on top of the onion in the pot, pour the remaining sauce over, and bake for 3 hours or until very tender when pierced with the tip of a knife.
	When the ribs are done cooking, pour the liquid and onion from the pot into a saucepan. Place the saucepan over medium-high heat and reduce the sauce by half, 5 to 7 minutes. Place the ribs on a cutting board, cut into sections, and transfer to a serving platter. Pour the reduced sauce over the ribs and serve warm.
	Store leftover ribs, covered, in the refrigerator for up to 3 days.

PORK CHOPS IN MUSTARD SAUCE WITH APPLES

Makes 4 servings

Mustard owes its very name to Roman cookery that mixed unfermented grape juice (must) with crushed mustard seeds. The Latin name, *mustum ardens* translates to "burning wine," and that combination of heat, acidity, and nasal-clearing kick lives on in mustards today. This dish is classically French in its flavors and technique and could work well for any other white meat, like chicken or rabbit. The small amount of Armagnac or Cognac used here contributes character that the white wine cannot achieve on its own. Apples, a quintessential fall fruit, are a seasonal accent fit for succulent pork. All that's needed to complete the meal is a vegetable simply prepared, such as green beans, English peas, or cauliflower, steamed and buttered. →

📖 All pork becomes more flavorful when salted ahead of time. The night before is ideal, but even a few hours ahead will do wonders.

2 (1-inch/2.5cm-thick) bone-in pork chops (about 1 lb/455g each), patted dry Sea salt Ground black pepper	The night before or several hours in advance, generously season the pork chops with salt and pepper on both sides.
2 oz/55g bacon, cut into $\frac{1}{4}$-inch/6mm pieces	Choose a pan large enough to accommodate both pork chops in a single layer. Set the pan over medium heat and cook the bacon pieces until they have a little color but aren't yet crisp. Transfer to a large plate.
	Increase the heat to medium-high. Add the seasoned pork chops to the pan and cook, flipping once, until nicely browned on both sides and cooked through to your desired doneness, about 12 minutes for medium. Transfer to the plate with the bacon. Pour off all but about 1 Tbsp of oil from the pan.
1 apple (such as Granny Smith or Pink Lady), peeled, sliced $\frac{1}{4}$ inch/6mm thick, and cut into 1-inch/2.5cm pieces	Add the apple to the pan and sauté until soft, 1 to 2 minutes. Transfer to the plate.
$\frac{1}{2}$ cup/120ml white wine 1 Tbsp Armagnac or Cognac	Pour the white wine and Armagnac or Cognac into the pan and use a wooden spoon to scrape up any browned bits.
$\frac{3}{4}$ cup/180ml Chicken Stock (page 32, or store-bought)	Add the stock and simmer until reduced in volume by about one-third. Decrease the heat to low.
$\frac{1}{2}$ cup/120ml heavy cream 2 Tbsp Dijon mustard 2 Tbsp chopped fresh tarragon 2 Tbsp chopped flat-leaf parsley	Stir the cream, mustard, tarragon, and parsley quickly into the pan juices, making sure the mixture doesn't come above a light simmer. Return the bacon, pork chops, and apples to the pan, and mix well. Cover the pan and let the chops heat through for 2 minutes. Slice the pork chops and serve immediately.

LAMB KOFTA
(SPICY LAMB SKEWERS)

Makes 4 servings

In many parts of the world, from the Middle East to South Asia, kofta are croquettes of meat, vegetables, or grains (or a combination thereof) that can take various shapes. I tend to favor the thinner kofta that are formed around a flat metal skewer, but what truly distinguishes them for me is the range of flavors possible in the spices used. This particular recipe takes inspiration from North Africa, using the spice mixture called *ras el hanout*, which translates to something close to "top shelf." Ras el hanout's standard ingredients are ground cumin, coriander, turmeric, ginger, and cardamom. But, according to country and preference, other spices and botanicals, such as cinnamon, rose petals, and lavender, may be added, too. A substantial amount of onions sweeten the meat, and the cooked quinoa is my way of adding moisture to the mix, as one would add fresh breadcrumbs to meatballs. Serve these kofta with the cucumber-rich yogurt sauce, Tzatziki (page 17), and Fattoush with Country Bread (page 151). If you have the grill going, eggplant would be a natural addition, too.

📖 To see if you've adequately seasoned the meat, fry a small piece of the kofta mix in a pan and taste it once it's cooked. Add more salt, pepper flakes, or ras el hanout if you find the flavor is lacking.

📖 If you don't have ras el hanout, grind together: 1 tsp fennel seeds, 2 tsp cumin seeds, 1 tsp black peppercorns, $\frac{1}{2}$ tsp dried lavender, $\frac{1}{4}$ tsp ground cloves, 1 tsp whole coriander, 1 tsp ground dried ginger, and $\frac{1}{4}$ tsp ground turmeric.

📖 For more about quinoa, see page 264 (Eggplant Parmesan Gratin with Fresh Tomatoes and Quinoa).

$\frac{1}{4}$ cup/45g quinoa

$\frac{1}{2}$ cup/120ml water

Large pinch of sea salt

Rinse the quinoa very well, 3 or 4 times. Combine the quinoa, water, and salt in a small saucepan over medium heat and bring to a boil. Cover and cook for 15 minutes. Remove the pan from the heat and let sit, covered, for 15 minutes. Uncover and let cool. (Quinoa can be cooked up to 3 days ahead and stored, covered, in the refrigerator.) →

1 lb/455g ground lamb

1 onion, finely chopped

1 tsp ground cumin

1 tsp sea salt

$\frac{1}{4}$ tsp ground
black pepper

$\frac{1}{4}$ cup/5g flat-leaf parsley
leaves, finely chopped

$\frac{1}{4}$ tsp ground cinnamon

1 Tbsp chopped
mint leaves

1 tsp ras-el-hanout
(optional) or add $\frac{1}{4}$ tsp
more of each of the
other spices

1 tsp red pepper flakes

In a large bowl, combine the cooled quinoa, lamb, onion, cumin, salt, pepper, parsley, cinnamon, mint, ras-el-hanout, and red pepper flakes. Gently mix just until the spices are evenly distributed, but take care not to overmix so the kofta are tender when cooked. (The meat mixture can be made up to 3 days ahead and stored, covered, in the refrigerator.)

8 bamboo or metal
skewers (optional)

The kofta mixture can be shaped around skewers and grilled or cooked as patties. For grilling, preheat the grill. If grilling and using bamboo skewers, soak the skewers in water for 30 minutes before forming the meat on them. To form the meat on skewers, place some meat in your palm and use your other hand to gently flatten. Place a skewer on top of the meat and close your hand, folding the meat evenly around the skewer, making the meat about $\frac{1}{2}$ to $\frac{3}{4}$ inch/12mm to 2cm thick. Repeat to add 1 to 2 more kofta to the skewer, and then set it on a plate and repeat with the remaining meat mixture and skewers. (Skewers can be prepared a day or two ahead and stored, covered, in the refrigerator.) If pan-frying, shape the meat mixture into patties that are 4 inches/10cm in diameter.

2 Tbsp olive oil, for
pan-frying (optional)

Heat the olive oil in a skillet over medium-high heat.

Grill the skewers or fry the patties until browned and cooked through, 6 to 10 minutes. Serve immediately.

Store leftover kofta in the refrigerator for up to 3 days.

DRY-RUBBED TRI-TIP

Makes 6 servings

Tri-tip is a small cut of beef from the bottom sirloin, with a fairly lean, quintessentially "beefy" flavor. Because of its size, which ranges from 1½ to 3 lb/680g to 1.4kg, tri-tip is my preferred cut to grill or pan-sear for a large party. I find that its triangular shape yields slices of beef that fulfill people's preferences for varying degrees of doneness—some are rare, others are well done, and most are perfectly in between. Tri-tip takes to spice or herb rubs well, and its leanness begs for a delicious, unctuous sauce to finish. I especially love serving tri-tip with Chimichurri Sauce (page 14), but most of the sauces in this book, from Romesco Sauce (page 29) to Bagna Cauda (page 12) and Aioli (page 10), complement tri-tip beautifully. If possible, plan to have a few slices left over; they make a satisfying sandwich the next day.

📖 Bring the meat to room temperature before cooking, which is especially important when you want rare to medium doneness. The best way to control for this doneness range is to temper the meat by slowly raising its overall temperature before truly cooking it. For cuts that are thicker than 1 inch/2.5cm, such as tri-tip, warm them in a 200°F/95°C oven to bring the internal temperature to about 100°F/35°C (use an instant-read thermometer to periodically monitor the temperature), about 30 minutes for tri-tip, depending on how cold the meat is when it goes into the oven. Tempering the meat this way relaxes the muscle so that the cut doesn't curl in the pan or oven or on the grill during cooking.

📖 Whether grilling or searing, make sure that the heat is hot enough, but not so high that the meat's surface burns. If using a thicker cut, get good color on the tri-tip's exterior and then lower the flame to prevent burning (or move the meat to a cooler spot of the grill). Ultimately, you're trying for a balance of the browning on the outside and the doneness level you prefer on the inside. Meat will continue to cook about 5 degrees once it is removed from the heat (or more, if you don't remove it from the hot pan). The United States Department of Agriculture recommends a minimum internal temperature for beef of at least 145°F/62°C. →

📖 Following are the temperatures at which you should remove the meat from the heat to achieve the corresponding levels of doneness.

Rare: remove the meat at 125°F/51°C, done at 130°F/54°C

Medium-rare: remove the meat at 130°F/54°C, done at 135°F/57°C

Medium: remove the meat at 140°F/60°C, done at 145°F/62°C

Medium-well: remove the meat at 155°F/68°C, done at 160°F/71°C

📖 The four ingredients in the dry rub form a versatile blend that goes well with all animal proteins—fish, poultry, pork, lamb, and beef.

$\frac{3}{4}$ tsp sea salt $\frac{1}{2}$ tsp ground black pepper 1 tsp ground cumin 1 tsp smoked Spanish paprika (pimentón)	To make the dry rub, combine the salt, pepper, cumin, and pimentón in a small bowl.
1 tri-tip (up to 3 lb/1.4kg)	Up to 3 hours before you plan to cook the meat, coat all sides of the meat with the dry rub and refrigerate. Remove the meat from the refrigerator 45 minutes before you want to cook it and let it come to room temperature.
1 Tbsp olive oil	If the tri-tip is large (3 lb/1.4kg) preheat the oven to 375°F/190°C. In a large heatproof pan, heat the olive oil until very hot. Add the room-temperature tri-tip and cook on all sides until well browned. If the tri-tip is large, place the pan in the oven to finish cooking, until the internal temperature reaches the desired doneness (see above). Let the beef rest, loosely tented with aluminum foil, for about 10 minutes. Slice the meat against the grain for the most tender slices and serve.
	Store leftover tri-tip in the refrigerator for up to 3 days.

CARBONNADE À LA FLAMANDE WITH CELERY HEART SALAD
(FLEMISH BEEF SHORT RIB STEW)

Makes 4 to 6 servings

This is one of my few recipes that includes cooking with beer. This stew is only slightly different from the Beef Daube (page 256), but the shift in a few ingredients gives it an entirely distinct feel. Instead of wine, a dark Belgian abbey-style beer is used as the braising liquid. A pinch of brown sugar and caramelized onions counter the beer's bitterness. The crunch of the celery adds a simple, refreshing bite. To round out the meal, serve with a straightforward accompaniment, such as mashed potatoes (page 197), boiled butter potatoes, or wide egg noodles.

📖 I prefer beef short ribs over stew meat, so that the cartilage and bone can contribute flavor to the broth. As the ribs are cut in half in this recipe, each person ends up with 2 good-size ribs.

3 lb/1.4kg beef short ribs (ask your butcher to cut them in half), patted dry Sea salt Ground black pepper 2 Tbsp olive oil 1½ lb/680g yellow onions, sliced	Preheat the oven to 250°F/120°C. Season the ribs with salt and pepper. Heat the oil in a Dutch oven or similar heavy-bottomed pot with a lid over medium heat. Working in batches, brown the ribs on all sides, 8 to 10 minutes per batch. Transfer the browned meat to a plate. Stir the onions into the fat left behind in the pot, scraping up any browned bits. Reduce the heat to low and cook the onions, stirring often to promote even browning, until caramelized, about 25 minutes.
6 cloves garlic, sliced	Add the garlic to the caramelized onions and cook for 1 minute.
3 cups/720ml Belgian strong dark ale	Pour the beer into the onions and garlic, increase the heat so that the liquid boils, and cook until reduced slightly in volume, about 5 minutes.

1 cup/240ml demiglace (if you don't have demiglace, mix $\frac{1}{4}$ cup/55g tomato paste into the beef stock)

2 cups/480ml beef stock

1 Tbsp brown sugar

2 tsp fresh thyme leaves, chopped

Add the demiglace, beef stock, brown sugar, and thyme to the pot and stir well. Return the browned short ribs to the pot. Bring to a simmer, cover, and transfer to the oven to cook until the meat is fork-tender, about 2 hours.

Remove from the oven, transfer the meat to a platter, leaving the onions in the pot, and put the pot back on the stovetop. Bring the cooking liquid to a boil and cook until slightly thickened, 10 to 12 minutes.

$\frac{1}{4}$ cup/60ml olive oil

1 Tbsp champagne vinegar

Sea salt

Ground black pepper

2 cups/40g celery leaves, picked from the inside a whole head of celery, chopped

1 small bulb fennel, thinly sliced

$\frac{1}{2}$ cup/10g chopped mixed fresh herbs (such as flat-leaf parsley, mint, and oregano)

Meanwhile, prepare the celery heart salad: Make the dressing in a bowl by whisking the olive oil into the champagne vinegar and season with salt and pepper to taste. Toss the celery leaves, fennel, and herbs in the dressing.

Champagne vinegar, as needed

Honey, as needed

Once the sauce has thickened, taste and adjust the seasoning by adding a splash of champagne vinegar if the sauce tastes a little too rich. It should also taste barely sweet; if not, stir in a touch of honey.

Return the meat to the thickened sauce. Serve with the celery heart salad on the side.

Store leftover stew in the refrigerator for up to 3 days.

BEEF DAUBE
(BEEF STEW)

Makes 6 servings

There are few ways to enjoy beef more than in a long-cooked braise, especially if you can wait till the next day when the flavors have had time to marry. Most regions in France have their unique interpretations of a daube, which is the catchall term for a meat braise. You'll find that when beef is involved, so too are tomatoes, red wine, carrots, and aromatics. Boeuf bourguignonne is one exception—a thick stew with mushrooms and lardons, but without tomato. The recipe here takes its cues from bourguignonne, using lardons (or bacon) for richness, but calls upon the classic daube for its use of tomato. To make the most savory sauce possible, I prefer ribs as opposed to cubed stew beef. When ribs are used, water suffices as the braising liquid, as the caramelization from browning combined with the bone's gelatin add so much body and flavor. Favorite combinations are with polenta, risotto, or Fried Potatoes and Roasted Oyster Mushrooms (page 206), but it is also great with heaps of grated fresh horseradish, sour cream or crème fraîche, and steamed potatoes.

📖 Lardons are made from salt-cured pork. Unlike bacon, it is cured pork that is not smoked. Your butcher may very well have lardons, otherwise bacon or pancetta will do just as well. If you can find bacon that is sold in chunks, rather than slices, you'll be able to imitate the baton shape of the lardons.

4 lb/1.8kg beef short ribs (ask your butcher to cut them in half), patted dry

Sea salt

Ground black pepper

2 Tbsp olive oil

Preheat the oven to 250°F/120°C. Season the meat with salt and pepper. Heat the oil in a Dutch oven or similar heavy-bottomed pot with a lid over medium heat. Working in batches, brown the meat on all sides, 8 to 10 minutes per batch. Transfer the browned meat to a plate and then pour off all but about 1 tsp of the fat in the pot.

8 oz/225g lardons or slab bacon cut into strips $\frac{1}{4}$ inch/6mm thick and $1\frac{1}{2}$ inches/4cm long

Add the lardons or bacon to the pot and cook, stirring often, until lightly browned and crisp but still tender and springy, 2 to 3 minutes. Using a slotted spoon, transfer to the plate with the beef.

1 onion, diced	Add the onion and carrots to the pot and sauté until lightly colored, 5 to 7 minutes.
2 carrots, scrubbed and diced	
1 (14$\frac{1}{2}$-oz/411g) can peeled, diced tomatoes	Pour the tomatoes and their juices into the pot, stirring and scraping along the bottom of the pot with a wooden spoon to pick up any browned bits.
1 (750ml) bottle red wine	Add the wine, beef broth or water, cinnamon stick, orange peel, garlic, thyme, and bay leaves to the pot. Return the browned meat and lardons to the pot and pour in water to cover the meat. Bring to a simmer over medium-low heat, cover, and transfer to the oven to cook for about 2 hours. After 15 minutes, check to make sure the liquid is at a lazy bubble and adjust the oven temperature as necessary. After 2 hours, test the meat by poking it with a fork; it should be very tender.
2 cups/480ml beef broth or water	
$\frac{1}{2}$ cinnamon stick	
2 strips of orange peel (peeled with a vegetable peeler)	
3 cloves garlic, crushed	
3 sprigs fresh thyme	
2 bay leaves	
Sea salt	Remove the stew from the oven, transfer the meat to a platter, and put the pot back on the stovetop. Bring the cooking liquid to a boil over high heat and cook until reduced in volume by one-half to one-third. Season the reduced cooking liquid with salt to taste. Return the meat to the pot, stir, and serve.
	Store leftover stew in the refrigerator for up to 3 days.

GATHER
INGS

I created these menus to give ideas for gatherings, one of the most satisfying aspects of home cooking. Cooking for a group can be daunting, mostly because of the quantity of food that needs to be produced but also because it's time-consuming to find just the right mix of dishcs plus a dessert that won't cut into the time be with guests. These menus are anchored by one of the large-scale recipes in this chapter and most are easily made ahead. Scale up the suggested recipes as needed according to the number of guests.

Holiday

Taco Night

Friends and Family Dinner

Celebration Dinner

PAN BAGNAT

Makes 6 to 8 servings

Sandwiches are an uncommon treat for me, made only possible (given my sensitivity to gluten) when I have Chad's bread, or any other bread made from a natural leaven. So when I'm making a sandwich, I want it to surpass all expectations. I want to satisfy not just one hunger, but the nostalgic hankering for all that a sandwich can be: a play of flavors and textures contained in each and every bite. It's a tall order, but this sandwich delivers. This is a sandwich we found throughout the south of France, always enjoyed with a glass of rosé.

1 Tbsp red wine vinegar

1 garlic clove, minced

$\frac{1}{4}$ cup/60ml olive oil

2 tsp Dijon mustard

Pinch of sea salt

Pinch of ground
black pepper

3 sprigs oregano, leaves
pulled from stems

3 sprigs marjoram,
leaves pulled from stems

In a small bowl, combine the vinegar, garlic, olive oil, mustard, salt, and pepper. Add the oregano and marjoram and whisk to blend.

$\frac{1}{2}$ red onion, thinly sliced

2 large tomatoes, cut
into wedges

$\frac{1}{3}$ cup/35g pitted Nicoise
olives

1 bunch/85g arugula

2 cucumbers, sliced
lengthwise into ribbons
with a peeler

5 radishes, thinly sliced

Combine the onion, tomatoes, olives, arugula, cucumbers, and radishes in a large bowl. Add the dressing and toss to coat. →

1 loaf rustic bread

4 hard-cooked eggs
(see 15-minute eggs,
page 95), sliced

8 oz/230g olive oil–
packed tuna, rinsed

6 olive oil–packed
or salt-packed
anchovies, rinsed

Split the whole loaf of bread lengthwise. Rip out some of the bread from middle of the top and bottom halves (to better fit the sandwich filling). Arrange half of the vegetables on the bottom half of the bread. Layer on the eggs, tuna, anchovies, and the remaining vegetables. Pour half of the dressing (left in the bowl that held the vegetables) over the sandwich filling. Pour the remaining dressing over the cut side of the top half of the loaf, and then place the top half over the filling to close the sandwich.

Wrap the whole thing snugly in plastic wrap, place it in the refrigerator, and weigh it down with a cast-iron pan or other heavy-bottomed pan. Refrigerate the sandwich for at least 2 hours and up to overnight. Cut in wedges and serve.

EGGPLANT PARMESAN GRATIN WITH FRESH TOMATOES AND QUINOA

Makes 6 to 8 servings (one 9 by 13-inch/23 by 33cm dish)

When tomatoes are plentiful, I've taken to making this lightened-up version of an eggplant Parmesan gratin, which relies on fresh tomatoes rather than a cooked sauce. Adding the uncooked quinoa soaks up the tomato water and thickens the gratin while avoiding the usual step of first cooking down tomatoes into a sauce. The result is a dinner that needs only a salad, like the Kale and Cucumber Salad (page 153), and garlic bread (page 186) to go with it.

📖 There has been much debate over the benefits of salting eggplants in order to rid them of bitterness. In my experience, as long as the eggplants are fresh and in season, I have rarely found this to be an issue. I tend to look for small to medium eggplants, of any color, that are firm.

Quinoa, a tiny seed closely related to beets, has a bitter coating of saponins, a naturally occurring chemical meant to protect the quinoa from pests. Boxed quinoa is often prerinsed, but I always take the extra step of rinsing it again. An easy method is to put the quinoa in a bowl of water, agitate it, and drain in a very fine-mesh strainer. Repeat a few times, making sure that water becomes clear.

Olive oil, for the pan	Preheat the oven to 400°F/200°C. Lightly oil the inside surfaces of a 9 by 13-inch/23 by 33cm baking pan. Line a baking sheet with a layer of paper towels.
$\frac{2}{3}$ cup/160ml olive oil, as needed 2 lb/910g globe eggplants, sliced into $\frac{1}{4}$-inch/6mm-thick rounds $\frac{1}{2}$ tsp sea salt	Heat your largest cast-iron skillet or heavy-bottomed pan over medium-high heat. Add a few Tbsp of olive oil and as many eggplant slices as will fit in the pan in a single layer. Cook until golden brown on the bottom, 2 to 3 minutes. Drizzle a little oil on top of the eggplant slices, then flip and cook the second sides until golden brown. Transfer to the prepared baking sheet and season with salt. Repeat the process until all of the eggplant is cooked.
1 cup/180g quinoa $\frac{1}{4}$ tsp sea salt	Rinse the quinoa very well, 3 or 4 times, making sure to completely drain any excess water. Transfer to the prepared roasting pan and shake the pan to spread the quinoa evenly. Season with salt.
$1\frac{3}{4}$ lb/800g tomatoes of any variety (about 4 large), cored and halved $\frac{1}{2}$ onion, sliced 2 cloves garlic, peeled 2 or 3 sprigs thyme, leaves pulled from the stems $\frac{1}{2}$ tsp sea salt, plus more as needed	Combine the tomatoes, onion, garlic, thyme, and salt in a blender and pulse to blend, stopping when the mixture is still very chunky. Taste and adjust the seasoning, adding more salt if necessary. →

1½ cups/360g soft cheese (such as goat cheese or ricotta)

4 or 5 sprigs marjoram, leaves pulled from stems, or ¼ cup/5g loosely packed, torn basil leaves

2 cups/200g grated firm cheese (such as fontina, Parmesan, Manchego, Gruyère, Gouda, or a combination)

To assemble the gratin, spoon about half of the tomato sauce over the quinoa. Dot with half of the soft cheese. Layer half of the cooked eggplant over the sauce. Sprinkle with about half of the marjoram or basil leaves and half of the grated cheese. Layer the remaining tomato sauce and follow with the remaining eggplant and marjoram or basil leaves. Scatter the remaining soft cheese evenly on top of the eggplant and then add the remaining grated cheese. Give the pan a gentle shake to spread the ingredients evenly.

Bake for about 45 minutes, until golden brown on top. (If the gratin is browning too quickly, cover it with aluminum foil. Remove the foil for the last 5 minutes of cooking to finish the browning.) Let rest for at least 10 minutes before serving to allow the quinoa to soak up any excess juices.

Store, covered with aluminum foil, in the refrigerator for up to 2 days. The gratin can be made ahead and reheated in a preheated 350°F/180°C oven for 10 minutes.

HOLIDAY TURKEY WITH TURKEY GRAVY

Makes 6 to 12 servings

We all celebrate Thanksgiving the same way, but that doesn't mean there has to be only one way to prepare a holiday turkey. Although the quintessential roasted bird looks beautiful upon presentation, let's be honest: it's a challenge to get all parts of the bird cooked just right. Just as for roasting a chicken (see page 228), it is the very anatomy of bird that makes roasted turkey so difficult to perfect, and so this past year I decided to spatchcock my turkey. I became convinced of this technique after much success with roasted chicken, for which the skin, breast, and legs all ended up roasted to my liking. This does require some compromise with presentation. The classic, upright roasted turkey is lost, but I'm convinced that you'll find it well worth the sacrifice. After all, the memory of a dry turkey lasts much longer than the brief sight of a golden, round bird. Once you've tried this technique, you may even find the ease of presentation a welcome advantage. Plus, the reduction in roasting time is phenomenal when juggling other dishes that need space in the oven. Our 10-lb/4.5kg bird took only 45 minutes to roast, and the pan drippings were not at all burnt (a hazard with hours of roasting). The small amount of brown sugar that I add to the rub helps intensify the browning, and the thyme and sage tucked between the skin and meat perfume the turkey, surpassing expectations for the holiday table.

📖 Gravy is too often used as a blanket to cover up meat that is less than ideally cooked. I use a turkey stock that is made the same way as the Chicken Stock (page 32), except for using roasted wings and a neck and turkey leg. This dark, rich stock gives body and flavor to the gravy without the heaviness that usually comes with overly thickened gravy.

📖 You will spatchcock the turkey, coat it with dry rub, and air-dry it in the refrigerator overnight, or at least from the morning of the day you plan to roast and serve it. Remember to remove the turkey from the refrigerator at least 1 hour before roasting. This ensures that the meat on the surface and the interior are at similar temperatures when the cooking process begins. As with all poultry and meats, be sure to let the roasted turkey rest for 10 to 20 minutes before serving, which allows the juices time to redistribute, making the meat evenly moist when sliced. This resting period is the perfect time to make the classic pan-drippings gravy, made from stock you will also prepare a day or more ahead (the stock can be frozen and thawed overnight in the refrigerator).

📖 Making pan gravy is simpler than you may think. After disposing of some of the fat in the roasting pan, the small amount of pan drippings that remain are deglazed over medium-high heat, using a cupful of water to loosen any bits stuck to the pan. I like to add giblets to my gravy, so I chop the giblets and toss them into the pan as I'm deglazing it. The flavorful liquid is then thickened with flour, hot stock is whisked in, and the gravy is cooked briefly to thicken. You can keep the gravy chunky by leaving the giblets in or pass it through a fine-mesh strainer for a smoother texture. →

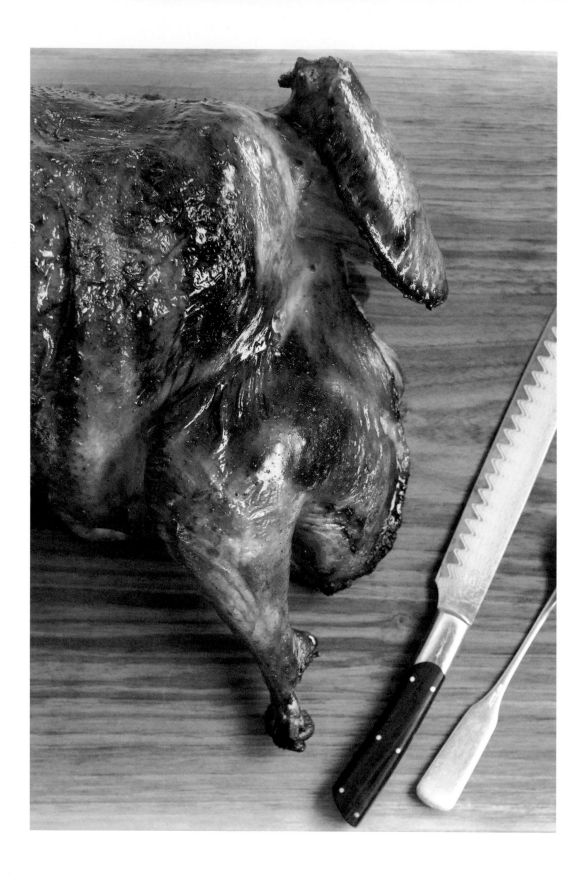

2 turkey wings and 1 neck (about 6 oz/170g)

1 turkey thigh and drumstick (about 1 lb/455g)

1 cup/240ml water

3 stalks celery with tops, coarsely chopped

3 carrots, coarsely chopped

1 yellow onion, quartered

$\frac{1}{2}$ cup/120ml water

Make the stock for the gravy the day before: Preheat the oven to 425°F/220°C. Place the turkey wings and neck, thigh and drumstick, celery, carrots, and onion in a small roasting pan and roast for 20 to 30 minutes, until the meat is crisp and golden brown and the vegetables have some color. Transfer the turkey parts and vegetables to a large saucepan and spoon out and discard most of the fat in the roasting pan. Set the roasting pan over medium-high heat on the stovetop and add the water, scraping the crusty bits from the bottom of the pan to deglaze. Scrape the deglazing liquid and bits into the pot with the roasted meat and vegetables.

2 qt/2L water

4 to 6 sprigs thyme

1 bay leaf

1$\frac{1}{2}$ tsp sea salt

1 tsp black peppercorns

Add the water, thyme, bay leaf, salt, and peppercorns to the saucepan. Over medium heat, bring to a gentle boil and then decrease to low and simmer for 1$\frac{1}{2}$ hours. Remove the saucepan from the heat and let the stock cool to room temperature.

Place a colander over a large bowl and strain the stock into the bowl, discarding the bones, meat, and vegetables in the colander. Transfer the bowl to the refrigerator for at least 2 hours or up to overnight.

When chilled, skim any fat off the surface. Turkey stock keeps, tightly covered, for up to 7 days in the refrigerator and for up to 3 months in the freezer.

1 whole turkey (about 10 lb/4.5kg)

Prepare the turkey for roasting the day before: Reserve the giblets for the gravy, storing the in the refrigerator until ready to use. Remove the backbone from the turkey, using a large, sharp knife or very sharp kitchen shears. Work on a secure cutting board. The best way to do this is to place a dampened towel on your work surface and set the cutting board on top of it. Hold the turkey upright, so that its back faces you. The back will come out in a long strip about 1$\frac{1}{4}$-inches/3cm wide, so place your knife a little more than $\frac{1}{2}$-inch/12mm to the right of →

the spine and cut down the length of the back. I find it easiest if you go down one side halfway, then the other side halfway, and so on, until the entire back is cut out. It generally takes a few cuts to do this. Discard the backbone. Lay the turkey flat, with the uncut side facing up. In some cases, the breastbone may need to be pushed on a bit to flatten it more. The legs should be pointing outward from the body rather than inward toward each other.

8 to 10 sprigs thyme, stemmed (optional)

$3\frac{1}{2}$ Tbsp sea salt

$3\frac{1}{2}$ Tbsp dark brown sugar

Separate the breast meat from the skin and slip about half of the thyme leaves under the skin on the surface of the meat. Repeat for the thighs with the remaining thyme. Combine the salt and brown sugar. Rub 1 Tbsp of the salt-sugar mixture over the underside of the bird and the rest on the uncut skin side, making sure to get some under the wings and thighs. Rub the uncut side with the remaining salt-sugar mixture. There should be a little less on the wings and a little more on the breast, legs, and thighs. Place the bird skin-side up on a platter and refrigerate, uncovered, or for at least 6 hours or up to 1 to 2 days.

About 1 hour before you are ready to roast the turkey, place a pizza stone on the floor of your oven and preheat the oven to 450°F/230°C for at least 30 minutes. Transfer the turkey to a baking sheet and let it come to room temperature, about 30 minutes.

Set the baking sheet directly on the stone and roast the turkey for 10 minutes, then lower the oven to 425°F/220°C. Roast for another 10 minutes and then rotate the baking sheet so that the bird cooks evenly. Use an instant-read thermometer, if you have one, to check for doneness after 30 minutes total cooking time. If the wing tips are browning too much, cover them with foil; if the turkey needs to brown more overall, raise the pan to the top oven rack. The center of the thigh should reach 170°F/76°C and the center of the breast should reach 150°F/65°C. When it does, after approximately 45 minutes total cooking time, remove the pan from the oven.

Transfer the turkey to a cutting board and let cool for at least 10 minutes and up to 20 minutes while you make the gravy.

6 Tbsp/85g unsalted butter

Giblets minced (reserved from the turkey, optional)

6 Tbsp/45g gluten-free or all-purpose flour

3 cups/720ml turkey stock (reserved from a previous step), simmering

Sea salt

Ground black pepper

To make the gravy, in a medium saucepan, melt the butter over medium-high heat. Add the giblets and sauté for 3 to 5 minutes, until cooked through. Using a slotted spoon, remove the giblets and set on a plate until ready to finish the gravy. If you are not making giblet gravy, skip this step. Decrease the heat to medium and stir in the gluten-free or all-purpose flour. Whisk in the turkey stock slowly, whisking until fully incorporated. Continue whisking until the mixture thickens to gravy consistency, about 15 minutes. Season with salt and pepper to taste. Stir in the giblets. Decrease the heat to low and keep warm, stirring occasionally, until ready to serve.

Slice and serve the turkey, spooning the gravy over the top.

Store roasted turkey, covered, in the refrigerator for up to 5 days, and the gravy, completely cooled and also tightly covered, in the refrigerator for up to 3 days.

Cornstarch Gravy: To use cornstarch instead of the gluten-free flour, skip the step of stirring in the flour. Instead, place $\frac{1}{4}$ cup/30g cornstarch in a bowl and whisk $\frac{3}{4}$ cup/180ml of the 3 cups/720ml of turkey stock into the cornstarch a few tablespoons at a time until fully incorporated. Pour this mixture into the pot with the remaining $2\frac{1}{4}$ cups/540ml of stock and bring to a simmer, whisking continuously. Proceed with the recipe as directed, beginning with seasoning with salt and pepper to taste.

CARNITAS

Makes 6 to 8 servings

Living in California, I've found some of the best takeout is the carnitas at any crowded neighborhood taqueria. This slow-cooked pork is traditionally made from large cuts, like a shoulder, and cooked in lard until tender. It is then crisped in its own fat to create a tantalizing play of textures. Orange zest or warm spices are sometimes added, but for the most part, flavorings are kept to a minimum. This recipe takes the best of this tradition while using a lighter touch, as quality lard is not as easily found. My approach to braising meat has been shaped by the French techniques I learned in culinary school. I immediately think of stews like boeuf bourguignonne, where the meat is browned before braising in liquid rich with diced and sautéed vegetables (known as mirepoix), stock, and wine. I love exploring the radically different techniques of Mexican cooking, where meat is not necessarily browned before it is braised, and something as basic as water coaxes a tough cut of meat into something divine. Following in the footsteps of Diana Kennedy, the renowned ambassador of Mexican cooking, this recipe uses just enough water to cover the meat. The result is meltingly tender pork that needs little embellishment. Cilantro, lime, and warm tortillas make an easy family meal. For larger gatherings, add a pot of beans and a cabbage salad. Don't hesitate to use a larger cut of meat, as the leftovers are to die for.

📖 If you begin this a day ahead, let the pork cool in the cooking juices after so that it stays moist overnight and absorbs the seasoning. The next day, after removing the pork from the refrigerator to come up to room temperature, place the Dutch oven or pot on a low flame just until the cooking juices liquefy. Remove the pork and set aside. Proceed with the recipe, reducing the juices until only $\frac{1}{4}$ cup/60ml remains.

📖 Though I call for Mexican oregano, in truth, many types of oregano are used in Mexico, just as there are many used in Mediterranean cooking. In general, Mexican oreganos are stronger flavored, so if you can find a dried source that seems relatively fresh, I suggest using it. Otherwise, fresh oregano is a worthy substitute.

3 lb/1.4kg pork shoulder, cut into 1½-inch/4cm chunks

1 qt/960ml water, plus more as needed

Combine the pork and water in a 4-qt/3.7L or 6-qt/5.6L Dutch oven or similar heavy-bottomed pot. Add additional water as needed to cover the meat. Bring to a boil and then adjust the heat so that the liquid simmers very gently. Look for lazy bubbles, like champagne bubbles in a glass, as opposed to many vigorous bubbles. Skim off any foam that rises to the surface.

½ navel orange, quartered

1 yellow onion, chopped

1 tsp dried Mexican oregano or fresh oregano leaves

5 cloves garlic, crushed

10 black peppercorns

1½ tsp sea salt

Add the orange, onion, oregano, garlic, peppercorns, and salt to the pot. Cook, uncovered, for 1½ hours either on the stovetop or in a 200°F/95°C oven.

1 to 2 Tbsp vegetable oil, as needed

Using tongs, transfer the meat and orange wedges to a plate. Bring the juices in the pot to a boil over medium heat and cook until reduced to approximately ¼ cup/60ml, about 45 minutes. Return the meat and orange quarters to the pot and continue cooking, stirring often, until no liquid remains and the meat is nicely browned in a few places, about 15 minutes. If the meat sticks to the pot and threatens to burn, add a little oil to facilitate browning. For extra-crispy carnitas, continue browning the meat for another 5 to 10 minutes.

24 small Corn Tortillas (page 62, or store-bought), warmed

Chopped fresh cilantro

1 small yellow or white onion, finely chopped

Lime wedges

The meat can be served as is, or if you prefer you can shred it using two forks. Take care not to overshred it—the pork will be very tender and a few larger pieces add nice texture. Serve with the tortillas, cilantro, onion, and lime wedges.

Store leftovers in the refrigerator for up to 3 days.

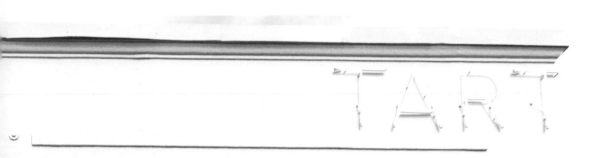

PORCHETTA

Makes 10 to 12 servings

We make porchetta—pork loin wrapped in skin-on pork belly—at Tartine Manufactory when we are hosting a party. Maybe it's the intoxicating smell of fennel, mustard, and garlic melting into the pork that makes me think of a celebration. Or maybe it's the memory of the eve of our wedding, when my parents roasted a whole pig in a pit. I have a hunch, though, that I'm tapping into something larger because a pig roast has always meant a gathering of community and celebration of plenty. Traditionally, the Italian recipe for porchetta calls for a young suckling pig to be deboned and stuffed. I've scaled down the recipe to feed a dinner party. Few dishes are simpler to prepare, feed as many mouths, and make people as boisterous as they reach for another bite. The pork tastes better if it has a chance to sit overnight (or for two nights) after it's seasoned. If the porchetta must be assembled the day it is cooked, it will still be cause for a party.

📖 If you begin this a day ahead, let the pork cool in the cooking juices so that it stays moist overnight and absorbs the seasoning. The next day, after removing the pork from the refrigerator to come up to room temperature, place the Dutch oven or pot on a low flame just until the cooking juices liquefy. Remove the pork and set aside. Proceed with the recipe, reducing the juices until only $\frac{1}{4}$ cup/60ml remains.

1 (6- to 8-lb/2.7 to 3.6kg) boneless pork shoulder roast with a thick ($\frac{1}{4}$-in/6mm) layer of fat, skin on	Using a very sharp knife or a retractable razor, carefully score the layer of fat every $\frac{1}{2}$ inch/12mm, cutting through the skin but not into the meat beneath the fat. A retractable razor is a good tool for this job because it allows you to control the depth of the incision.
2 Tbsp chopped rosemary	Combine the rosemary, sage, oregano, and fennel pollen or fennel seeds in a small bowl. →
2 Tbsp chopped sage	
2 Tbsp chopped oregano	
2 Tbsp fennel pollen or whole fennel seeds	

4 to 6 cloves garlic,
peeled

Pinch of sea salt

$\frac{1}{4}$ cup/60ml Dijon
mustard

Using a mortar and pestle, pound the garlic and salt
to a smooth paste. Alternatively, if you do not have a
mortar and pestle, use a microplane to finely grate
the garlic and stir in the salt. Add the mustard to the
mortar and blend together.

2 Tbsp sea salt

Ground black pepper

Generously season the pork with the salt and pepper,
sprinkling the salt more heavily on the meat than
on the fat. Smear the mustard-garlic mixture over
the pork and sprinkle with the herb-fennel mixture,
massaging it into the pork. Starting with one of the
long sides, roll the meat tightly into a cylinder, with
the layer of fat and skin on the outside. Secure the roll
with lengths of kitchen twine, tied at 1-inch/2.5cm
intervals. Cover with plastic wrap and refrigerate for
at least 1 hour and up to overnight.

At least 1 hour before roasting, remove the pork
from the refrigerator and let it come to room
temperature. About 20 minutes before roasting,
preheat the oven to 475°F/250°C.

Place the pork on a wire rack set inside a roasting
pan. Roast until the skin puffs and crisps and takes
on a deep amber color, 35 to 45 minutes. Once the
skin is golden, lower the temperature of the oven to
300°F/150°C and continue roasting until the internal
temperature reaches 135°F/57°C, about $2\frac{1}{2}$ to 3 hours
total time. Check the temperature after the first
$1\frac{1}{2}$ hours of cooking.

Remove the roast from the oven and let it rest,
covered loosely with aluminum foil, for 15 to
30 minutes. Carve the porchetta crosswise into
thick slices, making sure each slice has a little bit
of the cracklings, and serve.

The porchetta can be roasted ahead of time
(and then refrigerated) and the individual slices
rewarmed in a 350°F/180°C oven for about
5 minutes, until the skin is glistening and crisp.

Store leftovers, well wrapped, in the refrigerator
for up to 3 days.

LEG OF LAMB OVER POTATO-ONION GRATIN WITH MINT SALSA VERDE

Makes 10 to 12 servings

I love when I discover new ways to make a timeless dish. While reading Patricia Wells's wonderful *Bistro Cooking*, I came upon a lamb recipe, that roasted a whole leg on top of a rack that was fitted over a gratin. The idea came from her butcher, and it is one of those no-nonsense home-cooking techniques that seems ancient yet forgotten. Not only are space and dishes saved, but the gratin benefits from the delectable juices of the roast. I decided to take this one adventurous step further: I placed the leg on the actual oven rack (after wiping it clean of course). I wanted there to be ample hot air circulating all around the lamb, so that it could form a beautiful, rich crust on all of its surfaces. And it does not disappoint. The gratin recipe itself is so simple. With a cupful of white wine to help, the potatoes and onions become tender and browned, infused with juices of the lamb, in the same amount of time that the meat cooks. And though traditional mint jelly is far too sweet, the English were onto something. I like how the vividness of mint elevates the earthiness of the lamb and adds welcome brightness to this otherwise hearty feast.

📖 When buying the leg of lamb, ask your butcher to leave a layer of fat $\frac{1}{4}$ inch/6mm thick on the top.

📖 If the idea of roasting the lamb on the oven rack seems too far-out or messy for you, just prepare the gratin of potatoes in a dish upon which a cooling rack large enough to hold the lamb can sit. You won't get the full advantage of air circulation (the bottom of the lamb may steam slightly), but you will certainly come close. Just be sure to place a pan beneath any aspect of the lamb that may exceed the perimeters of the gratin dish. You don't want a burnt oven bottom! →

1 leg of lamb on the bone (6 to 7 lb/2.7 to 3.1kg) with a $\frac{1}{4}$-inch/6mm layer of fat 3 cloves garlic Olive oil Sea salt Ground black pepper	Pat the lamb dry. Using a mortar and pestle or the back of a large knife, crush the garlic to a paste. Spread it all over the lamb, and then rub the meat with olive oil and season with salt and pepper. Set aside at room temperature to temper for 2 to 3 hours.
	Preheat the oven to 400°F/200°C. Choose your largest baking dish or roasting pan to go under the leg of lamb and catch its drippings. If your dish isn't quite large enough, place a baking sheet or piece of aluminum foil under it to catch any errant drips.
1 clove garlic, halved	Rub the garlic all over the inside surfaces of the baking dish or roasting pan.
$2\frac{1}{2}$ lb/1.1kg russet potatoes, peeled and thinly sliced 1 tsp chopped fresh thyme 1 tsp sea salt 1 tsp ground black pepper 6 cloves garlic, finely chopped 2 tsp olive oil	Add the potatoes, thyme, salt, pepper, garlic, and olive oil to the baking dish. Toss to combine and then arrange the sliced potatoes in a neat layer.
2 yellow onions, thinly sliced 1 tsp chopped fresh thyme 1 tsp sea salt 1 tsp ground black pepper 2 tsp olive oil	In a bowl, toss together the onions, thyme, salt, pepper, and olive oil, and then lay on top of the potatoes.
$\frac{1}{2}$ cup/120ml dry white wine	Pour the wine over the potatoes and onions.

Place the baking dish on the lowest oven rack. Lay the prepared leg of lamb on the rack above the gratin. Make sure the gratin is positioned to catch all of the drips from the lamb. Roast for 15 minutes and then lower the oven temperature to 350°F/180°C. Continue roasting for another 1 hour to 1 hour 15 minutes, depending on the size of the leg. For medium-rare, the meat at the center of the leg should reach a temperature of 125°F/51°C on an instant-read thermometer; for medium, 135°F/57°C; and for medium-well, 145°F/62°C. Check the gratin after about 1 hour total roasting time; if the potatoes are tender, the gratin is done. If the roast needs more cooking time, put a pan underneath it to catch the drippings.

2 Tbsp chopped flat-leaf parsley

2 Tbsp chopped fresh mint

1 tsp chopped fresh thyme

2 tsp champagne vinegar

1 tsp honey

$\frac{1}{4}$ cup/60ml olive oil, plus more as needed

Pinch of sea salt, plus more as needed

Pinch of ground black pepper

While the leg of lamb and potato-onion gratin are roasting, prepare the mint salsa verde. Mix the parsley, mint, thyme, vinegar, honey, olive oil, salt, and pepper together in a bowl. Taste for seasoning, adding more olive oil and salt as needed.

Once the leg of lamb has reached the desired doneness, transfer it to a cutting board and let rest for at least 10 minutes before slicing. Serve with the gratin and the salsa verde.

Store leftover lamb, well wrapped, in the refrigerator for up to 3 days.

DES
SERTS

SHORTBREAD

Makes about 36 cookies

Shortbread is an ancient biscuit native to Scotland, based on a ratio of one part sugar, two parts butter, and three parts flour. Because Europe traditionally has softer flour, which means that it has less protein and produces a more tender crumb, the sought-after sandy texture of shortbread is more easily achieved. Where harder flour is used, as in the United States, a little added starch or starchy flour, such as rice flour, does wonders. The shortbread's characteristic melt-in-your mouth tenderness makes it a recipe perfect for gluten-free baking. After all, it is the butter that holds this cookie together, and gluten does not play a crucial roll. Shortbread is a natural partner to lighter desserts, like granita, sorbet, or a bowl of berries and cream. And nibbling shortbread with an afternoon coffee or tea feels like a civilized way to satiate your sweet craving.

📖 There is a pervasive myth that shortbread should never bake to the point of browning. I want to persuade you that a golden tint is not only okay but preferable. The buttery flavor will become more pronounced with a bit of color, and that is as essential an element to shortbread as its friable crumb.

$\frac{1}{2}$ cup plus 3 Tbsp/155g unsalted butter, at room temperature	In the bowl of a stand mixer fitted with the paddle attachment, beat the butter on medium speed until light and creamy, about 2 minutes.
$\frac{1}{3}$ cup plus 1 Tbsp/80g granulated sugar	Add the sugar to the butter and continue to beat until fluffy, about 3 minutes. Stop the mixer and scrape down the sides of the bowl with a rubber spatula.
$1\frac{1}{4}$ cups/150g almond flour $\frac{3}{4}$ cup plus 1 Tbsp/115g white or brown rice flour, or a combination $\frac{1}{2}$ tsp ground cinnamon $\frac{1}{8}$ tsp sea salt	In a large bowl, combine the almond flour, rice flour, cinnamon, and salt. Stir well and then add to the butter-sugar mixture. Mix just until incorporated.

Working on a large sheet of parchment paper, shape the dough into a log about 10 inches/25cm long and $1\frac{1}{2}$ inches/4cm in diameter. Wrap tightly in parchment paper or plastic wrap, twisting the ends, and place in the refrigerator for at least 1 hour.

Preheat the oven to 325°F/165°C. Line 2 baking sheets with parchment paper or silicone mats.

Unwrap the log. Using a sharp knife, slice the log into round cookies about $\frac{1}{4}$ inch/6mm thick. Arrange the cookies on the prepared baking sheets, spacing the cooking at least $\frac{1}{2}$ inch/12mm apart. Bake, rotating the baking sheets at the midway point, until the edges of the cookies are golden brown, about 15 minutes. Set the baking sheets on a cooling rack to cool for 5 minutes and then transfer the cookies to a wire rack and let cool completely.

The cookies will keep in an airtight container at room temperature for up to 4 days.

FRESH GINGER COOKIES

Makes 20 ($3\frac{1}{2}$-inch/9cm) cookies

These gluten-free ginger cookies bake up like any classic—both chewy and moist—and are scented with fresh and dried ginger and warm spices. Crystallized sugar, used on the dough's exterior, provides a crunchy contrast to the soft inside and offers momentary respite from the spice. If you do not have any on hand, regular granulated sugar will do. When I have Candied Orange Peel (page 355), I add it to the dough for an extra-special treat. You could add chopped, candied ginger as well. Although these delight in any weather, they are especially good if it is gloomy out, particularly when paired with a cup of strong black tea. →

¾ cup/165g unsalted butter, at room temperature	In the bowl of a stand mixer fitted with the paddle attachment, beat the butter on medium-high speed until creamy and smooth, about 1 minute.
1 cup/200g granulated sugar ¼ cup/60ml molasses	Add the sugar and molasses and continue to beat until light in color and fluffy, about 2 minutes. Stop the mixer and scrape down the sides of the bowl with a rubber spatula.
1 large egg 1 (2-inch/5cm) piece fresh gingerroot, peeled and finely grated	Add the egg and fresh ginger to the butter-sugar mixture and beat until incorporated.
2 cups/240g almond flour ¾ cup plus 2 Tbsp/110g oat flour 2½ Tbsp brown rice flour 2½ Tbsp sweet rice flour ¼ cup/30g tapioca flour/starch 2 tsp baking soda ½ tsp sea salt 1 Tbsp ground cinnamon 1 Tbsp ground ginger ½ tsp freshly grated nutmeg ½ tsp ground allspice ½ tsp ground cloves ¼ to ½ cup/10 to 20g Candied Orange Peel (page 355, or store-bought), or candied ginger, coarsely chopped (optional)	Combine the almond flour, oat flour, brown rice flour, sweet rice flour, tapioca flour/starch, baking soda, salt, cinnamon, ginger, nutmeg, allspice, cloves, and candied orange peel or candied ginger in a large bowl, and mix well, then add to the bowl of the stand mixer. Beat on low speed just until combined. Place in the refrigerator to chill until firm, 30 minutes to 1 hour.
	Preheat the oven to 350°F/180°C. Line 2 baking sheets with parchment paper or silicone mats. →

Large-crystal sugar

Using an ice cream scoop or a large spoon, scoop the dough into 20 golf ball–size balls (each about 50g). Roll the balls in sugar, and then place on the prepared baking sheets, spacing them at least 2 inches/5cm apart. You may bake 2 pans at the same time, but you will need to rotate them 180 degrees halfway through baking if the cookies are not baking evenly. Bake until the cookies no longer look wet and the edges are slightly darker than the centers, 12 to 15 minutes. If you prefer a cookie with a soft center, bake for only 12 minutes. For a crunchy cookie, bake for the full 15 minutes.

Set the baking sheets on a cooling rack to cool for 5 minutes, and then transfer the cookies to a wire rack and let cool completely.

The cookies will keep in an airtight container at room temperature for up to 2 weeks.

CHOCOLATE-BUCKWHEAT MADELEINES

Makes 12 cookies

Among my madeleine recipes, I turn to this one when I desire something chocolaty. I use a small amount of buckwheat flour, which gives these cookies a slightly warm, earthy flavor underpinning the chocolate. These fragrant chestnut-colored madeleines make for a beautiful plate when paired with winter citrus, like mandarin oranges, satsumas, or Candied Orange Peel (see page 355).

📖 Remember: A well-chilled batter, along with a pan that has spent 10 minutes in the freezer, helps the madeleines form their characteristic bump. Butter and flour the molded pan thoroughly, so that the madeleines do not stick.

6 Tbsp/85g
unsalted butter,
cut into pieces

2½ oz/70g 70 percent
cacao chocolate or
other chocolate of your
choice, chopped

Melt the butter and chocolate in a bowl set over a pot of barely simmering water. Stir until combined and then remove from the heat and let cool.

¾ cup plus 1 Tbsp/100g
confectioners' sugar

⅓ cup/40g almond flour

2 Tbsp white or brown
rice flour

2 Tbsp buckwheat flour

¼ tsp sea salt

¼ tsp baking powder

Sift the confectioners' sugar, almond flour, rice flour, buckwheat flour, salt, and baking powder together into a medium bowl.

3 large egg whites

In a large bowl, whisk the egg whites until frothy but not yet holding peaks. Using a rubber spatula, gently fold in the flour mixture, followed by the chocolate mixture. Cover and place in the refrigerator to chill for at least 1 hour and up to 5 days. If you are in a rush to bake, the batter can be placed in the freezer to chill briefly (I put my bowl in the freezer with the spatula in it so I can give it a few stirs). It should be sufficiently chilled after 15 minutes; don't forget about it! (The batter can be frozen in an airtight container for months; thaw in the refrigerator before using.)

Preheat the oven to 375°F/190°C.

1 Tbsp unsalted
butter, melted

1 Tbsp tapioca
flour/starch

While the batter is chilling, prepare the madeleine pan: Brush the melted butter across the inside surfaces of a 12-well madeleine mold, making sure to coat all the crevices. Sprinkle a little of the tapioca flour/starch into each well. Tilt and tap the mold to distribute the starch and evenly coat each well and then firmly tap out the excess. Place the mold in the freezer to chill for at least 10 minutes. →

Once the batter is well chilled, spoon it into the prepared pan, dividing evenly among the wells. There's no need to press the batter down; it will spread and fill the molds once it warms up in the oven. Bake until the madeleines are nicely puffed in the center and springy to the touch, 10 to 14 minutes, depending on how cold the batter was. Let them cool in the pan on a wire rack for a few minutes to give the chocolate a chance to set. Then turn the madeleines out of the pan by rapping it on the counter and using your fingers to gently release any that are stuck. These are best eaten the day they are made.

PISTACHIO MADELEINES

Makes 12 cookies

Though I don't claim a favorite among my madeleine recipes, the pistachio version is quite remarkable. If you've never had a cookie or cake made from the nut, I hope you give this a try. The elusive flavor is simultaneously delicate, piny, and sweet. The addition of almond extract has a surprising effect of enhancing the "pistachio" flavor. Pistachios' varying shades of green hinges on the harvesttime of the nut and the elevation at which they are grown.

📖 Remember: A well-chilled batter, along with a pan that has spent 10 minutes in the freezer, helps the madeleines form their characteristic bump. Butter and flour the molded pan thoroughly, so that the madeleines do not stick.

3 large egg whites

$\frac{1}{2}$ tsp almond extract

$\frac{1}{4}$ tsp sea salt

Combine the egg whites, almond extract, and salt in a large bowl and whisk until frothy but not yet holding peaks.

$\frac{3}{4}$ cup plus 1 Tbsp/100g confectioners' sugar	Add the confectioners' sugar, pistachio flour, rice flour, oat flour, and tapioca flour/starch to the egg whites and whisk to combine.
$\frac{1}{3}$ cup/40g pistachio flour or finely ground pistachios	
2 Tbsp white or brown rice flour	
1 Tbsp oat flour	
1 Tbsp tapioca flour/starch	

6 Tbsp/85g unsalted butter, melted	Add the butter to the flour and egg white mixture and whisk until completely incorporated. Cover and place in the refrigerator to chill for at least 1 hour and up to 5 days. If you are in a rush to bake, the batter can be placed in the freezer to chill briefly (I put my bowl in the freezer with the spatula in it so I can give it a few stirs). It should be sufficiently chilled after 15 minutes; don't forget about it! (The batter can be frozen in an airtight container for months; thaw before using.)

Preheat the oven to 375°F/190°C.

1 Tbsp unsalted butter, melted	While the batter is chilling, prepare the madeleine pan: Brush the melted butter across the inside surfaces of a 12-well madeleine mold, making sure to coat all the crevices. Sprinkle a little of the tapioca flour/starch into each well. Tilt and tap the mold to distribute the starch and evenly coat each well and then firmly tap out the excess. Place the mold in the freezer to chill for at least 10 minutes.
1 Tbsp tapioca flour/starch	

Once the batter is well chilled, spoon it into the prepared pan, dividing evenly among the wells. There's no need to press the batter down; it will spread and fill the molds once it warms up in the oven. Bake until the madeleines are puffed in the center and golden brown around the edges, 9 to 12 minutes. Immediately turn them out of the pan by rapping it on the counter and using your fingers to gently release any that are stuck. These are best eaten the day they are made.

JAM BARS

Makes 12 bars (one 9 by 13-inch/23 by 33cm pan)

Every year when there's a surfeit of jam in my pantry, I quickly run through the best ways to use it: with popovers, on toast, in yogurt, as a layer in trifles or cakes, and in these jam bars. With the three jams and an apple butter in this book (pages 50, 51, 56, and 60), you have a lot of options. The combination of rice syrup and almond butter make these bars less sweet, with a toothsome, more substantial savory quality than most other versions, which are more often than not merely sweet cookie dough made even sweeter with jam.

$\frac{1}{2}$ cup/110g unsalted butter or coconut oil, at room temperature

$\frac{1}{3}$ cup/85g almond butter

2 Tbsp brown rice syrup or maple syrup

Preheat the oven to 350°F/180°C. Line a 9 by 13-inch/ 23 by 33cm baking pan with parchment paper. Combine the butter or coconut oil, almond butter, and brown rice syrup or maple syrup in a large bowl and, using a wooden spoon, mix well.

$1\frac{1}{2}$ cups/150g rolled oats

1 cup/120g almond flour

1 cup/120g oat flour

6 Tbsp/90g granulated sugar

1 tsp baking powder

$\frac{1}{2}$ tsp sea salt

$\frac{1}{2}$ tsp vanilla extract

$\frac{1}{2}$ tsp almond extract

$\frac{1}{2}$ tsp ground cinnamon

Add the rolled oats, almond flour, oat flour, sugar, baking powder, salt, vanilla and almond extracts, and cinnamon to the butter mixture and stir until a soft dough forms. Divide the dough into thirds. Press two-thirds of the dough into the bottom of the prepared pan and reserve the remaining one-third for the topping.

1 cup plus 2 Tbsp/340g jam

1 tsp lemon juice

Pinch of sea salt

Stir together the jam, lemon juice, and salt and then spread the mixture evenly over the bottom crust.

Crumble the remaining one-third dough over the jam filling. →

Bake the jam bars until golden brown around the edges, about 35 minutes. Let the pastry cool completely in the pan on a wire rack before cutting into bars.

The jam bars will keep, well wrapped, at room temperature for up to 4 days.

Jam Bars with Chopped Nuts: If you're after textural contrast, chopped nuts added to the top layer give these jam bars extra crunch. After separating the dough, set aside the slightly larger portion to be used for the bottom. Add $\frac{1}{2}$ cup/40g sliced almonds or $\frac{1}{2}$ cup/50g chopped walnuts to the other third, which will be used for the crumble on top.

WALNUT PRALINES

Makes about 70 cookies (one 9 by 13-inch/23 by 33cm baking pan)

Years ago I was a culinary student at the Culinary Institute of America. I dare say that if anything made the freezing Hudson Valley winters worthwhile, it would be this very recipe, a perfected praline. The crust I use is my favorite Cream Cheese Dough (page 36), but you could use any pie dough or other shortcrust pastry as long as it does not contain a leavening agent. If you're one to make holiday confections, include this, as one tray makes many small treats that stay in pristine condition even when traveling in a tin or across the country in the mail. Different from a Southern praline candy of cooked sugar and nuts, this is a smooth, orange-scented caramel with nuts, poured over a crust and cut into small diamonds when set. It is one of the rare recipes that I don't have to pull out a candy thermometer to make because the proportions and cooking time are perfectly calibrated to render an easy-to-cut yet soft texture each time.

Cornstarch or tapioca flour/starch, for rolling

$\frac{1}{2}$ batch Cream Cheese Dough (page 36)

Lightly dust a work surface with cornstarch or tapioca flour/starch. Place the dough on the prepared work surface and roll to $\frac{1}{8}$ inch/3mm thick, rolling from the center evenly out in all directions. Dust with additional cornstarch as needed to discourage sticking. Cut out an 11 by 15-inch/28 by 38cm rectangle. Carefully lift and transfer to a 9 by 13 inch/23 by 33cm baking pan, easing the dough into the bottom and sides but not stretching or pressing too firmly, or it will shrink too much during baking. If the dough tears, just patch with a little extra dough, pressing gently to adhere. Trim the dough so it hangs $\frac{1}{4}$ inch/6mm over the edges of the pan, as the dough will shrink a bit while it bakes. Reserve any rolled dough scraps for patching the crust. Place the dough shell in the refrigerator to chill for 15 minutes.

Preheat the oven to 325°F/165°C.

Using a fork, prick the bottom of the dough shell approximately every 2 inches/5cm. For a partially baked shell, bake for 12 to 18 minutes, until golden brown. If there are any splits or holes in the crust, they can be patched with leftover raw dough scraps and baked for another 5 minutes. This is an essential step; the caramel filling will seep through any crack it finds and run under the crust.

Let cool completely on a wire rack. The pastry shell will keep, well wrapped, for up to 1 week in the refrigerator or for up to 2 weeks in the freezer.

$1\frac{1}{2}$ cups/300g granulated sugar

1 cup/220g unsalted butter

$\frac{1}{2}$ cup/120ml honey

$1\frac{1}{2}$ tsp sea salt

Preheat the oven to 350°F/180°C. In a medium saucepan set over medium heat, combine the granulated sugar, butter, honey, and salt. Melt the butter and bring to a boil, stirring to dissolve the sugar. Cook for 10 minutes and then remove from the heat. →

$3\frac{3}{4}$ cups/450g coarsely chopped walnuts

$\frac{1}{4}$ cup/60ml heavy cream

Finely grated zest of 2 oranges

Add the walnuts, cream, and zest to the sugar-butter mixture all at once, stir with a rubber spatula, and return to medium heat. Bring just to a boil. Pour the nut mixture into the pastry shell and smooth the surface with the spatula. Bake for 10 minutes, until the edges of the crust are dark golden brown.

Set the pan on a cooling rack to cool completely before cutting into $1\frac{1}{4}$-inch/3cm diamonds.

The walnut pralines will keep, well wrapped, at room temperature for up to 1 week.

Cardamom Pralines: Add $\frac{1}{2}$ tsp ground cardamom along with the walnuts and orange zest to the saucepan and then proceed with the directions.

DOUBLE CHOCOLATE SORGHUM BROWNIES

Makes 9 brownies (one 8-inch/20cm square pan or Pyrex dish)

Baking a perfect brownie is an exercise in nostalgia, with the ideal being the one each of us had as a young child. My standard was the recipe on the back of the Baker's Chocolate box—chewy, fudgy, and rich with dark chocolate. Use your favorite chocolate in these. You'll be able to tell the difference when you use good-quality chocolate. This recipe is unleavened, except for the eggs, and uses sorghum flour for its soft and almost imperceptible feel.

📖 While there's nothing more American than a brownie, I have once or twice baked the batter in a fluted tart pan. The formal shape makes this easy recipe into a perfectly delicious chocolate tart, made even better with a spoonful of unsweetened whipped cream.

Unsalted butter, for the pan

Preheat the oven to 350°F/180°C. Butter an 8-inch/20cm square baking pan or dish.

$\frac{1}{2}$ cup plus 2 Tbsp/140g unsalted butter, cut into pieces 8 oz/230g chocolate (70 percent cacao or higher; or bittersweet or semisweet, but the brownie won't be as dark)	Melt the butter and chocolate in a bowl set over a pot of barely simmering water. Stir until combined and then remove from the heat and let cool.
3 large eggs 1$\frac{1}{4}$ cups/250g granulated sugar	Add the eggs and sugar to the chocolate mixture and whisk to thoroughly incorporate.
$\frac{1}{4}$ cup/45g potato starch $\frac{1}{2}$ cup/70g sorghum flour Scant $\frac{1}{2}$ tsp sea salt 1 tsp vanilla extract 1 cup/120g shelled walnuts, chopped 6 oz/170g bittersweet or semisweet chocolate, chopped	Add the potato starch, sorghum flour, salt, vanilla, walnuts, and chopped chocolate to the egg mixture and mix well with a wooden spoon. Transfer to the prepared baking dish. Bake for about 25 minutes, until the surface no longer looks shiny and wet. The edges will appear slightly more matte than the center, which will remain fudgy even after cooling. Take care not to overbake. Set the pan on a cooling rack and let cool completely. Cut into squares and serve.

The brownie can be stored, tightly wrapped, at room temperature for up to 3 days.

APPLE BEEHIVE

Makes 1 beehive, cut into 6 to 8 servings

This dessert is built on apple slices shingled on top of one another. Layered with sugar and butter, this large domed stack resembles a beehive. As it slowly bakes, the layers condense and the top caramelizes, becoming unexpectedly complex for so few ingredients. For a similar effect, although different presentation, you can simply layer all of the ingredients in a pan and slice into portions after baking. →

298 TARTINE ALL DAY

Unsalted butter, for the pan	Preheat the oven to 400°F/200°C. Butter the bottom of an 8-inch/20cm tart pan. If you don't have one, line a baking sheet with parchment paper.
6 Granny Smith apples, peeled, cored, and very thinly sliced 6 Tbsp/85g unsalted butter, melted $\frac{3}{4}$ cup/150g granulated sugar 1 Tbsp plus 1 tsp ground cinnamon	Working directly on the prepared tart pan or baking sheet, arrange a layer of apple slices in an 8-inch/20cm circle, halfway overlapping each slice. Continue layering apple slices to form a beehive shape, saving some of the smaller slices for the top. Every 2 or 3 layers, brush lightly with the butter and sprinkle lightly with some of the sugar and cinnamon. Once you've assembled the beehive, brush the butter all over it. Arch aluminum foil over the dome, bake for 25 minutes, and then gently press down to help compact the layers. Remove the foil (to let the edges brown) and bake until soft all the way through when pierced with the tip of a knife, 20 to 35 minutes longer.
$\frac{1}{4}$ cup/60ml Quince Jelly (page 58), apple jelly, or strained apricot jam Lightly sweetened whipped cream (see page 319), cold, or vanilla ice cream, for garnish	Heat the jelly or jam to melt it and then brush it all over the baked beehive as soon as it comes out of the oven. Serve warm or at room temperature, cut into wedges, with a dollop of whipped cream or ice cream on the side.

SPICED APPLE-WALNUT CAKE

Makes 8 to 10 servings (one 10-in/25cm cake)

Just as there is a time of year to make gazpacho, there is a season for Spiced Apple-Walnut Cake. This is a cake to leave out on the counter for passersby to cut pieces from, to bring on a cold day's hike, or to eat with a glass of wine instead of dinner. It is moist and chunky because of the pound of apples folded into the batter.

⌒ On the East Coast, I have often made this cake with McIntosh apples. Granny Smith and Pink Lady apples are delicious in this recipe as well. If the apples are fresh and firm, there's no need to peel them.

Unsalted butter, for the pan

Tapioca flour/starch, for the pan

Preheat the oven to 325°F/165°C. Line the bottom of a 10-inch/25cm round cake pan with 3-inch/7.5cm sides with parchment paper cut to fit exactly. Butter and flour the sides of the pan, knocking out any excess flour.

1 cup/220g unsalted butter, at room temperature

2 cups/400g granulated sugar

In the bowl of a stand mixer fitted with the paddle attachment, beat the butter and sugar on medium-high speed until light and creamy, about 2 minutes.

3 large eggs

Add the eggs one at a time to the sugar-butter mixture, beating well after each addition. Stop the mixer and scrape down the sides of the bowl with a rubber spatula.

1 cup/140g rice flour

1 cup/120g almond flour

1 cup/120g oat flour

$\frac{1}{2}$ cup/60g tapioca flour/ starch, arrowroot flour, or cornstarch

1 $\frac{1}{2}$ tsp baking soda

1 tsp ground cinnamon

$\frac{1}{2}$ tsp grated nutmeg

$\frac{1}{2}$ tsp ground ginger

$\frac{1}{4}$ tsp ground cloves

$\frac{1}{2}$ tsp sea salt

Combine the rice flour, almond flour, oat flour, tapioca flour/starch or arrowroot flour or cornstarch, baking soda, cinnamon, nutmeg, ginger, cloves, and salt in a large bowl and mix well. Add to the butter-egg mixture and stir just until there are no streaks of flour.

1 lb/455g apples, cored and cut into $\frac{1}{2}$-inch/12mm chunks

$\frac{3}{4}$ cup/90g walnuts, lightly toasted and coarsely chopped

Stir the apples and walnuts into the batter. The batter will be very thick, so make sure to gently yet fully incorporate the apples and walnuts. →

Transfer the batter to the prepared pan and bake for about 1 hour and 40 minutes, until the top of the cake is dark golden brown and springs back when you press on it lightly.

Set the pan on a cooling rack to cool for 15 minutes. To unmold, run a butter knife around the sides of the pan to loosen the cake. Then invert the cake, lift off the pan, and peel away the parchment. Turn the cake right-side up and let cool completely on the rack before serving.

The cake keeps, tightly wrapped, for up to 3 days at room temperature and 1 week in the refrigerator.

Spiced Pear-Walnut Cake: Use pears, unpeeled, instead of apples and ¾ tsp ground cardamom in place of the ginger and cloves.

Applesauce Walnut Cake: Use the Applesauce (page 27), prior to blending and while still chunky, in place of the apple chunks.

LEMON POUND CAKE

Makes 8 to 10 servings (one 10-inch/25cm cake)

It seems that no matter where you go in London, a good lemon pound cake awaits you. An English original that became a standard in American kitchens, this recipe takes modern liberties, as I use a combination of non-wheat flours and olive oil in addition to butter to ensure that the cake's texture remains tender even after refrigeration (a thin slice of an ice-cold cake is a delicious treat). From start to finish, it takes only about an hour to make.

📖 Coconut flour is a nourishing by-product of coconut milk and quite useful in baking. The only thing to know is that it is extremely absorbent, so a one-to-one replacement with wheat flour is inadvisable. Mixing it first with water, as this recipe calls for, makes it easier to blend in evenly and creates a very moist cake.

Unsalted butter, for the pan	Preheat the oven to 350°F/180°C. Lightly butter the bottom and sides of a 10-in/25cm round cake pan.
4 large eggs, at room temperature $\frac{2}{3}$ cup/130g granulated sugar $\frac{1}{4}$ tsp salt	Combine the eggs, sugar, and salt in a large bowl. Using electric beaters or a whisk, beat on high speed until the mixture lightens in color and triples in volume, 2 to 3 minutes. Continue to beat at a medium speed for 1 more minute, until the air bubbles appear more uniform in size and the mixture forms satiny ribbons.
$\frac{1}{2}$ cup/110g unsalted butter, at soft room temperature 2 Tbsp olive oil	In another bowl, use a wooden spoon to stir together the butter and olive oil. (The butter must be very soft for this to work properly.)
1 Tbsp coconut flour $\frac{1}{4}$ cup/60ml water	In a small bowl, combine the coconut flour and water and then add to the butter and oil.
Finely grated zest of 1 lemon 3 Tbsp/45ml lemon juice $\frac{1}{4}$ tsp vanilla extract $\frac{1}{4}$ tsp sea salt	Add the lemon zest and juice, vanilla, and salt to the butter mixture.
3 cups/360g almond flour $\frac{1}{4}$ cup/35g brown rice flour 1 tsp baking powder	Stir together the almond flour, rice flour, and baking powder in a medium bowl. Gently fold the dry ingredients into the beaten egg mixture. Fold about one-quarter of the butter mixture into the egg mixture and then fold in the remaining three-quarters of the egg mixture. Transfer to the prepared pan, smoothing the top with a spatula. Bake until the edges are golden brown and a cake tester inserted in the center comes out clean, about 30 minutes. Let cool in the pan on a wire rack for at least 20 minutes before serving.
	The cake keeps, tightly wrapped, for up to 3 days at room temperature or 1 week in the refrigerator.
	Poppy Seed-Lemon Pound Cake: Add 3 Tbsp/25g poppy seeds to the almond flour mixture. →

Rhubarb-Lemon Pound Cake: Evenly spread $\frac{1}{4}$ cup/50g granulated sugar over the bottom of the pan. Cut 5 stalks of rhubarb to neatly fill the pan in a pattern. (I like to cut and fit the stalks in a star or chevron pattern but you could also lay them side by side.) Fit the rhubarb tightly into the bottom of the pan. Spread the batter evenly over the rhubarb and bake until a cake tester inserted in the center comes out clean, 45 to 60 minutes. Let cool in the pan on a rack for 5 minutes and then invert onto a serving plate to cool further before serving.

Cranberry Upside-Down Lemon Pound Cake: Scatter $1\frac{1}{4}$ cups/125g fresh or frozen cranberries across the bottom of the buttered pan and then proceed with the recipe and bake as directed. Once cool, invert the cake.

CORNMEAL-RICOTTA UPSIDE-DOWN CAKE

Makes 8 to 10 servings (one 10-inch/25cm cake)

Despite my affection for cornmeal, I often find that cakes made with it tend to be on the dry side. This recipe is inspired by one that uses ricotta and bakes at a low temperature, creating a cake reminiscent of a cheesecake. The cake lends itself to fruit toppings, baked at the bottom of the pan, the best being thinly sliced oranges, which cook to a marmalade consistency. Depending on the season, use any fruit suited for upside-down toppings. Peaches, apricots, and blueberries would be especially good in combination with the corn.

📖 Slice the oranges paper-thin, so that when heated in the layer of sugar syrup, they soften and slice well when cool. In addition to oranges (Valencia, navel, or Cara Cara), blood oranges and tangerines would also work just as well. Of course, remove any seeds before baking. →

Unsalted butter, for the pan	Preheat the oven to 325°F/165°C. Line the bottom of a 10-in/25cm springform pan with 3-in/7.5cm sides with parchment paper cut to fit exactly. Butter the sides of the pan.
$\frac{1}{2}$ cup firmly packed/90g light or dark brown sugar, or granulated sugar 2 Tbsp water 2 oranges, very thinly sliced	In a small bowl, mix the brown sugar or granulated sugar and water together to form a paste and then spread it across the bottom of the pan. Arrange the orange slices on top of the sugar paste, overlapping them with one in the center. Try to cover as much of the bottom of the pan as possible; the slices will shrink slightly during baking.
$\frac{1}{2}$ cup/110g unsalted butter, at room temperature $\frac{3}{4}$ cup/150g granulated sugar	In the bowl of a stand mixer fitted with the paddle attachment, beat the butter and sugar on medium-high speed until light and creamy, about 1 minute.
3 large eggs, separated (egg whites reserved for the next step) $\frac{3}{4}$ cup/180g Ricotta Cheese (page 33, or store-bought) Finely grated zest and juice of 3 lemons 1 tsp sea salt	Add the yolks one at a time to the butter mixture beating well after each addition. Add the ricotta, lemon zest, lemon juice, and salt. Beat to combine.
$\frac{1}{3}$ cup plus 1 Tbsp/55g stone-ground cornmeal 1 cup plus 1 Tbsp/130g almond flour	Mix the cornmeal and almond flour into the egg-ricotta mixture. Stop the mixer and scrape down the sides of the bowl with a rubber spatula.
	In another bowl, whisk the reserved egg whites to soft peaks. Using a rubber spatula, gently fold the beaten whites into the cake batter just until no white streaks are visible. (The batter will be very thick.) Immediately turn the batter into the prepared pan, smoothing the top with a spatula. →

Bake for 30 to 45 minutes, until the top of the cake is no longer shiny. Let the cake cool in the pan on a wire rack for 15 minutes. To unmold, run a butter knife around the sides of the pan to loosen the cake and then release and lift off the pan sides. Invert the cake, remove the pan bottom, peel off the parchment, and serve.

The cake will keep, well wrapped, for up to 4 days at room temperature or about 1 week in the refrigerator.

TEFF CARROT CAKE

Makes 8 to 10 servings (one double-layer 9-inch/23cm cake)

If teff flour had been available in medieval Europe, where carrot cake is thought to have originated, it definitely would have been used in this cake. It is a naturally nutty-tasting grain, most known for its use in the Ethiopian fermented flatbread injera. Teff makes this cake a slightly less guilty pleasure, due to its nutritional profile: it is gluten-free and high in protein, calcium, iron, and fiber. When ground into flour and used in cake batter, it holds moisture and creates a lovely, light crumb. I have always thought of carrot cake as distinctly American, although if you live in Switzerland or England you would rightly argue its immense popularity there (birthday celebrations in those countries often have this cake as its celebratory dessert).

Unsalted butter, for the pans	Butter the sides of two 9-inch/23cm round cake pans and line the bottoms with parchment paper.
	Preheat the oven to 350°F/180°C.
1 cup/200g granulated sugar 1 cup/140g coconut sugar 3 large eggs	Using a handheld mixer or a stand mixer fitted with the whisk attachment, whip the granulated sugar, coconut sugar, and eggs until thick and light in color, about 4 minutes on medium speed. When you lift up the whisk, the beaten egg mixture should fall back into the bowl in a ribbon.

$\frac{1}{2}$ cup/125g
Applesauce (page 27, or store-bought)

1 lb/455g carrots, grated

1 cup/200g coconut oil, melted

Juice of 1 lemon

Add the applesauce, carrots, coconut oil, and lemon juice to the egg mixture and mix well to combine.

$1\frac{1}{4}$ cups/170g teff flour

$\frac{1}{2}$ cup/70g sweet rice flour

$\frac{1}{2}$ cup/60g oat flour

$2\frac{1}{4}$ tsp ground cinnamon

10 gratings of nutmeg

$\frac{1}{4}$ tsp ground cloves

2 tsp baking soda

$\frac{3}{4}$ tsp sea salt

In a bowl, whisk together the teff flour, sweet rice flour, oat flour, cinnamon, nutmeg, cloves, baking soda, and salt. Add to the egg mixture and use a rubber spatula to fold just until combined.

$\frac{1}{2}$ cup/30g unsweetened shredded coconut

$1\frac{1}{2}$ cups/180g toasted walnuts

Gently fold the coconut and walnuts into the batter.

Divide the batter evenly between the prepared pans. Bake until a toothpick inserted in the center comes out clean, 35 to 40 minutes. Let cool in the pans on a wire rack for about 10 minutes. To unmold, run a butter knife around the edges of each pan, and then invert the cakes onto the wire rack and peel off the parchment paper. Let cool completely.

1 cup/227g (8 oz) cream cheese, at room temperature

6 Tbsp/85g unsalted butter, at cool room temperature

3 cups/360g confectioners' sugar, sifted

Juice of 1 lemon

$\frac{1}{4}$ tsp sea salt

To make the icing, using a stand mixer fitted with the paddle attachment, beat the cream cheese and butter on medium-high until fluffy and light, about 3 minutes. Add the confectioners' sugar, lemon juice, and salt and mix until smooth. →

Place one cooled cake layer on a serving platter. Spread about half of the icing on top of the cake layer, place the second cake layer on top, and frost the top with the remaining icing. Cut into slices and serve.

Store, covered, in the refrigerator for up to 3 days.

BIRTHDAY CAKE WITH FLUFFY MILK CHOCOLATE FROSTING

Makes 8 to 10 servings (one double-layer 8-inch/20cm cake or 24 cupcakes)

Before developing this cake I could count on one hand the number of times I've made a classic white cake, made light and pale with only egg whites. But after making this, I wondered why hadn't I made this beautiful and simple cake more often? It is a cake for frosting, and therefore in my mind, a cake for a celebration, perfect for a birthday or wedding. I've included a recipe for a chocolate frosting just dark enough for adults and milky enough for kids; whipped cream topped with copious berries would also be striking against the alabaster cake. The small amount of coconut flour might seem like an odd addition, but coconut flour holds moisture well. This is a cake that can be made ahead or, as instructed in the variation, baked into cupcakes.

📖 When using eggs in baking, particularly when making cakes, where they will contribute volume, try to start with eggs (or in this case, egg whites) at room temperature. They'll be easier to whip into full, fluffy peaks.

📖 This cake can be made as far as a day ahead. Cover and refrigerate it once it has cooled completely. Frost when it's still slightly chilled, as the cake's texture will be firmer, making it easier to frost.

Preheat the oven to 350°F/180°C. Butter the sides of two 8-inch/20cm round cake pans and line the bottoms with parchment paper cut to fit exactly.

$\frac{1}{2}$ cup plus 1 Tbsp/80g white rice flour

$\frac{1}{2}$ cup plus 1 Tbsp/80g brown rice flour

6 Tbsp/45g tapioca flour/starch

6 Tbsp/40g coconut flour

$\frac{1}{4}$ cup/30g oat flour

$1\frac{1}{4}$ cups/250g granulated sugar

$2\frac{1}{4}$ tsp baking powder

$\frac{3}{4}$ tsp sea salt

In the bowl of a stand mixer fitted with the whisk attachment, whisk together the white and brown rice flours, tapioca flour/starch, coconut flour, oat flour, sugar, baking powder, and salt. Alternatively, use a regular bowl and a handheld mixer.

$\frac{1}{2}$ cup plus 1 Tbsp/125g unsalted butter, at room temperature

6 Tbsp/90ml vegetable oil

Add the butter and oil and blend together with the dry ingredients.

6 large eggs, separated

Add the egg whites and beat until fully incorporated. Using a rubber spatula, scrape down the sides of the bowl, and then continue beating for another 1 to 2 minutes, until very smooth. Reserve the egg yolks for another use.

1 cup/240ml whole milk

$1\frac{1}{2}$ tsp vanilla extract

While whisking, gradually add the milk and vanilla to the bowl. Scrape down the sides of the bowl again and then mix for 30 seconds.

Divide the batter evenly between the 2 prepared pans. Bake until the tops spring back when lightly pressed or a toothpick inserted in the center comes out clean, 20 to 25 minutes.

Set the pans on cooling racks and let cool in the pans for 10 minutes. To unmold, run a butter knife around the sides of the pans to loosen each cake, invert the →

cakes onto the racks, lift off the pans, and peel away the parchment. Turn the cakes right-side up and let cool completely on the racks. If making ahead, the cooled cakes can be stored, tightly wrapped, at room temperature for up to 4 days.

Fluffy Milk Chocolate Frosting (page 357)

Transfer one cake layer to a serving plate. Spread about one-third of the frosting evenly over the cake layer. Top with the second cake layer and then spread the remaining frosting over the top and serve.

Frosted cake can be stored, covered, in the refrigerator for up to 3 days.

Birthday Cupcakes: Line 24 wells of a muffin tin with paper liners. Using an ice cream scoop or large spoon, portion the batter into the wells, filling each three-quarters full. Bake for 18 to 22 minutes, until the cupcakes are lightly browned and a toothpick inserted in the center of the largest cupcake comes out clean. Set the pan on a cooling rack for 5 minutes. Lift out the cupcakes and place them on the rack to cool completely before frosting. They will keep, well wrapped, in the refrigerator for up to 5 days.

TARTINE CHOCOLATE-ALMOND CAKE

Makes 8 to 12 servings (one double-layer 9-inch/23cm cake or 24 cupcakes)

Part of the fun and reward of recipe development is when you hit upon a method, ratio, trick, or particular combination of ingredients that makes all the failures worth it. This cake is one of those successes, with its surprisingly moist crumb, especially considering there is no butter or oil in the cake other than what naturally occurs in the almonds. The cake is dotted with jam before baking, an unusual step that creates little pockets of flavor and moisture throughout the cake and is a way to add a taste of fruit in the dead of winter. For a simpler approach, just cut the recipe ingredients in half to make one cake layer and serve slices with a spoonful of whipped cream on top.

📖 There can be confusion about the differences between almond flour and almond meal. They are one and the same and can be used identically.

📖 The quality of the cocoa you use matters. I often use Valrhona, which is one of the darkest and most full-bodied cocoas I have come across and gives the cake a deep chocolate color and flavor.

📖 I've used vinegar here because it helps to activate the baking soda, deepens the color of the cocoa, and enhances the chocolate flavor without leaving a hint of unwelcome acidity.

Unsalted butter, for the pans

Preheat the oven to 350°F/180°C. Butter the sides of two 9-inch/23cm round cake pans and line the bottoms with parchment paper cut to fit exactly.

---

4 cups/480g almond flour

$\frac{3}{4}$ cup plus 2 Tbsp/70g cocoa powder, sifted

1 tsp baking soda

In a bowl, combine the almond flour, cocoa powder, and baking soda and mix well, making sure that any lumps of almond flour are broken up.

---

4 eggs

6 Tbsp/75g granulated sugar

$\frac{1}{2}$ cup firmly packed/90g light brown sugar

$\frac{1}{2}$ tsp sea salt

Using a handheld mixer or a stand mixer fitted with the whisk attachment, beat the eggs, granulated sugar, brown sugar, and salt on high speed until very thick and pale in color, about 3 minutes. When you lift up the whisk, a ribbon of beaten eggs should trail back into the bowl.

---

2 tsp apple cider or distilled white vinegar

$1\frac{1}{2}$ cups/360ml whole milk

$\frac{2}{3}$ cup/200g raspberry, peach, strawberry, or apricot jam (optional)

2 to 4 tsp water

Whisk the vinegar and milk into the egg mixture. Pour the milk-egg mixture into the almond meal mixture and whisk until combined. Pour the batter into the cake pans. If the jam is too thick to drop off the spoon, slightly thin by stirring in the water. →

Evenly space dots of the jam over the tops of the cakes. Bake until the cake is set and a toothpick inserted into the center of the cakes comes out clean, 25 to 35 minutes.

Lightly sweetened whipped cream (see page 319)

Raspberries, blackberries, or a combination (optional)

Set the pans on a cooling racks and let cool in the pans for 10 minutes. To unmold, run a butter knife around the sides of the pans to loosen the cakes, invert the cakes onto another rack, lift off the pans, and peel away the parchment. Place a serving plate over the bottom of one cake layer and turn the cake right-side up, top with half of the whipped cream. Place the second cake layer over the whipped cream. Top with the remaining whipped cream and the berries. Serve warm or at room temperature.

The cooled cake can be stored, tightly wrapped, at room temperature for up to 3 days.

Tartine Chocolate-Almond Cupcakes: Line 24 wells of a muffin tin with paper liners. Using an ice cream scoop or large spoon, portion the batter into the wells, filling each three-quarters full. Bake for 18 to 22 minutes, until the cupcakes are lightly browned and a toothpick inserted in the center of the largest cupcake comes out clean. Set the pan on a cooling rack for 5 minutes. Lift out the cupcakes and place them on the rack to cool completely before frosting. They will keep, well wrapped, in the refrigerator for up to 5 days.

MOCHA-HAZELNUT CAKE WITH WHIPPED CREAM

Makes 8 to 10 servings (one double-layer 8-inch/20cm or 9-inch/23cm cake)

A light European-style nut torte (multilayered cake), with coffee and chocolate flavors in equal measure, this cake splits very well. →

I would cut it in as many thin layers as you're able to and fill with lightly sweetened whipped cream. If cutting each cake into many layers seems beyond your skills, just fill and top the two cakes with the cream.

📖 If you want a more pronounced hazelnut flavor, spread the hazelnut flour on a baking sheet and toast in a 350°F/180°C oven for 2 to 4 minutes, until fragrant and lightly browned.

Unsalted butter, for the pans	Preheat the oven to 350°F/180°C. Butter the sides of two 8-inch/20cm or 9-inch/23cm cake pans and line the bottoms with parchment paper cut to fit exactly.
$\frac{1}{2}$ cup/120ml very strong brewed coffee $\frac{1}{2}$ cup/100g granulated sugar	Combine the coffee and sugar in a small saucepan over medium heat, stir until the sugar dissolves, and then remove from the heat.
8 oz/225g chocolate (70 percent cacao or higher), chopped	Add the chocolate to the coffee mixture and stir until it has melted and is well incorporated.
$\frac{3}{4}$ cup/165g unsalted butter, at room temperature 8 large eggs, separated	In a large bowl, beat the butter with a wooden spoon until creamy. Add the yolks one at a time, beating well after each addition. Reserve the whites. Stir in the cooled chocolate mixture and set aside.
1 cup plus 2 Tbsp/140g hazelnut flour or finely ground hazelnuts $\frac{1}{4}$ cup/35g white or brown rice flour $\frac{1}{2}$ cup/40g cocoa powder	Combine the hazelnut flour, white or brown rice flour, and cocoa powder in another bowl and mix well.
$\frac{1}{2}$ tsp sea salt $\frac{1}{2}$ cup/100g granulated sugar	Using a handheld mixer or a stand mixer fitted with the whisk attachment, whip the reserved egg whites and salt until frothy. Gradually add the sugar and continue whipping until the mixture holds firm peaks. Sift the flour mixture over the whites and gently fold in with a rubber spatula to incorporate without deflating too much. Mix about one-quarter of the whites into the chocolate mixture and then fold the chocolate mixture into the rest of the whites.

Pour the cake batter into the pans. Bake until the tops spring back when lightly touched or a cake tester inserted in the center comes out with a few crumbs clinging to it, 25 to 35 minutes, depending on the size of the pans.

Let cool in the pans on a wire rack for 10 minutes. To unmold, run a butter knife around the sides of each pan to loosen. Then invert the cakes, lift off the pans, and peel away the parchment. Turn the cakes right-side up and let cool completely on the rack. If making ahead, the cooled cakes can be stored, tightly wrapped, at room temperature for up to 4 days.

1 cup/240ml
heavy cream

2 Tbsp confectioners'
sugar (optional)

To make the lightly sweetened whipped cream filling and topping, use a handheld mixer or a stand mixer fitted with the whisk attachment to whip the cream and sugar to soft peaks.

Transfer one cake layer to a serving plate. Spread about one-third of the whipped cream evenly over the cake layer. Top with the second cake layer and then spread the remaining whipped cream over the top. Alternatively, using a knife with a long blade, split each cake layer into 2 to 4 equal thin layers, layering them on the serving plate with whipped cream between each layer. Serve immediately or store in the refrigerator until ready to serve.

The whipped cream–filled cake, covered, can be stored in the refrigerator for up to 2 days.

PAVLOVA WITH CITRUS AND STONE FRUIT

Makes 8 to 10 servings (one 9 by 12-inch/23 by 3 cm cake)

The Pavlova, a cake made entirely of soft peaks of meringue and topped with pastry cream, whipped cream, and bright fruit, is →

always beautiful and doesn't require chef-level skills. Simultaneously crunchy and soft, tart and sweet, it is a study in contrasts and reminds me of a painter's palette with yellows, oranges, and pinks dotting the white surface. The sweet crispness of meringue makes it a natural foil for the tart fruit, and the tart fruit a foil for the rich creams.

📖 As in any recipe that uses egg whites to create volume, make sure that the whites are at room temperature, or even slightly warm before whipping. The vinegar aids the process (as would adding $\frac{1}{2}$ tsp of cream of tartar) of denaturing the eggs' protein, which creates more volume.

📖 The meringue can be made the morning of the day you plan to serve the Pavlova because the dessert should be assembled in just a few minutes before serving to keep its crisp exterior from softening when topped with the pastry cream.

5 large eggs, separated $\frac{1}{2}$ tsp sea salt 1 cup/200g sugar	Line an 13 by 18-inch/33 by 46cm baking sheet with parchment paper. Preheat the oven to 200°F/95°C. Using a handheld mixer or a stand mixer fitted with the whisk attachment, whip the egg whites and salt until frothy. Reserve the egg yolks for the pastry cream.
$\frac{1}{2}$ tsp distilled white vinegar or white wine vinegar	Decrease the mixing speed to medium and slowly add the sugar to the egg whites, streaming it down the side of the bowl. Add the vinegar. Increase the speed to high and whip until very thick and glossy, about 6 minutes.
2 Tbsp cornstarch or tapioca flour/starch	Turn off the mixer and sift the cornstarch or tapioca flour/starch over the surface of the egg white–sugar mixture. Using a large rubber spatula, fold in the starch until well incorporated.
	Turn the meringue out onto the prepared baking sheet and spread to approximately a 9 by 12-inch/ 23 by 30cm rectangle. Bake for $1\frac{1}{2}$ hours, until the outside is dry; the inside will remain soft. Set the pan on a cooling rack, or leave in the oven with the oven turned off, until the meringue is completely cool, at least 1 hour. If making the meringue more →

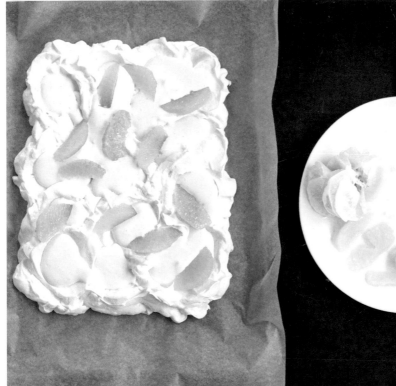

than a couple of hours ahead, when it is completely cool, wrap it tightly in plastic wrap to prevent it from absorbing moisture from the air before you are ready to assemble the Pavlova.

$1\frac{3}{4}$ cups/415ml whole milk

$\frac{1}{2}$ cup/100g granulated sugar

$\frac{1}{4}$ cup/30g cornstarch or tapioca flour/starch

Pinch of sea salt

$\frac{1}{2}$ tsp vanilla extract

$\frac{1}{4}$ cup/55g unsalted butter, cut into small pieces

To make the pastry cream, in a saucepan, warm the milk over low heat just until before it simmers. In a separate bowl, whisk together the sugar, cornstarch or tapioca flour/starch, and salt. Whisk the reserved egg yolks into the dry ingredients to form a paste. While stirring, add a few tablespoons of milk to the egg mixture, repeating until half of the milk has been stirred in. Return the mixture to the saucepan whisking over medium heat and cook until it thickens to a custard consistency, about 5 minutes. Don't let the mixture come to a full boil; you should see just a few bubbles. Remove the custard from the heat and stir in the vanilla and butter. Strain the custard through a fine-mesh strainer into a bowl. Cover with plastic wrap, pressing it down on the surface to create a seal so the pastry cream doesn't develop a skin as it cools. Transfer the pastry cream to the refrigerator to cool completely, about 2 hours. The pastry cream keeps in the refrigerator for up to 3 days.

1 grapefruit

1 nectarine

1 plum

For the grapefruit, cut a thin slice off the top and bottom (the stem and blossom end). Stand the grapefruit on one flat end on a cutting board. Using a very sharp paring knife, cut from top to bottom along the contour of the fruit, cutting away the peel and white pith and rotating the fruit as you go. Hold the remaining fruit in your hand one at a time and carefully slice between the membranes to release the segments. Pit and thinly slice the nectarine and plum.

Lightly sweetened whipped cream (see page 319)

$\frac{1}{4}$ cup/30g confectioners' sugar

1 tsp fennel pollen (optional)

Transfer the baked meringue to a large serving platter or board. Spoon the pastry cream over the meringue, spreading to distribute evenly. Drop drifts of whipped cream over the top of the pastry cream. Distribute the grapefruit sections over the top of the whipped cream. Dust the meringue with the →

confectioners' sugar. Distribute the nectarine and plum slices over the top of the grapefruit. Sprinkle the fennel pollen over the top. Cut into squares and serve immediately.

BLUEBERRY COBBLER WITH CORNMEAL BUTTERMILK BISCUIT TOPPING

Makes 8 servings (one 2-qt/2L baking dish)

During my East Coast childhood, few fruits signified summer as vividly as blueberries, which grew in my mother's garden alongside all of her other varieties of berries and fruit trees. The same could be said of blackberries, although those were so common growing wild all over the place that they were almost invisible. Unlike pie, cobbler offers the dual aspect of a crust on top and steamed dumplings in fruit juice on the bottom, where cold ice cream melts into swirls of hot fruit juices. There were never enough blueberries. After saving them up in the freezer, we'd make a pie or, most often, a cobbler. Cherries, sour or not, would be a very good substitution without making any adjustment to the sweetener or thickener in this recipe. Any other plump berries, such as huckleberries, blackberries, or strawberries (with or without rhubarb), would also make a fine substitute.

📖 It's important to let the batter rest while preparing the fruit. The interaction of the baking powder and acid in the buttermilk aerates the dough, and as the rice flour absorbs liquid, it thickens in a few minutes' time. It is because non-wheat flours vary in absorbency that one-to-one replacement of wheat flours often does not work. →

6 Tbsp/60g white
rice flour

6 Tbsp/60g brown
rice flour

6 Tbsp/60g cornmeal

3 Tbsp/25g almond flour

2 Tbsp arrowroot starch

$\frac{1}{2}$ cup/60g oat flour

$1\frac{1}{4}$ tsp baking soda

$\frac{1}{2}$ tsp sea salt

$\frac{1}{4}$ tsp ground cinnamon

Place a baking stone, if you have one, on the bottom of the oven and set a piece of aluminum foil on top of it to catch any drips. Preheat the oven to 375°F/190°C. Combine white and brown rice flours, cornmeal, almond flour, arrowroot starch, oat flour, baking powder, salt, and cinnamon in a large bowl and mix well.

5 Tbsp/75g unsalted
butter, melted

$\frac{1}{2}$ cup/120ml
buttermilk or kefir

2 large eggs

$\frac{1}{2}$ cup/100g
granulated sugar

In another bowl, whisk together the butter, buttermilk or kefir, eggs, and sugar. Add to the flour mixture, stirring just until incorporated. Set the mixture aside to rest undisturbed while you put together the filling.

6 cups/840g fresh
or thawed, frozen
blueberries

In a 2-qt/2L baking dish, gently mash half of the blueberries to release their juices.

2 Tbsp granulated sugar

2 Tbsp plus 2 tsp arrow-
root starch, tapioca
flour/starch, or quick-
cooking tapioca pearls

Finely grated zest and
juice of 1 lemon

Add the sugar, arrowroot starch or tapioca flour/ starch or quick-cooking tapioca pearls, and lemon zest and juice to the blueberries. Mix well.

2 to 3 Tbsp large-
crystal sugar or
granulated sugar

Without mixing or deflating the cornmeal batter, spoon it over the blueberry mixture. Sprinkle the sugar evenly over the top. Place the cobbler on the bottom rack of the oven or on the preheated stone placed on the bottom of the oven and bake until the cornmeal biscuit is golden brown and a cake tester inserted in the center of the biscuit comes out clean, about 45 minutes. The fruit should be bubbling around the edges. If the top is browning too fast, cover with aluminum foil.

Let the cobbler cool in the dish on a wire rack for a few minutes before serving.

APPLE PIE

Makes 8 to 10 servings (one 10-inch/25cm pie)

I use a combination of whichever quality apples are at the market so that the filling will have a range of sweetness and texture. I precook the apples so that they cook down before they go in the piecrust, which ensures there's little space between the filling and top crust of the finished pie. As I sauté the apples, I reduce the juices to a near caramel. This concentrates the flavor and means less starch is needed. I've paired the filling with the Cream Cheese Dough (page 36), which has a slight tang from the cream cheese and goes very well with apples.

Cream Cheese Dough (page 36), rolled out to two 12-inch/30cm circles.	Place a baking stone, if you have one, on the bottom of the oven and set a piece of aluminum foil on top of it to catch any drips. Preheat the oven to 425°F/220°C. Drape one dough circle across a 10-inch/25cm pie plate and place in the refrigerator to chill. Place the other dough circle on a large plate and place in the refrigerator to chill while you prepare the filling.
$\frac{1}{4}$ cup/60g unsalted butter 4 lb/1.8kg Granny Smith and Pink Lady apples, peeled, cored, and sliced	Melt the butter in a Dutch oven or similar heavy-bottomed pot set over medium-high heat. Add the apples and stir to coat them in the butter.
$\frac{1}{2}$ cup firmly packed/90g brown sugar $\frac{1}{8}$ tsp sea salt Finely grated zest and juice of 1 lemon	Add the brown sugar, salt, and lemon zest and juice to the apples. Increase the heat to high and cook, stirring often with a wooden spoon, for 1 minute. Cover the pot, decrease the heat to low, and cook for 10 to 15 minutes, until the apples have softened and released their juices.
	Using a slotted spoon, transfer the apples to a bowl, leaving their juices behind in the pot. Increase the heat to high and cook the juices until they have reduced in volume and are very thick, almost like caramel, about 5 minutes. Pour the cooked juices into the bowl with the apples. →

1½ tsp ground cinnamon

½ tsp freshly
grated nutmeg

1 Tbsp tapioca flour/
starch, arrowroot flour,
or cornstarch

Add the cinnamon, nutmeg, and tapioca flour/starch
or arrowroot flour or cornstarch to the apple filling
and mix well. Let the filling cool to room temperature.

Remove the pie plate with the bottom crust from the
refrigerator and fill with the cooled apple mixture.
Transfer the top dough circle from the plate to the
pie and place it over the apples, pressing the edges
of the dough circles together and then crimping them
with a fork or with your fingers. Cut small, decorative
steam vents in the center of the top dough circle.
Place the assembled pie in the freezer to chill for 5 to
10 minutes, until the outer crust is firm.

1 large egg

Pinch of sea salt

Large-crystal sugar or
granulated sugar

Whisk together the egg and salt. Remove the pie
from the freezer and brush the egg wash across the
top crust. Sprinkle the top crust with the sugar.

Bake the pie directly on the bottom of the oven for
35 minutes. Decrease the oven temperature to 375°F/
190°C, move the pie to the center rack, and bake
for another 30 to 40 minutes, until the juices are
bubbling slowly up through the steam vents and the
crust is dark golden brown. If the crust is browning
too quickly, place aluminum foil over the top of
the pie. Remove the pie from the oven and let cool
on a wire rack for at least 3 hours before serving.

The pie can be stored at room temperature for up
to 2 days and in the refrigerator for up to 5 days.

BOYSENBERRY PIE

Makes 8 to 10 servings (one 10-inch/25cm pie)

If you are lucky and come across enough boysenberries to make a pie, do it. Floral and sweet, boysenberries were once quite popular, especially in California, where they were first bred, but their fragility in traveling has made them a niche crop and a regional treat come summertime. Because the boysenberry is an ingenious cross between a raspberry and three native blackberry species, if you cannot find boysenberries, I'd recommend using either blackberry, olallieberry, or loganberry (another blackberry-raspberry cross) in its place. The purple juice that the pie gives off during baking is majestically fragrant and exquisitely dark. It's important that the pie rests once out of the oven, as the juice needs time to set.

Cream Cheese Dough (page 36), rolled out to two 12-inch/30cm circles.

Place a baking stone, if you have one, on the bottom of the oven and set a piece of aluminum foil on top of the stone to catch any drips. Preheat the oven to 400°F/200°C. Drape one dough circle across a 10-in/25cm pie plate and place in the refrigerator to chill while you prepare the filling. Place the other dough circle on a large plate and place in the refrigerator to chill until firm, about 10 minutes.

3 lb/1.4kg boysenberries

3 Tbsp/30g quick-cooking (instant) tapioca

$\frac{1}{2}$ cup/100g granulated sugar

$\frac{1}{8}$ tsp sea salt

Combine the boysenberries, tapioca, sugar, and salt in a large bowl and lightly mash the fruit to release the juices.

Remove the pie plate with the bottom crust from the refrigerator. Fill the pie shell with the boysenberry mixture. Transfer the top dough circle from the plate to the pie and place it over the fruit, pressing the edges of the dough circles together and then crimping them with a fork or with your fingers. Cut out small, decorative steam vents in the center of the top dough circle. Place the assembled pie in the freezer to chill for 5 to 10 minutes, until the outer crust is firm. →

1 large egg

Pinch of sea salt

Large-crystal sugar
or granulated sugar

Whisk together the egg and salt. Remove the pie from the freezer and brush the egg wash across the top crust. Sprinkle the top crust with the sugar.

Bake the pie directly on the bottom of the oven for 35 minutes. Lower the oven temperature to 375°F/190°C, move the pie to the center rack, and bake for another 30 to 40 minutes, until the berry juices are bubbling slowly up through the steam vents and the crust is dark golden brown. It's very important that the filling bubbles; only then will the tapioca be able to gel and thicken the berry juices. If the crust is browning too quickly, place aluminum foil over the top of the pie. Set on a cooling rack to cool at least 3 hours and up to overnight before serving.

The pie can be stored at room temperature for up to 2 days and in the refrigerator for up to 5 days.

CHERRY-FRANGIPANE GALETTE

Makes 6 servings (one 9-inch/23cm galette)

I like galettes for the same reason I like any handmade, free-form item: It shows the hand of the maker. Adding frangipane flavors the fruit and absorbs the juices; frangipane also goes exceptionally well with all stone fruit. Cooking this on the bottom of the oven on top of a baking stone ensures a crisp bottom crust.

$\frac{1}{2}$ batch Cream Cheese Dough (page 36), rolled out to a 10-inch/25cm circle approximately $\frac{1}{8}$ inch/3mm thick

Line a baking sheet with parchment paper. Place the dough circle on the prepared baking sheet, cover, and chill in the refrigerator until firm, about 10 minutes.

$\frac{1}{4}$ cup plus 2 tsp/60g
granulated sugar

$\frac{1}{4}$ cup/55g unsalted
butter, at room
temperature

Meanwhile, prepare the frangipane: In the bowl of a
stand mixer fitted with the paddle attachment, beat
the sugar and butter at medium speed until creamy,
about 3 minutes.

1 large egg

$\frac{1}{2}$ tsp almond extract

Add the egg and almond extract to the butter
mixture and mix well. Stop the machine and, using
a rubber spatula, scrape down the sides and bottom
of the bowl.

$\frac{1}{2}$ cup/60g almond flour

2 tsp tapioca
flour/starch

$\frac{1}{4}$ tsp sea salt

Add the almond flour, tapioca flour/starch, and
salt to the butter mixture and beat until fully
incorporated. (If not using the frangipane right
away, store, covered, in the refrigerator for up to
1 week.)

Remove the dough from the refrigerator and spread
the frangipane in the center of the dough circle,
leaving a 2-inch/5cm border.

1 lb/455g fresh or frozen
cherries, pitted

2 to 3 Tbsp/45g
granulated sugar or
brown sugar

Taste the cherries for sweetness to determine
how much sugar you want to use to sweeten them.
Scatter the cherries evenly over the frangipane
and then sprinkle with the sugar.

Fold in the sides of the dough to cover the cherries
partially, making sure not to create any valleys
where the fruit juice can run out. Chill until firm,
about 15 minutes.

While the galette chills, preheat the oven to
425°F/220°C. If you have a baking stone, set it on
the bottom of the oven to preheat.

1 large egg

Pinch of sea salt

1 Tbsp large-crystal
sugar or granulated sugar

Whisk together the egg and salt. Brush the egg
wash over the pastry edges and then sprinkle the
galette with the sugar. →

Bake the galette on the baking stone or directly on the bottom of the oven for 20 minutes. Lower the oven temperature to 375°F/190°C, move the baking sheet to the center rack of the oven, and continue baking until the pastry has a nice, dark golden brown color and the fruit is bubbling, 25 to 30 minutes.

Lightly sweetened whipped cream (see page 319), cold, or vanilla ice cream, for garnish

Remove from the oven and serve hot, or let cool on a wire rack. Serve warm or at room temperature with a spoonful of whipped cream or a small scoop of ice cream.

The galette can be stored at room temperature for up to 2 days and in the refrigerator for up to 5 days.

CHAMPAGNE GELÉE WITH STRAWBERRIES

Makes 4 to 6 servings (3 cups/720g gelée)

Beautifully simple, wine gelée relies on a single ingredient—champagne—for its flavor. The Champagne, lightly sweetened and just barely set, is a simple, refreshing dessert and somehow very sophisticated, which, compared to most gelatin desserts, makes it an anomaly. Serve it with just berries or add a touch of whipped cream as well. When cut and scooped into serving dishes, as it is in this recipe, it looks like a bowl of shimmering diamonds. It is divine on the hottest of days, though a word of caution: the alcohol remains—a fact easily forgotten when devouring it.

$\frac{1}{4}$ cup/60ml Champagne, Prosecco, or Cava

$4\frac{1}{2}$ tsp powdered unflavored gelatin

Pour the Champagne into a small saucepan and sprinkle the gelatin evenly over the top to bloom. (It will become soft and absorb the liquid.) Heat the mixture over low heat, stirring constantly, until the gelatin dissolves completely. →

6 Tbsp/90g granulated sugar $2\frac{3}{4}$ cups/650ml Champagne, Prosecco, or Cava	In a large bowl, mix the sugar into the Champagne. It will foam, but the bubbles will subside after a minute. Stir in the gelatin mixture, making sure it is evenly incorporated. Pour into a square or rectangular container so that the liquid is about 1 to 2 inches/2.5 to 5cm deep. Cover and chill in the refrigerator until set, about 1 hour. The longer it chills, the more set it will become.
12 oz/240g strawberries 2 tsp granulated sugar	Just before serving, hull and slice the strawberries. Toss with the sugar and let macerate for a few minutes. The sugar will pull some juice out of the berries. Toss a few times to coat in the juices.
	Once the gelée is set, use a knife to cut the gelée in a crosshatch pattern in order to create small cubes. Arrange the cubes in dessert glasses or small serving bowls. Top with the strawberries and serve.

Lillet and Orange Gelée: In place of the Champagne, use a combination of 1 cup/240ml freshly squeezed orange juice that has been strained through a coffee filter and 1 cup/240ml Lillet Blanc. Bloom $1\frac{1}{4}$ tsp of gelatin in $\frac{1}{4}$ cup/60ml of the orange juice-Lillet mixture. Then add 4 tsp granulated sugar to the remaining liquid and proceed as directed in the recipe.

Campari and Raspberry Gelée: In place of the Champagne, make a raspberry puree by blending $\frac{3}{4}$ cup/90g fresh raspberries with $\frac{1}{2}$ cup/120ml water and then straining through a fine-mesh strainer. Add $\frac{3}{4}$ cup/180ml Campari to the raspberry puree for a total liquid volume of $1\frac{1}{4}$ cups/300ml. If you have less, add water to make up the difference. Bloom $1\frac{1}{4}$ tsp of gelatin in $\frac{1}{4}$ cup/60ml of the Campari-raspberry mixture. Then add 4 tsp granulated sugar to the remaining liquid and proceed as directed in the recipe.

DARK CHOCOLATE AND TOASTED ALMOND SEMIFREDDO

Makes 10 servings

Thanks to the semifreddo, exceptional frozen dessert can be made at home without an ice cream machine. Semifreddo, meaning "half frozen," is an Italian dessert made from cream, eggs, and a flavoring. Closely related to the French parfait, it contains only cream. Because of its low moisture content, as compared to ice cream, it freezes to the smoothest consistency with fewer ice crystals, which is also due to the fact that air is whipped into two components—the cream as well as the eggs—and folded together. This is my back-pocket frozen dessert; it can be put together quickly, even days ahead, and held in reserve until you're ready to serve.

📖 If you would like to slice the semifreddo, line a 9 by 5-inch/23 by 13cm loaf pan with plastic wrap. If you plan on scooping the semifreddo, there is no need to line the pan.

$\frac{1}{2}$ cup/100g granulated sugar 3 large eggs 2 large egg yolks Pinch of sea salt	In a heatproof bowl set over a pan of simmering water, whisk the sugar, whole eggs, egg yolks, and salt until very pale and thick, 4 to 6 minutes. Remove from the heat.
2 cups/480ml heavy cream	In the bowl of a stand mixer fitted with a whisk attachment, beat the cream to soft peaks. Set aside $\frac{2}{3}$ cup/160ml of the whipped cream for serving; store the whipped cream, covered, in the refrigerator until needed.
8 oz/225g semisweet chocolate (63 percent cacao or higher), melted	Using a rubber spatula, fold the chocolate into the egg mixture and then quickly but gently fold in the whipped cream, stopping when the cream is about three-quarters of the way mixed in. →

¾ cup/90g toasted
and coarsely
chopped almonds

Add the almonds to the chocolate mixture and
quickly but gently fold until completely incorporated.
Transfer the mixture to the prepared pan, cover, and
freeze for at least 4 hours.

To slice the semifreddo, turn it out onto a serving
platter and peel off the plastic wrap. (You can do this
step ahead of time and store, covered, in the freezer
until you are ready to serve.) Slice and serve with
a dollop of the reserved chilled whipped cream.

CHOCOLATE POTS DE CRÈME

Makes 4 servings (four 6-oz/175ml ramekins)

Pot de crème is a dessert to make when you want an elegant end
to a meal. Lighter and silkier than a pudding, it is like an omelet in
that it relies almost more on the cook's touch than the ingredients
themselves. This is because, like many egg dishes or a flan, carry-over
cooking is inevitable, so the baker needs to remove the pot de crème
from the oven just before it is cooked through. The edges should be
firm, while the center should still be wobbly. If you are worried that
you're taking it out too early, have confidence that the chocolate will
assist in firming up the custard as it cools.

Preheat the oven to 300°F/150°C. Choose a baking
pan for a water bath large enough to accommodate
four 6-oz/175ml ramekins without touching and
deep enough to hold water that will reach three-
quarters of the way up the sides of the ramekins
when added. Pour enough water into the pan to
reach about halfway up the sides of the ramekins,
and place the pan in the oven while it is heating.

¾ cup/180ml heavy cream	Combine the cream, milk, sugar, and salt in a small saucepan set over medium heat. Stir with a wooden spoon until the sugar has dissolved and then remove from the heat.
¾ cup/180ml whole milk	
2 Tbsp granulated sugar	
Pinch of sea salt	
4 large egg yolks	In a large bowl, whisk the egg yolks to break them up. Pour a little of the warmed milk into the yolks, whisking to incorporate, and then gradually whisk in all of the milk mixture.
3 oz/85g bittersweet chocolate, melted	Pour a little of the melted chocolate into the milk-yolk mixture, whisking to incorporate, then gradually whisk in all of the chocolate. Divide among the ramekins and set the ramekins inside the larger pan in the oven. Pour more water into the pan if necessary to reach three-quarters of the way up the sides of the ramekins. Bake until only the center of each pot de crème is still wobbly, about 45 minutes. The pots de crème will continue to cook after they are removed from the oven. Let cool, and then refrigerate to chill, 2 to 3 hours. Serve chilled with a spoonful of the whipped cream.
Lightly sweetened whipped cream (see page 319), for garnish	
	Store, covered, in the refrigerator for up to 4 days.

KABOCHA CUSTARD

Makes 6 servings (six 6-oz/175ml ramekins)

I know I'm not alone in my preference for pumpkin pie's custard over its crust. This recipe came about to indulge my love of all things pudding and my inability to eat most crusts. In this recipe, I wanted to make a custard that pays homage to the classic pumpkin pie filling but is slightly more rich. Warmed with spices, this dessert is a beautiful orange-gold and very creamy; you might find yourself making this not just for holidays but for many winter evenings. →

1 small kabocha squash, cut into 8 pieces	Preheat the oven to 375°F/190°C. Place the kabocha and oil in a bowl and toss to coat the squash well. Transfer to a baking sheet and roast in the oven for 45 minutes, until the tip of a knife is easily inserted. Cool on the sheet. Remove the skin and process the flesh in a food processor or blender until smooth.
2 tsp olive oil	

Decrease the oven to 350°F/180°C. Choose a baking pan for a water bath large enough to accommodate six 6-oz/175ml ramekins without touching and deep enough to hold water that will reach three-quarters of the way up the sides of the ramekins when added. Pour enough water into the pan to reach about halfway up the sides of the ramekins and place the pan in the oven while it is heating.

1 large egg	Whisk together the whole egg, egg yolks, and salt in a large bowl.
3 large egg yolks	
Pinch of sea salt	

1 cup/240ml whole milk	Combine the milk and granulated and brown sugars in a small saucepan. Warm over medium heat, stirring until the sugar has dissolved.
$\frac{1}{4}$ cup/50g granulated sugar	
2 Tbsp brown sugar	

While whisking the egg mixture, add a ladleful of the warm milk mixture and whisk to incorporate. Gradually add the remaining milk mixture in a slow, steady stream, whisking continuously.

1 cup/240ml heavy cream	Set a fine-mesh strainer over a separate large bowl. Add the cream, squash puree, vanilla, cinnamon, nutmeg, and allspice to the egg-milk mixture and whisk until fully combined. Pass the mixture through the fine-mesh strainer, using a rubber spatula to scrape and press along the bottom of the strainer in order to push the squash puree through the strainer and into the bowl.
$\frac{3}{4}$ cup/170g kabocha puree (from the first step)	
1 tsp vanilla extract	
1 tsp ground cinnamon	
$\frac{1}{4}$ tsp freshly grated nutmeg	
Pinch of ground allspice	

Divide the custard among six 6-oz/175ml ramekins and set the ramekins inside the larger pan in the oven. Pour more water into the pan if necessary to reach three-quarters of the way up the sides of the ramekins. Bake until only the center of each pudding is still wobbly, 40 to 50 minutes. The custards will continue to cook slightly after they are removed from the oven.

Serve warm with a dollop of the whipped cream.

Lightly sweetened whipped cream (see page 319), cold, for garnish

Store the custard, covered, in the refrigerator for up to 3 days.

FLAN

Makes 6 servings (one 2-qt/2L soufflé dish)

What originated in France as crème caramel became flan when it crossed the Spanish border. It became one of Spain's famed desserts, later spreading to Mexico and much of Latin America, acquiring the habit of sweetened condensed milk along the way. Wherever there has been Spanish or Portuguese colonial influence (Chile, the Philippines, and coastal towns in India, such as Goa), there exists some version of a flan often enhanced with dulce de leche, additional egg yolks, or flavorings such as coconut. In this recipe, I wanted to make the simplest of custard true to its original form, warmed with vanilla and ethereal in texture. I like a flan that barely holds its shape when turned out of the mold and has a lot of jiggle, yielding to the slightest pressure of a spoon.

📖 The contrast of dark caramel against delicate custard makes this dessert remarkable. When making the caramel, cook the sauce until it becomes a deep shade of mahogany. Watch constantly, as the process goes quickly. The sauce may even smoke a little, but take it as far as you are comfortable, keeping in mind that once you take if off the heat its color will continue to deepen. Use a stainless steel or enamel pot (as opposed to cast iron) so that you can see →

the caramel color. And if you let it get too dark, don't fret. This sauce is simple in ingredients but rich in subtlety and its success comes from practice, so just try again.

$\frac{1}{2}$ cup/100g granulated sugar 1 tsp lemon juice $\frac{1}{4}$ cup/60ml water	Preheat the oven to 350°F/180°C. Choose a baking pan for a water bath large enough to accommodate a 2-qt/2L soufflé dish without touching and deep enough to hold water that will reach three-quarters of the way up the sides of the dish when added. Pour enough water into the pan to reach about halfway up the sides of the dish and place the pan in the oven while it is heating.
	Combine the sugar, lemon juice, and water in a small saucepan and place over medium heat. Bring to a boil, stirring with a wooden spoon to dissolve the sugar. Cook, without stirring, until the caramel turns dark amber, 5 to 8 minutes. Remove from the heat and immediately pour into the soufflé dish, quickly swirling the dish to coat the bottom evenly.
3 cups/720ml whole milk 6 Tbsp/90g granulated sugar	In a small saucepan, heat the milk and sugar to almost boiling, stirring with a wooden spoon to dissolve the sugar.
3 large eggs $\frac{1}{8}$ tsp sea salt 1 tsp vanilla extract	In a large bowl, whisk together the eggs and salt. While whisking, slowly ladle about one-third of the hot milk into the whisked eggs and then gradually whisk in the remaining milk. Stir in the vanilla.
	Set a fine-mesh strainer over the soufflé dish. Pour the custard through the strainer into the soufflé dish and set the dish inside the larger pan in the oven. Pour more water into the pan if necessary to reach three-quarters of the way up the sides of the soufflé dish. Bake until only the center of the flan is still wobbly, 45 to 55 minutes. It will continue to cook after it is removed from the oven. Let cool or chill in the refrigerator. Place a serving plate over the baking dish and invert onto the plate. Serve at room temperature or chilled.
	Store, covered, in the refrigerator for up to 3 days.

LEMON PUDDING CAKE

Makes 6 servings (one 2-qt/2L soufflé dish or six 6-oz/175ml ramekins)

If you've never made a pudding cake, start with this one. This is a ridiculously easy recipe, especially when you consider how tasty it is. (I've even heard the word "magic" uttered while describing it.) When whipped egg whites are folded into such a wet batter, a natural separation occurs in the baking process, resulting in two tiers, a pudding on the bottom and the most tender and fluffy cake on top. Just out of the oven, at room temperature or chilled, the play of textures is exciting and comforting. All sorts of flavors are possible, but tangy lemon is one I return to again and again. The only thing to add is a spoonful of unsweetened whipped cream.

Unsalted butter,
for the ramekins

Preheat the oven to 325°F/165°C. Choose a baking pan for a water bath large enough to accommodate a 2-qt/2L soufflé dish or six 6-oz/175ml ramekins without touching and deep enough to hold water that will reach three-quarters of the way up the sides of the dish or ramekins when added. Pour enough water into the pan to reach about halfway up the sides of the dish, and place the pan in the oven while it is heating. Butter the bottom and sides of the soufflé dish or the ramekins.

$\frac{3}{4}$ cup/150g
granulated sugar

2 Tbsp white rice flour

2 Tbsp arrowroot flour

2 Tbsp oat flour

$\frac{1}{8}$ tsp sea salt

In a large bowl, using a wooden spoon, stir together the sugar, white rice flour, and arrowroot flour, oat flour, and salt and make a well in the center.

---

4 large eggs, separated

$1\frac{1}{2}$ cups/360ml whole
milk or buttermilk

$1\frac{1}{2}$ tsp finely grated
lemon zest

$\frac{1}{2}$ cup plus 2 Tbsp/150ml
lemon juice

In another bowl, stir together the egg yolks, milk, and lemon zest and juice, and then pour into the well of the dry ingredients and mix to incorporate. Reserve the egg whites.

¼ cup/50g granulated sugar	Using a handheld mixer, whip the reserved egg whites and sugar together until they hold stiff peaks. Using a rubber spatula, fold about one-half of the beaten whites into the buttermilk batter and then fold in the second half.
	Transfer the batter to the prepared dish or ramekins and set the dish inside the larger pan in the oven. Pour more water into the pan if necessary to reach three-quarters of the way up the sides of the soufflé dish or ramekins. Bake for 25 to 35 minutes, until lightly browned and the top springs back when touched.
Confectioners' sugar, for dusting	The cake can be served straight out of the oven, at room temperature, or chilled. Just before serving, dust the top surface with the confectioners' sugar. This cake should be eaten the same day it is made.

PERSIMMON PUDDING

Makes 8 to 10 servings (one 2-qt/2L pudding)

I first had this pudding when Karen Waikiki, a friend and talented chef in Northern California, made it for us one December evening. There are persimmon trees in many backyards in California, and every store here carries the two main varieties in the fall and winter: Fuyu persimmons, characterized by their flat bottoms and squat shape which are eaten crisp like an apple, and Hachiya persimmons, the larger variety, which are elongated and oval and are the ones used for this recipe. The Hachiya is astringent when unripe, so be sure that it is so soft that it nearly bursts open, like an overripe tomato. They are usually purchased firm and will ripen when left on a windowsill, anywhere from one to three weeks, depending on when it was picked. If you have perfectly ripe persimmons on hand but want to make the dessert in a couple of weeks, cut the stem off and freeze the fruit (the skin may be used as well; no need to discard it) and use when ready. →

I should confess that every time I make this recipe I hold my breath because it only unmolds perfectly about half of the time and is vexing to me every holiday. For this reason, if you want a perfectly unmolded, sure-thing dessert, steam the pudding in a metal bowl instead of the pudding mold. Just fit foil on top, crimping to create as good a seal as you can.

📖 The lemon might seem odd here, but the acid provides a jump start for the baking soda's leavening and adds a little tang to cut the persimmons' sugary flavor.

	Preheat the oven to 350°F/180°C. Grease a 2-qt/2L steam pudding mold. Choose a saucepan for a water bath large enough to accommodate the pudding mold without touching and deep enough to hold water that will reach three-quarters of the way up the sides of the mold when added. Pour enough water into the saucepan to reach about halfway up the sides of the mold and place the pan in the oven while it is heating.
2 cups/500g persimmon pulp (from about 4 squishy-soft Hachiya persimmons) 2 tsp baking soda	In a medium bowl, using a wooden spoon, stir together the persimmon and baking soda.
$\frac{1}{2}$ cup/110g unsalted butter, at room temperature $1\frac{1}{2}$ cups/300g granulated sugar	Using a stand mixer fitted with the paddle attachment, beat the butter and sugar together on medium-high speed until creamy and smooth, about 4 minutes.
2 large eggs	Add the eggs one at a time to the butter-sugar mixture, beating well after each addition. Stop the mixer and scrape down the sides of the bowl with a rubber spatula.
2 Tbsp lemon juice 1 Tbsp vanilla extract 2 Tbsp brandy	Add the lemon juice, vanilla, and brandy to the persimmon mixture, stir well, and then add to the egg mixture and beat on low speed to incorporate.

$\frac{1}{3}$ cup plus 1 Tbsp/50g tapioca flour/starch

$\frac{1}{3}$ cup plus 1 Tbsp/50g oat flour

$\frac{1}{4}$ cup plus 1 heaping Tbsp/50g brown rice flour

1 cup/140g raisins

1 $\frac{1}{2}$ cups/180g walnuts, toasted and coarsely chopped

1 tsp ground cinnamon

$\frac{1}{2}$ tsp sea salt

Combine the tapioca flour/starch, oat flour, rice flour, raisins, walnuts, cinnamon, and salt in a medium bowl and mix well. Stir the dry mixture into the batter.

Transfer the batter to the prepared mold, cover tightly with the lid, and set the mold inside the saucepan in the oven. Pour more water into the pan if necessary to reach three-quarters of the way up the sides of the mold. Bake for 2 $\frac{1}{2}$ hours. Let the pudding cool in the mold on a wire rack for 10 minutes before turning it out onto a serving platter.

Whipped cream (see lightly sweetened whipped cream, see page 319, minus the sugar), cold, for garnish

Serve the pudding hot with a dollop of the unsweetened whipped cream.

CATALONIAN RICE PUDDING

Makes 6 servings (one 2-qt/2L baking dish)

This recipe comes from Alen Ramos and Carolyn Nugent, two very talented pastry chefs who work with us and have traveled and worked extensively in kitchens around the world. They learned this recipe in Catalonia, from a small pastry shop in Rosas. It is the loveliest rice pudding I've ever had, like a golden-hued, vanilla-scented cloud. The original →

recipe doesn't use egg yolks—they are Alen and Carolyn's addition and closer to American rice puddings; try it the Catalonian way without egg yolks for a less rich version. I like keeping with regional tradition and original recipes so I include both methods here.

📖 Arborio rice varies greatly in starch content. If the pudding seems too thick add a splash of cream. If too thin, cook for 5 to 10 minutes more. The pudding will continue to thicken as it cools.

$\frac{3}{4}$ cup/150g Arborio rice

$\frac{2}{3}$ cup plus 2 Tbsp/160ml heavy cream

$3\frac{3}{4}$ cups/900ml whole milk

1 vanilla bean

Combine the rice, cream, and milk in a saucepan. Cut the vanilla bean in half lengthwise and, using the dull edge of your knife, scrape all the tiny black seeds into the pot. Add the scraped vanilla pod as well. Bring to a simmer over medium heat and cook until the rice is very soft and looks like it is almost bursting, about 25 minutes.

$\frac{1}{4}$ cup/50g sugar

$\frac{1}{4}$ tsp sea salt

Add the sugar and salt to the rice mixture and stir to incorporate. Remove the pot from the heat.

6 large egg yolks (optional)

$1\frac{1}{2}$ cups/200g mixed chopped fruit (optional)

Whisk the egg yolks in a small bowl. While stirring continuously, add about a small ladleful of yolks to the hot rice pudding. Once combined, stir the rest of the yolks into the pudding, mixing well to incorporate. Cook over medium heat for 2 minutes, stirring constanly to prevent the yolks from curdling. Transfer the rice pudding to a serving bowl and let cool to room temperature. Place in the refrigerator to chill until completely cold. Serve chilled with a spoonful of fruit on top.

Store, covered, in the refrigerator for up to 3 days.

Eggless Rice Pudding: To make this the Catalonian way, don't finish the recipe with egg yolks. Instead, stir $5\frac{1}{2}$ Tbsp/100g of Crème Fraiche (page 37, or store-bought) into the pudding at the end of cooking, stirring until warmed through and creamy. To serve, place a small handful of diced apricots in the bottom of each serving bowl, ladle in the pudding, and top with grated orange zest. Serve with madeleines (pages 288 and 290, or store-bought).

STICKY DATE PUDDING WITH HOT TOFFEE SAUCE

Makes 6 servings (one 9-inch/23cm pudding)

Though it originated as a steamed pudding, a classic English dessert similar to a jam-roly poly (also known as a dead man's arm, so named for the shirt sleeve it would be steamed in), I find it moist enough to forgo the steaming. This dessert, made sweet by the toffee sauce, yet not terribly sweet on its own, has a light texture punctuated by sweet bits of dates dotted throughout. The variety of date you use will alter the flavor. Medjool is a favorite of mine, but try others, such as Barhi or Deglet Noor.

📖 For the flour blend, cornstarch or arrowroot can replace the tapioca flour/starch with no effect on the final pudding.

2 cups/340g dates, pitted and coarsely chopped 2 cups/480ml water	Preheat the oven to 350°F/180°C. Butter the bottom and sides of a 9-in/23cm-baking pan with 2-in/5cm sides. In a medium saucepan, cook the dates in the water at a low simmer for 5 minutes.
1½ tsp baking soda	Add the baking soda to the saucepan, turn off the heat, and let sit for 20 minutes, or until cool.
¾ cup/90g almond flour ⅓ cup plus 1 Tbsp/50g tapioca flour/starch 1½ cups/180g oat flour ½ tsp baking powder ½ tsp ground cinnamon ½ tsp ground ginger ½ tsp sea salt	In a large bowl, combine the almond flour, tapioca flour/starch, oat flour, baking powder, cinnamon, ginger, and salt. →

6 Tbsp/85g unsalted butter, at room temperature

1 cup/200g granulated sugar

3 large eggs

In the bowl of a stand mixer fitted with the paddle attachment, beat the butter on medium-high speed until light and creamy, about 1 minute. Add the sugar and continue to beat until fluffy, about 1 more minute. Add the eggs one at a time, beating well after each addition. Stop the mixer and scrape down the sides of the bowl with a rubber spatula. With the mixer on low speed, add the flour mixture and the date mixture, beating just until combined. (Beating longer will yield an overmixed batter, which produces a dense pudding.) Pour the batter into the baking pan. Bake for 45 to 60 minutes, until a cake tester inserted in the center comes out clean. Let cool in the pan on a wire rack while you make the toffee sauce.

$\frac{3}{4}$ cup/165g unsalted butter, cut into pieces

$1\frac{1}{2}$ cups firmly packed/270g dark brown sugar

1 cup/240ml heavy cream

$\frac{1}{2}$ tsp vanilla extract

$\frac{1}{2}$ tsp sea salt

1 Tbsp lemon juice

To make the toffee sauce, combine the butter, brown sugar, cream, vanilla, salt, and lemon juice in a small saucepan. Bring to a boil and cook for 5 minutes. Remove from the heat.

Confectioners' sugar, for dusting

Just before serving, dust the top of the pudding with the confectioners' sugar. Cut the warm pudding into wedges and serve each topped with hot toffee sauce.

Hubbard Squash Sticky Date Pudding: Although not traditional, Hubbard squash adds a surprising element. Fold in 6 oz/170g of cooked Hubbard squash, cut into $\frac{1}{4}$-in/6mm cubes, into the creamed butter and egg mixture just before adding the flour. Bake as instructed.

CANDIED ORANGE PEEL

Makes 4 cups/600g

During the holidays when oranges are abundant, I like finding ways of using the peel as well as the flesh. If you've never candied your own citrus, a few steps are required, but the results are endlessly useful and so much better than store-bought versions. A little chopped candied peel added to scones, a pound cake, or to a ginger-molasses cookie (page 285) adds dimension and texture. When served after dinner, dipped in chocolate (or not), it makes a simple but stunning ending, reminiscent of a digestif's bittersweet notes. My rule of thumb in using the peel is that wherever the zest of orange or the texture of candied ginger would work, candied orange peel can't go wrong. It is a treat that will last for months, and the syrup is its own bonus: try adding a splash to sparkling water or to cocktails. You'll note that this is one of a few recipes in which I call for corn syrup. There are very few uses for corn syrup that I can think of where I don't look for a healthful substitute, but this is one exception. Corn syrup is an inverted syrup, whereby sucrose, or table sugar, is split into glucose and fructose. When these simpler component forms are created, a syrup is much less likely to crystalize. You may have experienced this when cooking sugar with water only to see it crystallize—but the addition of an acid such as lemon juice or cream of tartar will prevent this crystallization. In candying peel, if an invert sugar is not used, you will find after a week or two that the peel has turned gritty because it has recrystallized.

📖 The secret to moist candied peel is to keep some of the pith on. Some recipes advise you to take all of it off, but a small amount of it is necessary to hold the peel's softness while it is candying in the sugar syrup. Once cooked through, the pith and peel will together become translucent and seem to be one pliable, tender piece.

---

2 cups/400g granulated sugar

2 cups/480ml water

$\frac{1}{4}$ cup/80g corn syrup

Combine the sugar, water, and corn syrup in a medium saucepan set over medium heat. Stir until the sugar has dissolved and then remove from the heat. →

4 Valencia or navel
oranges

Trim the ends of the oranges. Using a small knife, score the orange peel into quarters, pressing the knife through the peel but not cutting into the fruit. Peel off the rind. If the white pith stuck to the rind is very thick, trim some off. However, make sure to leave a small amount of the pith on, since the candied peel will be tough if there isn't enough left on. Cut the peel into $\frac{1}{4}$-in/6mm-wide strips.

Place the strips in a medium saucepan and cover with plenty of water. Bring to a simmer over medium-low heat, cook for 2 minutes, and drain. Repeat twice more, refilling the pot with fresh water each time. After the third draining, with a slotted spoon, transfer the peel to the pot with the sugar syrup. Cook at a gentle simmer over low heat until translucent, 1 to 1$\frac{1}{2}$ hours, depending on how thick the pieces are. If the water is evaporating too quickly and the peel is no longer submerged, pour in enough water to return to the original level.

When the orange peels are translucent, increase the heat to medium and cook the syrup until the temperature reaches 230°F/110°C on a candy thermometer. Using a slotted spoon, transfer the candied peel to a wire rack set over a plate or parchment paper to catch any drips. (Once cool, store the orange syrup in a jar with a tight-fitting lid in the refrigerator for up to 3 months.)

1 cup/200g granulated
sugar (optional)

While the candied peels are still sticky, you can toss them in sugar for an extra-sweet, crunchy texture. If not, let the peel dry on the rack overnight, until no longer tacky to the touch. Store in an airtight container at room temperature for up to 6 months.

FLUFFY MILK CHOCOLATE FROSTING

Makes about 4 cups/900g, enough for one double-layer 8-inch/20cm cake

My favorite frosting is buttercream. I much prefer its texture to those that use confectioners' sugar—cream cheese frosting being the one exception. In making this, I wanted an easy frosting with a buttercream-like texture that was chocolaty but not too dark. Archer, like many kids, hates dark chocolate frosting and will go so far as to refuse cake altogether. This is an unusal but wonderful technique that is far simpler than a traditional buttercream because it doesn't require the technical step of making a sugar syrup cooked to a specific density. I heat the cream, sugar, and chocolate gently and then whip it, adding the butter in as I continue to work the ganache. The frosting becomes smooth, pliable, and possesses just the right amount of chocolate to gratify both me and Archer.

📖 A wide range of chocolates can be used, from 64 percent cacao milk chocolate to a really dark chocolate. What you choose to use will affect the flavor but not the technique.

1 cup/240ml heavy cream $\frac{3}{4}$ cup/150g granulated sugar Large pinch of sea salt	In a medium saucepan, heat the cream, sugar, and salt over medium heat, stirring until the sugar has dissolved and the cream is hot but not boiling. Remove from the heat.
12 oz/340g milk chocolate, chopped	Add the chocolate and stir until completely melted and smooth. Set aside to cool completely or transfer to a bowl and place in the refrigerator or freezer, stirring with a rubber spatula every 7 to 10 minutes, or more often if chilling in the freezer.
1 cup/220g unsalted butter, cut into chunks, at room temperature	When the chocolate mixture is completely cool, transfer to the bowl of a stand mixer fitted with the paddle attachment. Beat on medium speed and add tablespoon-size pieces of the butter, one at a time, mixing until completely incorporated before →

adding the next piece. Once you have added all the butter, stop the machine, scrape down the sides and bottom with a rubber spatula, and beat for a couple minutes more, until light and fluffy.

Use immediately or store, covered, in the refrigerator for up to 4 days. If storing, allow the frosting to warm to room temperature and then mix until smooth again before using.

MARSHMALLOWS

Makes 48 (1½-inch/4cm) marshmallows

If there is one candy worth making, for me it is the marshmallow. If you've never had marshmallows made from scratch, you should know that they are vastly different to the store-bought bagged variety. The fairy-tale name comes from the eponymous plant, whose root produces a gummy juice, which, when combined with egg whites and sugar, makes an aerated confection, once used to treat sore throats. Today gelatin takes its place, but I swear that half the love affair with the marshmallow is because of its playful name. This recipe doesn't take much effort, and the marshmallows keep well. They are a most welcome treat for all seasons: sweet potatoes in autumn, hot chocolate in winter, fillings for candies, and of course, over the campfire with s'mores.

📖 If you don't have a candy thermometer, the cold-water test can be used instead. To test, remove the saucepan from heat so that the syrup does not continue to cook. Have a small bowl of cold water ready. Spoon out ½ tsp of the syrup and drop it into the water. Work the syrup with your fingers for a few seconds. It is at the hard ball stage when it forms a hard, but pliable ball. If it is not yet firm, return the syrup to the heat and test again after 30 seconds or so. If the syrup forms into separate threads in the water, it has gone too far.

Butter or vegetable oil, for the pan

Grease a 9 by 13-inch/23 by 33cm pan, making sure to coat the sides and corners.

$\frac{1}{3}$ cup plus 1 Tbsp/ 55g cornstarch	Combine the cornstarch and confectioners' sugar in a medium bowl and mix well. Use about half of the cornstarch mixture to evenly dust the bottom and sides of the prepared pan. Set the other half aside for coating the top of the marshmallows.
$\frac{1}{2}$ cup/60g confectioners' sugar	
7 Tbsp/105ml cool water	Pour the water into the bowl of a stand mixer fitted with the whisk attachment. Sprinkle the gelatin evenly over the water and let bloom for a few minutes.
$2\frac{1}{2}$ Tbsp powdered gelatin	
2 cups/400g unbleached granulated sugar	Combine the sugar, water, and corn syrup in a saucepan. Fasten a candy thermometer to the side of the pan so that the tip of the thermometer is submerged in the sugar mixture but is not touching the bottom of the pan.
$\frac{3}{4}$ cup/180ml water	
3 Tbsp/45ml corn syrup	
1 vanilla bean, or 1 tsp vanilla extract	Split the vanilla bean lengthwise and, using the dull edge of the knife, scrape all the vanilla seeds into the saucepan. (Alternatively, if you are using vanilla extract, add it to the saucepan.) Bring the sugar mixture to a boil over high heat. Cook, without stirring, until the temperature reaches 250°F/120°C. As soon as it does, remove the pan from the heat.
	While mixing the gelatin at medium-low speed, gradually pour in the hot sugar mixture and beat for 1 minute.
2 large egg whites	Add the egg whites and salt. If making one of the variations, add the flavoring ingredient (strawberry, matcha, peppermint, rosewater, or whiskey) at this stage. Increase the mixer speed to high, and beat for 5 to 7 minutes, until the mixture has tripled in volume and turned fluffy, glossy, and pearly white. →
$\frac{1}{4}$ tsp sea salt	

Using a lightly oiled spatula, spread the marshmallow evenly in the prepared pan and do your best to smooth the surface. Dust the top with some of the reserved cornstarch mixture. (For an easy way to dust evenly, scoop the cornstarch-sugar mixture into a fine-mesh strainer and tap the sides of the strainer while holding it above the marshmallow.) Let stand, uncovered, at room temperature until set, at least 3 hours or up to overnight.

Once the marshmallows have set, cut them into individual pieces. It helps to use a chef's knife that you've dipped into water, otherwise the knife will stick as you draw it through the marshmallow. (Some people like to cut them with kitchen scissors instead.) For s'mores, I like them to be about the size of a walnut. For hot cocoa, I cut them smaller. The cut sides will be sticky and can be dusted with the remaining cornstarch-sugar mixture. Marshmallows will keep, stored between sheets of parchment paper, in an airtight container at room temperature for about 2 weeks.

Strawberry Marshmallows: Place 1 cup/20g freeze-dried strawberries in a food processor and process into a powder. Add to the egg whites before whipping.

Matcha Tea Marshmallows: Omit the vanilla bean and add 2 Tbsp matcha tea to the egg whites before whipping.

Peppermint Marshmallows: Substitute $\frac{1}{2}$ tsp vanilla extract for the vanilla bean and add $\frac{1}{4}$ tsp peppermint extract to the egg whites before whipping.

Rose Marshmallows: Substitute $\frac{1}{2}$ tsp vanilla extract for the vanilla bean and add $\frac{1}{4}$ to $\frac{1}{2}$ tsp rosewater to the egg whites before whipping.

Whiskey Marshmallows: Add 2 Tbsp whiskey to the pan with the sugar, water, and corn syrup.

Coconut Marshmallows: Preheat the oven to 350°F/180°C. Place 3 cups/240g unsweetened shredded coconut on a baking sheet and toast in the oven, stirring occasionally, until golden, 5 to 7 minutes. Cool on the baking sheet. Substitute the toasted coconut for the cornstarch and confectioners' sugar mixture. Spread 1½ cups/120g of the coconut in the prepared pan and continue with the recipe. Of the remaining coconut, top the marshmallows with ½ cup/40g and place 1 cup/80g in a bowl to use for dredging the cut marshmallows.

ACKNOWLEDGMENTS

Thanks to: Chad, my taster, always; my editor, the patient, wonderful Lorena Jones; the team at Ten Speed Press; the staff of Tartine Bakery and Manufactory; my agent Kitty Cowles, the absolute best; Juliette Cezzar, a whiz in design and the best to hang out with; Paige Green and her team, with whom I'd always go through Groundhog Day; Maria Zizka, always there to test just one more recipe; and Jessica Washburn, partner in the countless cups of tea and conversations about food and history that have shaped this book.

Also thanks to: Mia Manamea, Bridge Grant, Launa Conti, Valkyrie Modesto, and Gillian Masland. And many thanks to Camryn Mothersbaugh, for her good humor, joke telling, drawing skills, and dedication in spending so many afternoons with Archer so that I could accomplish this book and so much more.

Thank you to all of the women I have worked for and with, and those I have gotten to know along my way in the business of food and drink—writers, farmers, chefs, vintners, bakers, educators, and makers of all kinds. You each create a better place for more women to find their space and a louder, clearer voice. Keep doing that, and keep stepping it up.

INDEX

Published in the United States by Ten Speed Press, an imprint
of the Crown Publishing Group, a division of Penguin Random House LLC,
a Penguin Random House LLC Company, New York.
www.crownpublishing.com
www.tenspeed.com

Ten Speed Press is a registered trademark of Penguin Random House LLC.

Lorena Jones Books and the Lorena Jones Books colophon are trademarks of
Penguin Random House LLC.

Library of Congress Cataloging-in-Publication Data
Names: Prueitt, Elisabeth M., author.
Title: Tartine all day : modern recipes for the home cook / Elisabeth Prueitt.
Description: First edition. | California : Ten Speed Press, 2017. |
    "Lorena Jones books." | Includes bibliographical references and index.
Identifiers: LCCN 2016049912 (print) | LCCN 2016051149 (ebook) | Subjects:
LCSH: Cooking, American--California style. | Tartine (Bakery) |
    BISAC: COOKING / Regional & Ethnic / American / California Style. |
    COOKING / Courses & Dishes / Bread. | LCGFT: Cookbooks.
Classification: LCC TX715.2.C34 P78 2017 (print) | LCC TX715.2.C34 (ebook) |
    DDC 641.59794--dc23
LC record available at https://lccn.loc.gov/2016049912

Hardcover ISBN: 978-0-399-57882-3
Ebook ISBN: 978-0-399-57883-0

Printed in China

Recipe testing by Maria Zizka
Design by Juliette Cezzar

10 9 8 7 6 5 4 3 2 1

First Edition